Nickels and Nightingales

Per ardua ad astra.

B/Gen (R) J. V. WATTS DSO DFC*CD.

Jack Watts

GSPH

Published by

GSPH GENERAL STORE
PUBLISHING HOUSE

1 Main Street, Burnstown, Ontario, Canada K0J 1G0
1-800-465-6072 or Fax: (613) 432-7184

ISBN 1-896182-13-5
Printed and bound in Canada.

Cover Design and Layout by Tammy L. Anderson

General Store Publishing House gratefully acknowledges the
assistance of the Ontario Arts Council and the Canada Council.

Canadian Cataloguing in Publication Data

Watts, Jack
    Nickels and Nightingales

ISBN 1-896182-13-5

    1. Watts, Jack 2. World War, 1939 - 1945—Aerial
operations, British. 3. World War, 1939 - 1945—Personal
narratives, Canadian.
I. Title.

D811.W37 1994   940.54'4941   C95-900056-9

First Printing April1995

Contents

Introduction

In introducing this book, I feel that it is important to tell you I am writing this story in an attempt to rectify an oversight which has persisted for many years now, that is, the lack of recognition of the part played by those thousands of airmen who wore the single wing: the observers, air gunners, wireless operators, flight engineers and later in the war, the navigators and bomb aimers. So much has been written about the pilots in the Air Forces that it has tended to hide the roles played by those other members of aircrew. Let's face it, without those single-wing wonders, there would have been no Bomber Command! Perhaps my story will help to restore the public image, a little bit anyway.

At the same time I would like to dedicate my story to my wife for her abiding love and unstinting support in this and in all my efforts, as well as to our eldest daughter, Linda, for her endeavours in the editing and production of the final manuscript.

With no more ado, I give you "Nickels and Nightingales," an account of one young Canadian's life in RAF Bomber Command during World War II.

Chapter 1

It was 2030, the twilight hours of November 10, 1942 . . . and my twenty-second birthday. I was supposed to be in Cairo, celebrating in the company of some delightful South African WAAFs whose official wartime duties included staffing the communications section of Middle East Air Headquarters. Unofficially, in our minds at least, their greatest contribution to the war effort was not in MEAHQ but in entertaining the troops on leave from the desert front.

But I was not in Cairo. I was in the cold nose compartment of Halifax Bomber DT498 watching the runway slide from beneath me as we left on a mission to bomb Tobruk, Rommel's shipping and supply centre in his drive to claim Egypt for the Axis. It wasn't supposed to happen like this. Where was the party and the fun?

The irony of the situation was that 10 Squadron, of which I was the longest surviving member and its navigation and bombing leader, had flown out from our base in Yorkshire via Gibraltar to the Middle East "to provide short term, heavy bomber support to the Russians in the area of the Black Sea." We had left in complete secrecy after being confined to base and being kept incommunicado for the previous couple of weeks while ground crew, spares and ground handling equipment were organized to ensure our independence on arrival, and the aircraft were modified for operation in warmer climes. Everything went like clockwork, and if it didn't fool the enemy, it certainly took us for a ride.

And to think I almost missed it . . . I had been screened, taken off active duty after my last mission from our base in Leeming, just before the squadron was stood down to prepare for a "special assignment." But because of the unusual nature of the assignment, as we then knew it, I requested to remain with the squadron as its navigation leader, to ensure continuity in command and in morale which was so important to mission success. What I didn't say in my request was that, in all honesty, I simply didn't want to miss out on such an exciting adventure.

On our arrival in the Middle East, we learned that we had been diverted from our presumed assignment to a support role in the buildup of the coming desert campaign. By this time, Rommel had reached the area of El Alamein where the British forces under Alexander and Montgomery awaited him. Confrontation was inevitable and both sides raced against time and geography to be the first and best prepared. Since we had the only four-engined heavy bombers in the Desert Air Force, it became apparent that our role in the plan of operations would be to prevent Rommel's supplies from reaching his forces in the field. If our forces could achieve and maintain superiority, we stood a chance of turning back the threat to Egypt and mounting an offensive to clear the Axis out of Africa. So, although no one ever officially told us, it was obviously goodbye Black Sea, hello Africa.

We had been in the desert since July, already more than one hundred days over our "temporary" eighteen day assignment. For the most part, we had run so many attacks on Tobruk supply routes, that we came to call our flights the Tobruk Milk Run. When death is your daily companion, it's easier to learn to laugh, especially when you're so young and, therefore, immortal. Though the tides appeared to be turning in our favour in the desert, it was still too soon to be optimistic. We made two attacks in direct support of ground operations, one at Tobruk and one at El Alamein. With them came a welcome relief from the "Milk Run" and a surge of morale-building excitement for the whole squadron. There was still, however, a deep feeling of insecurity among both air and ground crews. We were suffering losses, fewer than would have been the case had we remained operating over Europe, but losses none the less, compounded by our hasty and secret departure from England and the fact that no one had any definite information about our status or our term of commitment. Apart from the many and varied rumours, we seemed to be operating in a sort of emotional vacuum.

Morale, particularly as it relates to air crew, is a vital though fragile state of mind, and the success of the air effort was as dependent on personal high morale as it was on technical proficiency. Perhaps even more. Morale, faith, giving the finger to death, call it what you want, was what kept the bomber crews going. Night after night, in defiance of the statistical certainty of not surviving a tour of missions, the crews searched out their targets, fighting not only the enemy's defences but also their own deficient equipment and, worse, the weather. To many, it was like taking a deep breath before plunging into icy water. You set your sights on the safe completion of a specific tour length, some thirty missions. An unexpected extension of the tour would be like running out of breath in the middle of that icy plunge — daylight and air unbearably out of reach — and that, for some, was intolerable. We had left the orderly, though hazardous, life in Bomber Command under the impression that we would be away only for a matter of days. Four months later, we were floundering, mentally at least, in an unpredictable and seemingly endless scenario. The strength, the morale that was our unity and our efficiency was being sapped.

In an attempt to improve overall cohesion of our group, we had agreed to break up the more senior crews and allow less-experienced airmen to operate more frequently. It became painfully evident to squadron personnel, particularly to those anticipating more action, that this policy was not being honoured by all. This only created more ill feeling and discontent since one of the offenders was a flight commander. The failure of anyone to break up his crew was interpreted by his critics as an indication that he had something to cover up, like waiting for others to attack first, or dropping his bombs short to keep clear of enemy defences. With the squadron already unsettled by circumstances beyond our control, there was no way we could allow this state of affairs to also elude our control. Something should and would be done about it.

As "senior survivor," I had seen too many results of losing the competitive edge and I acquainted the flight commander in question with the gossip surrounding him and his crew as well as the effect it was having on the squadron. We met alone in his office and I suggested at the same time that he could put these rumours to rest by flying the next sortie with a mixed crew. I did not make these accusations lightly, nor did he take them that way. After a shocked silence, he exploded. "If that's what the bastards are saying, I **will** fly tonight and I'll take a **mixed** crew, but **you** choose the crew. I have only one stipulation: I want my own flight engineer. I don't care a bugger who else you choose." I knew he was a good man, and feeling somewhat ill at ease about the role I had taken upon myself, I told him that I would be his observer and that we would make up the rest of the crew, with the exception of his flight engineer, from the newest squadron members.

And so it was that on this November evening, as the disappearing sun made way for the chill of the desert night, I sat at the navigation table of someone else's faithful Halifax en route to Tobruk. Happy Birth Day, Jack . . . this is one surprise party you might want to skip.

Chapter II

Typical of our desert operations, we took off with a full load of high explosives from our base at Fayid and set course for Tobruk. Our objectives were the dock installations, stores and any shipping which might be in the harbour when we arrived.

Navigation conditions were ideal. The skies were clear for astro observations and the by now familiar, though few, landmarks stood out below us to confirm our track and ground speed.

Inside the aircraft, we were comfortable in our khaki shirts and slacks, flying boots and white roll-neck sweaters that warded off the chill at altitude; our oxygen masks hung idle since we were flying below the critical 10,000 foot level. We all wore our helmets to protect our ears from the heavy drumming of the engines and because they housed the ear-pieces of the aircraft intercom system. Regulations dictated that you wore your parachute harness and your Mae West throughout any operational flight. On this occasion, however, both of mine lay at my feet on the floor of the observer's compartment. I was the Old Pro, working in maximum comfort you could say. And besides, birthdays are lucky days . . .

It was almost midnight when we turned onto the target heading. I passed Ray, the flight commander, our course home from the target, as was my practice, before leaving the plotting table for the bombing position in the nose of the craft. With my Mickey Mouse and bombsight set up for the attack, I began studying the ground as we approached Tobruk, letting my eyes adjust for night vision and getting ready to guide the pilot to the aiming point. Tobruk stood out clearly against the sea as the desert slid behind us. All was quiet ahead. We must have been the first to reach the target area.

No musical chairs for us; we skimmed the built-up area, heading straight for the docks. Regardless of what his critics may have said about him, there was no question or hesitation in Ray's determination to prove them wrong. We flew straight and we flew level as I called out minor heading changes to bring the docks steadily down the drift wires of the bomb-sight. It was a perfect run.

By now, the shocking, incandescent glare of the searchlights filled the hull with moving shadows and flak from the anti-aircraft batteries below began clawing at the sky around us. The moment had arrived; the aiming point was centred in my sights. I pressed the tit.

No sooner did I see the bombs begin to fall in a short-stick heading for the docks than the whole aircraft shook violently, rocked by an explosive wave.

My first thought, as I lay on my stomach in the nose, was that an anti-aircraft shell had struck and detonated one of the falling bombs beneath us. Instinct took over. I checked the bombing panel to confirm that all the bombs had been released and called for the bomb bay doors to be closed. They wouldn't. The hydraulic system had been damaged and there was no pressure. Smoke began drifting through the aircraft. Acrid, rubbery smoke pervaded the fuselage; our electrical systems were compromised. Suddenly, the IFF (Indicator Friend or Foe), which was a self-destruct system to prevent capture intact, exploded. All hell broke loose and warning lights flashed ominously all over the instrument panel. The port outer engine burst into flame. Ray shouted, "Bail out!"

Crew drill on a Halifax called for the observer to jettison the escape hatch in the floor of the aircraft at his position, at the foot of a couple of steps below and ahead of the co-pilot's seat. The observer was then to bail out, followed by the flight engineer, the mid-upper gunner, the wireless operator, and finally, the pilot. The tail gunner was to bail out of his turret by rotating it fully so that his entry doors opened to the rear.

When Ray ordered bail-out, I grabbed my parachute harness from the floor, slipped it on along with my chest pack chute and jettisoned the hatch. As I straightened up, I could see the three crew members assembling on the steps behind the hatch, ready to go and waiting for me to jump. We had no co-pilot that night and Ray and I were the only officers. I couldn't bring myself to abandon Ray as we seemed to be holding a steady line even though we were losing altitude. I stepped back from the hatch and signalled the others to go.

After they disappeared, I crossed the gap and climbed the steps to join Ray in the cockpit. He hadn't moved. He seemed stunned, but unharmed. Both port engines were now ablaze. I picked up Ray's parachute chest pack and clipped it onto his harness. We were still heading straight out to sea, but we seemed to be losing altitude much more rapidly. I thought it might be a matter of strength to regain some control of the aircraft and stepped behind Ray to grab the stick. I pulled back, hard. The column fell into my hands with the resistance of a flower petal. I realized, partially at least, why Ray was doing nothing. The control cables had been severed by the explosion. The sea seemed to be rushing towards us.

Another explosion! The heat from the burning port engines finally ignited the fuel tank. The port wing tore off, flames spewed into the cockpit and the Halifax was thrown into a deadly, irreversible spin. "Get out!" Ray screamed. As I struggled down the steps to the escape hatch, I could see him getting out of his seat to follow me.

It's strange how the mind works in such moments, and how, in retrospect, those events and actions seem so improbable. As I sat on the floor of the aircraft to put my feet through the hatch, I noticed the heating tube, thick like an elephant's trunk, looping down through the opening. Instantly, I pictured myself dangling helplessly, my feet tangled in the loop of that tube as the Halifax plunged its flaming mass into the sea. No way! It was like my butt had hands of its own, gripping the edge of the hatch as I took a few more precious seconds to pull that death loop free. And then, I had an eerie feeling, as if I were in a vacuum, neither floating nor falling, not knowing which way was up and which was down, spread-eagled, boneless and helpless.

I don't remember pulling the parachute release handle, but my nothingness was suddenly replaced by pain, sickening and cruel. My parachute had opened. Because I had left my Mae West on the floor, my parachute harness was too big for me and when the chute opened, I fell those few inches of slack as the chute grabbed the harness and ripped the cross straps up, between my legs. I can't describe the pain; I just know that I never want to experience anything like it again. It flashed like a lightning bolt right to the hair on my head and I am sure that, had I not already had survival on my mind, I would have blacked out. Instead, I was jerked upright. Not far below me, I caught my last sight of our flaming aircraft, a red-orange spectre, just before it hit the dark waters and disappeared . . . I was alone, dangling beneath my chute in the darkness, somewhere above a black abyss that everyone else called the Mediterranean Sea.

I had never parachuted before, but instinct told me that a quick release from my chute and harness would be essential if I were to survive ditching. I had just managed to get off my flying boots and socks when I began to swing like a drunken pendulum. My plans to hold the chute release button in my hand when I hit the water went up in smoke; I needed both hands to grab the parachute risers to try and get some control over what seemed to be very violent and dangerous oscillations. How I wished I had stuck to my first plan. It was impossible to judge my height above the uniform, glassy black surface of the water and as soon as I reached up to find the risers, I hit the sea. It was a terrifying shock. First, I wasn't expecting it and second, I had no idea how hard the impact would be.

There was no time to think. One moment I was reaching desperately upward to control my chute — had I but known, it was the effect of the warmer air currents near the surface of the sea — the next instant I was plunging deep and deeper beneath the surface. I fought my arms back down from over my head to my chest, in what seemed like nightmarish slow motion, to find the release button of my harness. God, Oh God, it wasn't there. Frantically, I felt for the harness straps, desperate to trace them to that precious button. Finally, though it was probably only a matter of seconds, I found the release just as I reached the bottom of my plunge. It had been dragged over my head by the water. I don't think I ever squeezed anything so hard in my life and the timing must have been just right because as I struggled upwards in the dark, the death trap of my life-saving harness fell away, freeing me to reach for the surface, for air. By the time I felt my head clear the water, I was gasping, choking on the sea that had almost claimed me, only vaguely conscious of the single white strip that was the last of my chute sinking quietly away. In the silence, I listened. Over the blackness of the sea, I looked and looked. No one else was there.

***

I could see the glow of fires in one spot on the horizon, nothing else. That had to be Tobruk. I had no way of estimating the distance but knew it was going to be a long swim. Getting rid of my slacks and shorts was pretty easy, but it was a struggle to get out of my heavy sweater and shirt. As soon as I was stripped, I turned towards the glow on the horizon and started to swim. I had always been a strong swimmer, but it wasn't long before the adrenalin wore off and the effects of everything else and the swimming began to take their toll. I had made no apparent progress and I was tired. To make matters worse, I tried to take my bearings again, but discovered that the glow of the fires had disappeared. There was, in fact, nothing to be seen, absolutely nothing . . . except the horizon, the meeting of sea and sky, identical no matter where I turned. Somewhere out there was a shoreline, but which way?

This was a moment of despair, if not panic. But I wanted to live, I didn't want to give up, not having gone that far, and suddenly my mind cleared. Of course, I was a navigator and this was my biggest challenge yet. I could visualize the chart I had been working on for the flight and I knew my general position. To reach the shore I would have to head south. So, I lay on my back in the water and searched the sky for the North Star. When I found it, I lined myself up, with my feet to the star, my head to the south, and began the most gruelling experience of my life.

For a long time I stubbornly tried to maintain an exact southerly heading despite the fact that I was taking the chop of the sea in my face. Finally, though, in tired desperation, I tested the run of the sea while I was reassessing my direction. What a relief to find that it was actually taking me very close to my southerly course. I found that I could swim more comfortably then and swallow less water.

Time seemed to stand still. As the hours dragged on, my swimming became so automatic that I stopped thinking about it with near fatal results. I suddenly came to my senses, motionless and deep under the water. I was drowning, simply because I was no longer commanding my arms and legs to function and had let my mind slide towards oblivion. Yet my instinct for self-preservation was still at work. It had made me hold my breath until I could hold it no longer and the shock of breathing in the salty water brought me back. In a daze I struggled for the surface, and again I began to swim. This didn't happen only once. Three times during that agonizing swim I awakened to find myself drowning. Three times I fought back up to the surface, each time having to set my course again to find the shore.

There were times I had to swim through schools of jellyfish. At any other time this would have revolted me, but then it was meaningless. For a while my mind was absorbed by the play of the phosphorescence of my own hands stroking through the water. I swam every stroke known to man, maybe more. I swam on my side, on my stomach, on my back. Anything to break the monotony, anything to shift the aching of my muscles. And when my mind was working, it was my imagination. Through those long hours in the water and the hours of loneliness that followed, I entertained myself with visions of a triumphal welcome on my return to base.

After what seemed like an eternity, my attention was attracted by a change in the darkness ahead. I couldn't understand, at first, what it was that was creating this impression. But my experience of a year earlier came to my mind. We had run out of fuel crossing the North Sea. Low-lying clouds had misled us then and had raised our hopes of reaching the coast. I knew that, in my present state of exhaustion, false hopes and disappointment would be more than I could take. So I refused to believe that the shore might be near. I just continued to move in my robotic state until I could no longer close my mind to what surely sounded like breaking surf.

I should have been elated, ecstatic that land was so close, that the end of my nightmare was tangible. But I wasn't. I saw the surf as another obstacle, something that my body might finally bow to. But if my body was only just functioning automatically, suddenly my mind was not. It had come very much alive again, and assessing my chances, made me go on. Fortunately, there was nothing to do other than continue to paddle until my knees and my hands touched the sand and the rocks of the shore. I think I paddled myself right out of the water onto the beach, into a cleft in some larger rocks where I finally stopped. My mind switched off the instant my body stopped moving. It was a time for everything and nothing, and nothingness won.

Chapter III

It was midnight when I bailed out, and it was dawn when I dragged myself ashore. How far I had swum I will never know. But it had taken me three lifetimes and at least five hours.

When I regained consciousness, it was to a momentary blankness. Where was I? What had happened? The sun had eclipsed the shade in my rock cleft and was shining in my face. That and the flies buzzing around me must have awakened me. Then I knew where I must be; it all came back. The flies had been attracted by the blood caked in my crotch and the memory of that flash of pain which had followed the opening of my chute washed over me just as the sea had done. I knew that, although I had escaped the flames and the water, I was down in enemy territory. All the stubbornness of my twenty-two years welled up inside me. There was no way I was going to throw away my victory over the sea by giving up and becoming a POW. I was going to make it all the way back to base and I was going to have that heroic welcome, the thought of which had lifted my head out of the water each time I found myself going under.

But there was no escaping the difficulties facing me. I knew, more instinctively than rationally, that I had to keep on believing, that I had to be positive. The very thought that my parachute harness might have emasculated me would have made me crawl back into the sea or at least given myself up. Both were abhorrent, so I convinced myself that, as long as I didn't know the extent of my injury, I could fight and maybe survive. I lay there awhile, waving the flies away, adamantly refusing to look at or to touch my injury. Perhaps I was only fooling myself, but my self-preservation was at stake.

Except for a waterlogged RAF issue wristwatch and a bracelet of seven Canadian nickels, I was naked. Neither would keep me warm during the night or protect me from the sun during the day. Since it was early November, the days were not oppressively hot and I already had the better part of an all-over tan. The nights would be the most uncomfortable. Most importantly though, food and drinking water were non-existent. I had to admit to myself that there was certainly not much of anything in my favour.

Cautiously, I rolled myself onto my stomach and raised my head above the sheltering stones to look around. Well back on the rise of the shore was a small tower that I presumed looked seaward. To the west, I could see nothing but sand dunes and barbed wire. On my east, I could just make out what appeared to be a blockhouse type of building and maybe some washing on a line. They were too far away to identify, but I could also see figures moving about near the building. They didn't look like locals to me, so I had to assume they were German soldiers attached to Tobruk. Obviously I was in a rather delicate position. If the tower ahead of me was manned, I could not chance any movement in daylight. There was nothing to be gained by moving westward, and to the east the Germans blocked the way. The only sensible course seemed to be to remain hidden where I was. They hadn't found me yet, so maybe for the time being I would be safe. My body certainly didn't argue, only too relieved just to lie there quietly.

It was no punishment that first day in the warm sun among the sheltering rocks and even that night. It was cold but it didn't bother me as I watched our bombers attack Tobruk again. The sound of our aircraft overhead, the sharp bursts of the German anti-aircraft guns and the duller blasts of bombs exploding kept my mind off my problems and let me forget about the chill of the desert night. The next two days passed like the first.

I could see, and almost hear, the Germans. During that time I saw several small ships sail from where the harbour must have been. But increasingly, my need for water and my more rested condition began to intrude on my lethargy. I started to plan my escape. I knew that the first overwhelming need would be for water. I didn't stand a chance without it.

As soon as the fourth night fell, I began scouting my immediate area, looking for anything that could possibly hold, and better still contain, water. I was looking for the garbage of war, bottles, tins, radiators of shot-up vehicles. It was pretty hopeless in the dark, but it was still the only time I could move about safely. After a fruitless search, I had to give up and return to my refuge in the rocks, suffering more and more from thirst, but entertained once again by a grandstand view of another attack on Tobruk.

The rising sun meant being warm again. The nights were getting harder to take. My mouth and throat had become very dry and my tongue seemed to be swollen in my mouth. Not painfully, just uncomfortably. I realized that I was rapidly dehydrating and, if it wasn't critical yet, it would shortly be so. Despite having not eaten for four days, I wasn't the least bit hungry. I was going to need water long before I was going to need food. My wound had stopped bleeding and there was no pain to prevent me from putting it out of my mind.

So far, no one had discovered me and it seemed wise to remain hidden during the day. As the sun grew warmer that morning, I imagined again my return to base and my welcome. That the news of my being missing might be sent to my family in Canada, and cause shock and sorrow to my mother, never crossed my mind. I guess the struggle to reach land and then my determination to get back to my squadron had focused all my thoughts along positive lines, leaving no room for the negative. At any rate, in spite of the situation I was in, naked and alone in naturally inhospitable terrain behind enemy lines, I planned to simply walk back. As the hours of sunshine passed, my need for water became more and more urgent. I knew that my choice to remain hidden had a definite time limit. If I didn't move soon, I was going to die.

At first light on the 15th, I crawled away from shelter and began a cautious hands-and-knees approach on the blockhouse. I hid in and behind every gully and dune on the way, staying flat on my belly in the open areas. To be discovered now would be heartbreaking. I left the beach area I had scouted during my nights and slid under some barbed wire. Hanging on it was a sign that said "Minnen." There was no turning back now.

By the time I reached the blockhouse, it was broad daylight. It was a square, windowless, one-floor cement building. A thin plume of smoke was rising from a small outdoor fire in front of it, but there were no other signs of life. It was ominously quiet as I left the last sheltering gully and circled around to the front of the building. What a sight I must have been, a stark naked, brown, tousled figure. Nothing stirred. I crept up the concrete steps to a partially open door. Still no sound. I slipped through the door into a large, square room. There was a big table on which mail had been sorted and stacked and as I raised my eyes I found myself face to face with a huge portrait of General Rommel, staring back at me.

The room was otherwise empty, but the effect of Rommel's portrait gave it a presence, one of impending danger. My position was desperate. If anyone came, there would be no other way out. I simply had to press on. What I would have, or could have, done if a German happened to be in the building, I do not know, but it became obvious that no one was there. I thought that the soldiers who lived there must have been out on patrol and that I was indeed lucky. There would be little time, though, to find what I needed and get out.

More purposefully now, I searched the back rooms. In one of them I found a German uniform of summer-weight shirt and slacks and a pair of desert combat boots with canvas uppers and solid, studded composition soles. This would serve for the next step in my escape. Now, water and food. I had seen a stock of Jerry cans beside what looked like a portable water filtration plant, but I couldn't be sure that any such water was potable. I left it there and continued to search for something safe. I found a machine pistol and ammunition, a large hunting type of knife and a vicious-looking bayonet. Just as I picked up a handy over-the-shoulder satchel for my find, I saw a row of shelves on which stood a number of tin cans. All were unopened and without labels. I picked them up, shaking them one at a time until I had one which obviously contained liquid. The rest I put in my knapsack. With the can on the floor, I hammered the bayonet through the top to open it. Tomato juice! This, I was certain, would be safe. I had never experienced such satisfaction as that moment when I tipped up the can and drank every drop. I don't remember tasting anything. It was the simple pleasure of feeling the liquid in my mouth and throat after what seemed like such a long time without.

I was now clothed. I had had something to drink, had food in my bag, and was now equipped to get on my way before my unintentional benefactors returned. But my efforts were not without cost. My wound had started to bleed again because of my activity, and I felt weak and uncertain as to how long I could last. I remembered seeing a storeroom with a number of wicker-covered Chianti bottles on the floor. I made my way back and found that many of them were full. For some confused reason, I didn't trust the full bottles. I thought they might have been poisoned. Why, I will never know, but I opted for one of the bottles with only a little left in it. This would be the stimulant for my long walk home. I returned to the large central room and, with knapsack and weapons at my feet, I drank it all.

It shouldn't come as any surprise that the effect of the wine was the complete opposite of my expectations. I might just as well have hit myself over the head with the bottle. I collapsed across the top of the table, under the watchful eyes of Rommel, and passed out.

The next thing I knew, I was coming to in the dim light of the room, not sure where I was or what had awakened me, but certain that something had. I lay still, instinct, not reason, making me listen and wait. What was the alarm? Then I heard it. The sound of a starter. I still had not moved, straining my senses to find the warning, hoping beyond hope that, whoever it was, was leaving not arriving. The motor caught. It was a truck. The sound came closer and the motor stopped again, right outside the door. I heard voices that I couldn't identify and my heart sank as I pictured the Germans returning from patrol. Was my run of luck over? Was my heroic return a delusion?

The noise stopped again. I still had not moved. Only my eyes went to the door I had left ajar as I found it. Suddenly, the door swung violently open as if someone had kicked it from outside. They had come back, yet still I waited. Someone was coming through the door. There was a flash of sunlight on a steel helmet, my fate was near. Then, as he moved further into the doorway, I saw a red band on his arm. A red band with the letters MP. I jumped off the table onto the floor. My studded boots hit the concrete with a terrible clatter that sounded much louder than my excited croaks, "You're British! You're British!"

I don't think either of us was more startled than the other. The MP came to a sudden halt, his hand reaching to unbutton the flap of his holster as I skidded past him out the open door. I wasn't going to stand there and be shot by mistake! I arrived in the bright sunlight at the top of the steps only to look down into the business end of a rifle and bayonet in the hands of a British army sergeant planted at the bottom. Alerted by the sudden commotion inside the quiet building, he was just rushing the steps to his companion's aid as I arrived outside. Thank God he didn't shoot before he asked in an English bobby's accent, "'Ere, wot's goin' on up there?" My studded boots clattered again as my dash to safety stopped. A bayoneted rifle in front and the muzzle of the MPs pistol shoved brutally into the middle of my back.

As it turned out, the tanks of the 8th Army had by-passed Tobruk during the night, cutting it off. The Germans had evacuated rather than be trapped there. My move from the beach had coincided with their departure. The MPs who found me were in the vanguard of the main body, and their role was to take prisoners of any Germans remaining behind. They were under orders not to enter Tobruk itself, since suicide squads, particularly of wounded Germans, were expected to be holding out in protected positions. But the MPs couldn't resist first pick of souvenirs and had disregarded their orders. Little were they expecting a Canadian flyer to be their first major souvenir.

However, at that moment, I was staring into the bore of a very grim sergeant's rifle and feeling my skin prickle where the other's pistol pushed into my back. To make matters worse, I was of course in a German uniform, was very deeply tanned, and my hair was sun-bleached and wild. I didn't know it then, but the seat of my slacks was bloodstained from my leaking wound. Had I realized how angry the MP behind me must have felt because of his embarrassing carelessness, I might have talked even faster than I did. The words tumbled out of my mouth; I was Canadian, I had been shot down in the sea. At this point the rifle-bearing bobby interjected, "Any identification?" — I was devastated. I never wore my ID discs. God I wished I had them then. I had to say no and start explaining my presence again. Not once did that rifle waver in its aim at my head or the pressure of the gun in my back ease until suddenly, without changing his expression, the sergeant said, "Had anything to eat, son?"

My knees must have finally given way because, before I could answer, he said, "Sit down lad." Then he told the MP behind me to get me a coat; I must have started shivering. By this time the truck driver had joined us and he was told to "brew up" and make some breakfast for everyone. With hot tea and finally some food, we sat on the steps and talked. The sergeant told me they had received reports of parachute sightings on the night of our attack, but that they had not expected to find any survivors. The Germans made every effort to capture any airmen who escaped from their aircraft and to send them immediately to Germany as POWs. The members of my crew who had bailed out successfully ahead of me must have landed on or near the shore and been captured. They could even have been on any of those ships I had watched sail from Tobruk while I was hiding. It had taken me so long to reach the shore that the Germans had probably assumed there were no more survivors.

The coat which the MP had found for me in one of the back rooms of the blockhouse was a British army greatcoat, most likely a memento someone had left from an earlier occupation of the building by the British army. Since the beginning of the war, Tobruk had been captured, defended, fallen, and recaptured a number of times.

Because of their assignment, the sergeant apologetically explained that they could do no more for me than offer me a drive back into the desert behind Tobruk where there was an airfield. He was certain the RAF would be taking it over now that the Germans had abandoned it. He would hand me over to them and carry on with his task of picking up prisoners. He assured me that his driver, an old regular soldier, had been in the desert since before the war and could find his way over the sands like a homing pigeon. There would be no difficulty in finding the airfield. At this, we set off across country, keeping off the roads to avoid the land mines the Germans would have planted to slow any pursuit.

Even in my state of mind it was an eerie ride. In the vicinity of Tobruk we saw groups of African soldiers who had been prisoners of the Germans and who now found themselves abandoned and masterless. They wandered like lost souls. We witnessed one of our own vehicles blown to bits at a mined crossroad, mute testimony to the wisdom of my saviour sergeant and his driver. And, dispersed in the desert, small quiet campfires burned, around which squatted handfuls of 8th Army veterans, brewing their tea. They seemed to be dressed indifferently for soldiers, a motley collection of pieces of uniforms, apparently selected more for comfort than for military smartness. But for all their appearance in their silent watch, nothing belied the deadly gleam of their clean and ready weapons. Except for my greatcoat, I was the only one in a German uniform.

My driver was as good as his reputation. After a few hours of driving through the unmarked desert landscape, we arrived at an airfield where several RAF fighters sat on the strip and a small party of RAF personnel waited. Only the main landing strip had been swept of mines. More aircraft and personnel would be arriving when all the mines had been cleared. Wishing each other well and with my thanks for all the help, my escort and I parted.

The RAF fellows welcomed me with enthusiasm but could not do much to help me. They happily opened a tin of that ubiquitous bully beef for me to chew on and thrust a bottle of whisky into my other hand for something to drink. Neither was exactly what I needed though the fellowship was welcome. They finally decided to send me down to the main road where another MP was on point duty. There they vouched for me and wished me good luck before they returned to their new airfield to prepare for the arrival of their squadron.

It wasn't long before a RAF Humber station wagon came along. The MP stopped it and explained my predicament to the two officers being driven in it. They happily had me join them. They were on their way back to Gambut, one of the advance bases where transports were bringing fresh water from Alexandria for the army. It seemed very likely that I would be able to get a flight out of there to speed me on my return to base.

The road we were on paralleled the coast and we made good speed for quite some time before turning off into the desert to reach the airfield. As they had said, it was an advance transport base and a hive of activity, with Hudsons, Dakotas, trucks and people in profusion. The staff officers who had brought me this far took me straight to the air commodore who was in command. As soon as we were introduced, he wasted no time. He had hardly welcomed me back into friendly hands than he looked about him. "F/O Brown," he called, "when are you taking off?" Brown saluted, "Almost immediately, Sir." "Then you have a passenger," the air commodore said. Turning back to me, he wished me well and sent me to join F/O Brown at his nearby Hudson. We took off at approximately 1500 hours and landed at Amorea, just outside Alexandria at about 1715.

Whatever qualities youth might possess, it is obvious to me in retrospect that patience was not one of mine. With a kind of drunken single-mindedness, the only thought that drove me on was of getting back to my base. Alexandria was no good to me; it still wasn't home. There was yet another leg in my journey. So I walked off the airfield onto the highway hoping to hitch a ride. The night we left for the attack on Tobruk, we had been based in the Nile Delta at Fayid. But we were supposed to decamp the following day for a more advanced airfield known only as LG 40. With all the days that had passed, I knew that I would have to make for the new base, not Fayid.

It was growing dark by the time a lorry stopped. The airman on the passenger side leaned out of the cab to ask where I was heading. "You haven't got a hope in hell of getting there tonight," he said. "Come along with us for the night and start again in the morning." Having little option, I climbed into the cab with the driver and his passenger. They were on the ration run and headed for their own base, LG 99. It was dark when we finally turned off the coastal highway into the airfield and they asked me where they could drop me. "The Offi-cers' Mess," I replied as they did a double-take, obviously even more surprised by my dishevelled hair, my unshaven face, and my army is-sue greatcoat. However, in unspoken disbelief, they stopped the truck in front of a large tent.

I climbed down, thanked them for the lift, walked straight up to the tent and through the flap into what was obviously the bar. Only two officers were there, sitting with their backs to me on bar stools. They both swung around simultaneously with glass in hand to see what had startled the barman. "Who the hell are you and what do you want here?" I was asked in a voice which didn't know whether to be irritated or curious. As soon as I identified myself though, and told them I was returning from enemy territory after being shot down, they scrambled down from their stools and welcomed me with open arms, inviting me immediately to have a drink. I refused their offer with thanks and asked instead if I might have some food and a bed. With embarrassed and apologetic sympathy, they set about raising someone in the kitchen and alerting the CO.

I was eating the quickly rustled-up meal when the CO arrived. He was Lt Col Marsden of the South African Air Force, in command of the SAAF Squadron of Boston light bombers of LG 99. They were part of the Desert Air Force providing daylight tactical support for the 8th Army. He was immensely pleased to welcome me and, by the time I was being escorted to a tent where there was an empty bed, had ar-ranged for me to meet him at operations the next morning following briefing. His last words to me were music. "It's about time I had a night in Cairo," he smiled, "I'll drop you off at LG 40 on the way."

Chapter IV

I had made no effort to clean up before going to sleep. It was late and I was too exhausted, mentally and physically, so I just flopped onto the cot and passed out. When I finally woke up the next morning, it was time to meet the CO at operations. As soon as he had finished briefing his crews, we drove out to his aircraft. He showed me to the rear of the Boston where the open hatch of the belly gun invited me to ride. We were no sooner inside than he started the engines, taxied out and roared down the runway without breaking his roll. In only half an hour we were over LG 40 where I could see the Halifaxes parked in the dispersals. Again, he wasted no time and went straight in for a landing. We touched down and came to a stop at the runway intersection. Here, with the engines still running, he let me clamber down from the hatch and left me as he roared off again, not wasting another minute of his forty-eight hour pass to Cairo.

Unshaven, in my German uniform under the British greatcoat, I stood in the middle of this strange airfield as a couple of RAF airmen came by. They were somewhat taken aback by this apparition asking them directions to the CO's tent and pointed speechlessly to a group of tents on the nearby perimeter. Equally mute, I plodded across the intervening sand strip. They just watched.

As I reached the pathway to the CO's tent, the flap opened and out stepped the CO, W/C Seymour-Price. A tall man, he had his head down as he started out along the path, completely unaware of my approach. When he did raise his head, I could tell that he saw me and watched his face change from a baffled question mark to a surprised but happy recognition. But it wasn't until he actually reached out his hand and touched me that he exclaimed, "Jack, my God, it is you."

He clasped me in his arms saying, "Oh boy, wait until the lads hear this," and literally pulled me along to his van which was parked at the end of the pathway. He started up immediately and drove wildly, slowing only each time he came across any of the squadron air crew, shouting, "Look who's here!"

But before any of them could reach us, he roared off again to find more of the lads, yelling back each time, "Meet us in the mess. Spread the word. Get everybody there." On and off the road we drove, in and out of sand holes until my discomfort became hard to mask. "My God, what an idiot I am," he said, "I completely forgot to ask if you were all right." As soon as I admitted that I did indeed have a small problem sitting comfortably, he abandoned our triumphal tour, wheeled around, and headed for sick quarters instead.

Seymour-Price escorted me into the tent where F/L Astley, our medical officer, had just two words for me after hearing my story. "Drop them." A quick inspection sufficed and, as I was straightening up and doing up my pants, he was already writing out a Casualty Tag which he subsequently pinned to my shirt like a ticket on a piece of luggage. When the CO heard him tell me that I would have to go to the hospital in Cairo, he put in his oar. "OK, Doc, I'll take Jack to the hospital in my van, but before we leave can we stop in the Officers' Mess? Everyone's waiting there to see him." Doc replied, "Right, with two provisos: we stay for a half hour only and I go to the hospital with you." No one had asked my opinion, but I didn't care. I was so happy just to be back in friendly hands.

Just as we were leaving sick quarters, Doc asked us to wait for a moment. He ran back inside to get his camera and took a picture of me to preserve that special moment in my life.

We piled into the van and took off for the mess. It was all my imagination had clung to, and more. When we entered, the bar was already open. I was perched, carefully, on a pile of cushions like a sheik in his harem with my admiring squadron pals gathered all around me begging to hear the details of my escape. It was pretty heady stuff for a young fellow, but I was so happy and so exhausted, I couldn't tell my story coherently. The atmosphere was too jovial and

Happy to be back behind British lines.

too party-like for that to have mattered anyway. As soon as the welcome had been expressed and I had answered the immediate questions, Doc imposed his curfew. "Sorry, gentlemen, it's time to go." The CO needed no second urging and we rose immediately, leaving the mess and the bar full of jubilant officers.

It was on the way to Cairo that the CO told me that he had had to report me as missing in action. They had all been so convinced that the Germans wouldn't catch me that he had delayed the report three days. But, he hastened to tell me, news of my safe return would be dispatched quickly. Even at this late stage, the implications didn't really register. The mental block I had developed against personal involvement was still intact. The squadron had become my "home" and I had made it safely back. Canada, and my family, still seemed too far away, too remote, to be involved.

When we reached the emergency entrance of the RAF hospital in Heliopolis, the three of us walked in — a wing commander pilot, a flight lieutenant medical officer and a ragamuffin in German uniform. The duty doctor heard what had happened, read my Casualty Tag, and repeated the same embarrassing examination I had already undergone. As I pulled my trousers back up, again, he ordered the nurse to take me up to the ward and said to me, "You probably think that swim you had to make was a bad experience. Well, thank your lucky stars you had to do it. The long immersion in the salt water cauterized the wound and prevented almost certain blood poisoning. That swim might have risked your life on the one hand, but it certainly saved it on the other."

After a bath, I was put to bed in a ward with a half dozen other injured airmen. I didn't know it at the time, but there was also a conference in the hospital commander's office between my CO, a BBC correspondent, and the hospital authorities. Word of my escape had reached Middle East HQ and the BBC correspondent who thought an interview with me would be a good human interest story for inclusion in his midnight broadcast to London. Since my treatment specified that I remain bedridden, the hospital authorities were unwilling to let me leave the hospital, regardless of the reason. The impasse was resolved when the correspondent agreed to interview me in the hospital and the doctors agreed that I could be moved to the commander's ground-floor office for an interview.

I was therefore very surprised that evening to be lifted out of my bed onto a gurney and wheeled into the commander's office. The window was open, a cable for a microphone system was already hooked up through it, and the waiting BBC correspondent hardly let me get over my surprise before starting his interview. He wanted me to tell him my experiences when I was shot down and how I had avoided capture. When the interview was over and the correspondent had signed off, there was a sudden hullabaloo outside. A crowd of my squadron mates jumped out of hiding beneath the window to barrack me in typical RAF goodfellowship with shouts of, "Oh, what a line shooter," "The band played 'Believe It If You Like'," and "Bullshit was all the band could play."

Seymour-Price had rushed back to the airfield after the interview had been arranged and had organized a squadron trip into Cairo to eavesdrop so they could all hear my story firsthand. It was very thoughtful and considerate of him, and one very happy young man was wheeled back to bed that night. Not only was my story being told in Britain, but my fellow airmen had shown me heartwarming respect and admiration. Such feelings are infrequently, if ever, displayed, never lightly given or received. It was an unusual occasion and one I knew I would always treasure.

The next morning as I lay awake savouring the whiteness of my bed in the stark cleanliness of the ward, I was startled by a young, dark head peering round the doorway and a lilting, Welsh-accented female voice. "Well, where is he? Where's our hero?" It was an RAF nursing sister, our ward nurse. She had caught the BBC interview and read the account of my escape in the local English daily. Now, she was coming to see for herself and to be sure, she said, that none of her charges suffered from pampered egos. There I was, deeply tanned by the desert sun, with a heavy growth of sun-bleached hair on both my head and my face, a disgustingly healthy figure against the white backdrop of my sheets. She was so right when she greeted

me with, "Well, there you are. You must be here under false pre-
tences; you look like you've just returned from a holiday!"

My treatment called for saline baths and new dressings three and
four times a day. Since I was bedridden, the standard procedure was
to encircle my bed with screens, have me roll onto my stomach and
raise myself on my hands and knees, legs well-parted, so the nurse
could clean and dress the wound. After three days of this less-than-
appealing routine, I was beginning to accept it in spite of the repeated catcalls of my jealous ward mates. Then, on this one
particular morning, as I waited on my hands and well-parted knees
with my butt in the air, everything stopped. Nothing was happening,
and for a while there was no sound either. I turned my head to look
back over my shoulder and heard a sort of snigger. I was somewhat
irritated that anyone could find this predicament of mine amusing. It
was my little Welsh nurse simply bursting with suppressed laughter.
Seeing my indignation, she spluttered an apologetic explanation. "Do
you realize that this is your fourth day here? I am your ward nurse and
yet this is the first chance I've had to do your dressing. You have had
a different nurse for every treatment!" Well, what is a twenty-two year
old supposed to think or say? The novelty must have worn off,
though, because as the treatments continued, I soon became familiar
with the nurses who were my regulars.

The doctor supervising my care became dissatisfied with the way in
which the wound was healing. Besides the tear in the perineum, a
chunk had been gouged out by the metal ring in the crossed leg
straps of the parachute harness. The tear was healing nicely, but it
was closing over the cavity caused by the gouge. He felt that, if it
were left to heal this way, it would create an abscess. The doctor decided, therefore, to remove the growing flap of new flesh surgically
and to pack the hole decreasingly day by day to allow it to heal progressively from the bottom up.

Although it was only minor surgery, I was given the usual pre-op
treatment — shaving of the targeted area and sedation. When the attendants came for me, I called the ward nurse over and asked her
quietly and confidingly if she would be kind enough to do me a fa-

vour. She was a kind young woman with a soft heart that only added to her professionalism and she asked immediately what she could do for me. Still in a quiet and serious tone of voice, I said to her, "Sister, when I come out of the anaesthetic, will you please ask me how I am? If I reply (and here I changed my voice to a high mincing tenor) 'Oh, fine thank you,' (going went back to my normal voice) then just leave me in my misery." She almost flattened me where I lay. She had really been taken in, but it was my only retribution for the unfair advantage she had taken of me when I first arrived.

My treatment after surgery continued much as before. But as the healing progressed, I was finally allowed to give up the bedpan. Though my walking was at first limited to going to the nearest bathroom, it was not long before one of the nurses said, "Enough of this. I am tired of setting up those screens. Come with me." To the hoots of my ward mates, I dutifully followed her into the hall and into a nearby bathroom. "OK," she said, "Drop your pyjamas, put your hands on the edge of the tub, lean over and spread your legs." In this ignominious position, I couldn't resist looking back over my shoulder and saying, "Well, Sister, this is the first time I've had it this way." Fortunately for me, she had a good sense of humour because she was quite a big woman and I was in no position to defend myself! I might have paid a high price for my loose lip.

My wound had to be dressed at all times, and now that I was becoming more ambulatory, the dressing had to be kept in place by a large T-binder that went around my waist and under my crotch. After weeks of continuously wearing this contraption, I must say that I became much more sympathetic of women and their burdensome sanitary napkins.

The British doctors on the hospital staff were extremely well qualified, some of them having given up Harley Street practices to serve their country. Now, plying their skills in the RAF, they encountered challenge and reward, frustration and discouragement. The death ward was just down the hall from me. Any patient who entered that ward came out only one way. It was never empty; the flow of Desert War casualties was endless.

One night after I had been granted walking-out privileges, my doctor and one of the orthopaedic surgeons had a night off. They invited me and a young RCAF pilot, F/O Ruskell, to join them in a bar tour. "Junior" Ruskell had been a patient of the orthopaedic surgeon and was now mobile with a walking cast on one foot. The four of us ended up in a very friendly bar where I drank Cuba Libras for the first time and, as the saying goes, was feeling no pain. As a matter of fact, none of us was particularly sober when the doctors came up with a "bright idea." Apparently, there had been an investiture that day in the hospital. The American Air Corps had not been in the Middle East for very long at that time, and one of their pilots had been brought to the hospital with anti-aircraft shell fragments in one leg. He was the first, and only, American casualty in the hospital. His commanding general had visited him that same day to pin the Purple Heart on his hospital gown. It was perhaps a reflection of the times and the grim injuries these surgeons had witnessed over the years of warfare that they looked upon this investiture as a bit of a joke. In their rather relaxed frame of mind, they decided to hold their own investiture, with Junior and myself as the recipients!

Somewhere, the barman came up with a couple of safety pins and a piece of purple-coloured cardboard. After they cut the paper into two over-sized purple hearts, the doctors called for the attention of the bar patrons and had the two of us climb up onto the bar. To his captive audience, my doctor extolled my heroics, DFC and all, and said that he was now going to award me the purple heart for a publicly-unmentionable wound received in action against the enemy, a wound to which he would pay only mute testimony while pinning on the award. He then ceremoniously pinned the big purple heart to the seat of my pants! Not to be outdone, his orthopaedic friend told the audience about the bravery of his patient and awarded Junior his purple heart by pinning it to the cast with the words, "Gentlemen, I give you the man with the longest screw in the Middle East!" What most of them didn't know was that Junior had crash-landed his damaged Kittyhawk on the shore near the front lines right on top of a land mine. The explosion had sent a large fragment into the cockpit and into Junior's foot where it severed the heel bone from the rest of the foot. When the swelling had finally gone down, the surgeon had opened up Junior's foot like a boot and had pinned the heel in place with the "longest screw" in the Middle East.

While I was still in hospital, I received word from the Irvin Airchute Company in England that my successful bail-out had qualified me for membership in the Caterpillar Club. Since I had bailed out of a "flamer," they sent me a gold caterpillar with ruby eyes along with my membership card. At about the same time, Middle East HQ (Air) advised me that my return on foot from enemy territory in the desert qualified me for membership in the Order of the Winged Boot. For this, I also received a membership card accompanied by a metal pin in the shape of a flying boot with a wing on the heel. I was now a member of the three clubs recognized by the RAF: the Winged Gold-fish, for an earlier ditching in the North Sea, the Caterpillar, and the Winged Boot. As if this were not enough, I also received an invitation to an investiture at Buckingham Palace for the DFC. Unfortunately, it reached me too late for me to send my regrets for "being un-avoidably detained."

By now, Christmas was approaching. Those of us who were ambulatory were charged with obtaining the bar supplies as we prepared to celebrate the festive season in a traditional manner. Every ward was involved in some form of celebration and it looked as if everyone who could would have a good time. Liquor was, of course, taboo, but with only a skeleton staff to supervise. . . . They were kind enough to turn a blind eye to the bars we had set up. It was all in good fun, as long as excesses were avoided. We did succeed in getting one of the duty nurses to drink a little bit too much, but we didn't realize our error until it was too late. This nurse made her rounds late in the day looking a little strange, but very kindly and generously offering chocolates to one and all. What a painful surprise it was for those who accepted her kindly treats to discover that what they had taken for chocolate was actually cascara, a laxative whose nickname was "dynamite." The next morning, we had to climb over a latched lavatory door to rescue one unfortunate patient who had finally collapsed on the toilet.

When the casualty report of my being missing in operations had gone out through Middle East HQ (Air), one of the South African WAAFs on duty recognized my name and notified my girlfriend. When word of my safe return came through, that message too was passed on. For some reason, my girlfriend chose to ignore it. There was apparently an exchange of words among the girls when they found out she was not going to visit me in hospital, and one of her acquaintances, whom I had never met, was particularly incensed. She decided that the least she could do would be to visit me to compensate for her friend's disregard. Her name was Mari. She was tall, slim, blond, and very attractive. I couldn't help but think that, compensation or not, she was much better than the original. Not only was Mari more attractive, she was also more outgoing and mature. We never seemed to lack subjects to discuss during her visits and we rapidly developed a relationship that had nothing to do with the original sympathy she had felt when her comrade deserted me. As the weeks of my enforced idleness slipped by, she came more and more frequently. By the time my hospitalization was coming to an end, we had agreed to spend as much of my two weeks' recuperation leave together as we could. It was a trying time for me, and probably an unsettling one for my nurse. On each of those last nights, I had very erotic dreams of the pleasures I anticipated.

The day of my release came and Mari was there, waiting for me. She took me straight to the pension where she had made our reservations. It was run by a woman of mixed Arab and European blood who would have been a casting director's dream of a Madam. When the Arab servant had guided us to our room and bowed his way out the door, we were finally alone, for the first time since we had met. It was late afternoon by then, and Mari had obtained tickets for an early evening show. But as we held each other and indulged in the small intimacies we could only think about before, it became obvious to both of us that we had to make a choice. Would we go to the show or go to bed? There was no disagreement. To hell with the show. With a shared urgency, we found ourselves in bed.

Mari was even lovelier nude than I had fantasized. She was lightly tanned all over that slim body, with small, firm breasts and long, shapely legs. And she was a real blond too. For a while it was enough to feel Mari's softness against me, to sense her warmth and willingness on my skin as I held her. But it wasn't long before all those erotic dreams and Mari's own obvious desire threatened to drive me beyond control. She sensed my predicament and drew me over her, strong and hard, as ready to take her as she wanted to be taken. And then, it happened; my erection simply folded. I was devastated. From a vigorous and obviously aroused male I had changed to a limp dishrag. Was my injury worse than they had told me? Visions of impotency raged in my head.

Obviously Mari knew all about my accident. Fortunately for me, she was very sympathetic and understanding. She must also have been sexually experienced, though this did not occur to me then. I could not have been in better hands. She calmed me, encouraged me, and kept me from feeling any embarrassment. In spite of her own desires, she did not pressure me to perform or to prove myself and she was able to get me to lie back and relax.

A little later in the evening, it looked as if Mari was right. I became aroused, and once again she opened herself to me. And again, I folded. This time I was really devastated and all my fears seemed confirmed. I was reduced to tears. What would I do? Where would I go? What was left for me?

Thank God for Mari. That remarkable, caring young woman came to my rescue again. In the growing darkness, she held me, a seemingly useless hunk of man, and soothed me. Never was there any sign of disappointment or criticism in her manner. She treated me as warmly and as lovingly as if I had satisfied her every desire instead of leaving her completely and totally without pleasure again. When I think of the relatively short time we had known each other and the absence of any previous physical relationship between us, I can only be thankful that this very special young woman was there to see me through that frightening sequel to my escape.

Because of her initial patience and understanding, our two weeks turned into a wonderful, recuperative holiday. Mari and I enjoyed each other boundlessly and my confidence returned. It was on New

Year's Eve that I was snapped back into another reality. We were attending a big dance party at the luxurious Gezira Club which had opened its doors to the Allied officers for the duration of the war. It was probably caused by the combined effects of the festivities, the gaiety of the crowd, and the impact of the coming of midnight and the New Year I almost hadn't lived to see. Without warning, in the middle of the dance floor with Mari in my arms, I was overcome by emotion. "Mari," I said desperately, "get me out of here. Anywhere, just out." She took one quick look at me, grabbed my arm and pushing through the crowd, led me across the dance floor through the French doors and out onto the lawn. There, in the middle of the lush tropical grass, under a sky full of stars, I sat and cried. Finally, my insulation was cracking. I thought about home. I called for my mother. I felt so far away, so terribly alone and so helpless. It was everything that I should have been feeling but had blocked out of my mind while I was out there in the sea and then while I hid for my life in the rocks. I don't know how much Mari understood or if she understood at all what was going through my head, but she was there. She cradled me in her arms, not trying to stop me from crying. She mothered me, and calmness returned. We didn't return to the dance. Instead, we went back to the privacy of our room.

There is something pitiless about youth, something which war and duty make more callous, something which is difficult to understand even as we try to justify it. I was no different. As my holiday drew to a close and my physical condition so obviously improved, I began to think more and more about rejoining my squadron. It had left LG 40 to follow the advancing army while I was in hospital. I wasn't certain how I was going to find its new location, but I was determined to do so. As this determination grew, I guess I was already distancing myself from Mari, but I was not conscious of it at the time. I had recovered and it was time to go back into action.

Just before my leave terminated, Mari and I were pleasantly surprised by a group of exuberant visitors to our pension. They were some of my squadron mates who had tracked me down from the hospital. They brought great news with them. Our squadron had been temporarily removed from the Order of Battle to permit a wholesale changeover in personnel and the obtaining of replacement Halifaxes. The revamped squadron would then be transferred to Italy except for the "old timers," including me. We were to report to the Heliopolis airport on the outskirts of Cairo for repatriation to Britain! After seven months, our eighteen-day "temporary assignment to special duty in Russia" was finally over. While I was heading back for the war in Europe, Mari's duties in the SAAF bound her to Cairo. I never saw her again.

Chapter V

We left Heliopolis on the 24th of January at 0710, in a RAF Lockheed Lodestar flown by a P/O Roberts. We flew south and refuelled at Wadi Haifa on the Sudan/Egypt border, then on to the airfield at Khartoum, Sudan, where we were billeted for the night. At 0600 the following morning we boarded a relatively luxurious DC 4 flown by a civilian American pilot, Capt Flowers. About noontime we landed on an isolated strip in the middle of the jungle near a place called Maidugri in Northern Nigeria. There, we were met by an American military bus and driven away from the strip for lunch at a newly built tropical encampment while the aircraft was being refuelled. To us, the conditions in this camp cut out of the jungle were almost a miracle. The roads were excellent, all of them wide and hard-surfaced. The barracks were roomy, comfortable and fully screened, including the porch attached to each barrack hut where shiny white refrigerators bulged with cold Cokes and other soft drinks. The dining mess was large, airy and also fully screened, equipped with ceiling fans for maximum comfort. After our many months of RAF living, what a sight the kitchen was for Canadian eyes. It was sparkling clean, a bright vision in stainless steel and white enamel. But best of all was the food. The bread was fresh from the oven and every table had its own supply of real butter, jams, jellies, and peanut butter. They all sound so ordinary now, but, for young Canadians who had forgotten the sight and taste of such North American delights, it was a dream come true. Who would have believed you could have all this in the middle of an African jungle? After our steady diet of bully beef concocted in every conceivable way, what a pity this interlude was so brief. In all too short a time we were airborne again, this time for the Gold Coast and Accra, now the capital of Ghana. We were met there by local African officials whose precise Oxford diction was almost disorientating and put quickly into vehicles destined for Takoradi, a port city about 100 miles west of Accra. There, the officers were accommodated in a bamboo-hutted encampment just outside Takoradi and the NCOs were billeted in a hotel within the city itself.

Living in the bamboo huts was quite an agreeable experience: a little like being in a summer camp, once we got used to hearing the lizards scuttling about in the dry bamboo and learned ingenious ways to defeat the incursions of unwelcome rodents. We were enthralled to watch the natives arrive in the camp carrying large platters of fresh fruit on their heads and cut bite-sized portions of pineapple or coconut with their razor-sharp machetes. The abundance and small cost of this fresh fruit was another welcome break from the stodgy wartime food served to us in the RAF messes and in this camp.

Food, however, was far from preoccupying the thoughts of our NCOs. The proprietor of their hotel had obtained the contract for billeting troops by promising to run a "clean" establishment. That meant no prostitutes. In a subtle, but legal way, he was true to his promise. He set up a sort of nightclub in the roof garden of the hotel where clients could dance to records and enjoy drinks from the bar. There was one unwritten law: any liaison that happened after the dancing and drinking would not take place in his hotel. So, in theory, the girls came to drink and dance at his club, nothing more. In fact, the girls came, encouraged the drinking and dancing, took the boys to another nearby hotel, and presumably gave a cut of their take to our friendly and obliging, but observant, proprietor. I must say, though, that watching the young African girls dance was a feast for the senses. None of our boys could match them in rhythm or in style and often the girls would dance together as much to please themselves as to please us.

While we remained in the camp awaiting the arrival of a troop ship, I met a doctor who was in the RAMC and several of the Army Nursing Corps sisters who were stationed in Takoradi. In its earlier days, the Gold Coast had earned the reputation of being the Governor-General's graveyard and it was still an unhealthy place for the unwary. Malaria-carrying mosquitos abounded and regular prophylaxis against the disease was mandatory. We had to take one tablet of Atabrine daily, the only medication available to us at that time, but the side effect of its prolonged use made you look as if you had jaundice. Yellowed skin and eyes did nothing to make the personnel feel healthy or attractive. Though the nurses were anxious to leave, none wanted to return home looking the way they did. Even the medical officer, Washington, who was an American Negro, and a very fine and fit man, looked ill because of the Atabrine's effects. He had attended post-graduate studies in Edinburgh and was there when the war broke out. The RAF had turned him down when he promptly volunteered for service but the Army accepted him and sent him to Africa. I never heard him complain, but I could sense he had been disillusioned. None of the personnel was enjoying this assignment in spite of its relative security. Like us, they had volunteered for active duty, not for comfort.

After about a week, we were finally dispatched to the beach with our baggage; the ship had arrived and was lying offshore. The harbour was too shallow for deep-draught vessels to berth at the dock, so loading and unloading had to be effected by lighters. It was incredible to see the Africans, carrying unbelievably heavy loads on their heads, wading to and from the lighters through the surf. When a particularly heavy item had to be moved, two of these marvellously-muscled men would lift the piece while a third positioned himself beneath it. With only a small pad to protect his skull and the piece balanced on it, he would deliver it through the water to the lighter or the shore. Each one of them rippled and gleamed with health. Never have I seen such superbly- developed men.

Only one small hurdle was yet to be overcome before we embarked. We had been warned that venereal diseases were so rampant as to be almost endemic in the local population and particularly virulent for the imprudent outsider. Because of this, there was a mandatory health check before permission to board would be granted. We were, therefore, a little worried about our NCOs and the possible consequences of their "nightclubbing." We didn't want to leave anyone behind at this stage. All went well, however. Everyone passed inspection and we boarded the *Andrepora* together. She was a Dutch passenger liner which had been at sea when Holland fell and was now operating as a troop carrier, with her same Dutch crew, between England and South Africa. She was returning to Southampton now, via Takoradi and Freetown.

Our ship sailed alone, without benefit of convoy or escort. For some reason we did not let ourselves worry about it even though we knew the dangers lurking in the Bay of Biscay and knew there was no way to avoid it on our passage north. Instead, we diverted ourselves as best we could and relieved the monotony by playing endless hours of poker. We should have baptized it the Champagne Game. The liner had run out of liquor on its way to Takoradi and all that remained for us was South African champagne, a bottle of which stood ceremoniously in the centre of our table at all times to quench our thirst.

One day, while we were still off the African coast, the old battleship *Rameles*, with an escort of three destroyers, passed us on her way North. This imposingly armoured vessel literally drove herself through the water, not appearing to rise or fall with the swell. The waves parted before her, broken by her prow and washed over her deck to the massive forward gun turret. She looked just like what she was, an unyielding weapon of war, purposeful but graceless. It was almost as if the power of her mighty engines alone kept her afloat, as if she would sink should her forward thrust be stopped. Though we were unarmed and unescorted, none of us envied those who sailed with her.

Finally, and uneventfully, we docked at Southampton and were sent immediately by train to London. Still dressed in our light desert uniforms, we had no more to keep us warm than our tans. We had left England in such haste and under such strict security, thinking that we would be back in a matter of days, that we had simply walked out of our rooms in Leaming and left everything as usual in our quarters. When it had become evident that we were not returning, our personal gear had been inventoried, collected, packed, and shipped to the RAF Depository in Slough, near London. This was our destination so we could pick up our gear and dress more suitably for the winter climate. I personally wasted no time!

Chapter VI

Now that I was back in England, the reality of everything that had happened to me hit home. Although most of my squadron mates had returned with me aboard the *Andrepora*, there were many who had not. Among those was the crew with whom I had flown that fateful night to Tobruk. I was the only survivor. I suppose it was inevitable that eventually I would ask why me? And of course I had no answer. But perhaps equally inevitably, in the absence of an answer, there came a feeling that I was living on borrowed time and that I had an outstanding debt to pay, in the name of those who had paid the price instead of me. This was a philosophical question far beyond me at that time though these feelings remained with me for many years.

My mind drifted back to September 4, 1939, when Canada loyally and immediately followed Britain's lead in declaring war on Germany. The small permanent forces of the Royal Canadian Army, Navy, and Air Force were placed on a war footing and their reserve elements were mobilized. Though rich in resources and possessing vast industrial and agricultural potential, Canada had only a small population. She could never be the source of large-scale military forces simply because she did not have the numbers on which to call. She was blessed, however, with glowing achievements in the field of aviation as well as the space, the weather, and the tranquility to support aviation training, even on the grandest scale ever imagined.

From the onset of hostilities, the farsighted leadership of the Commonwealth had understood the need for previously unheard of numbers of trained airmen. Hence the birth of the British Commonwealth Air Training Plan (BCATP), situated on Canadian soil. Trainees flocked in from most of the Commonwealth nations. In the early stages, the Royal Air Force provided some of the training aircraft and a nucleus of senior personnel. The bulk of the effort, however, to build the many training units and aerodromes, to man these stations, and to provide the flow of recruits for Air Force training fell upon Canada. The BCATP and its graduates were one of Canada's major contributions to the Allied success in World War II. It is a proud testimonial to the Royal Canadian Air Force which shouldered the primary responsibility for this almost uniquely Canadian effort.

Relief from the debilitating experiences of the Depression had scarcely manifested itself before war was declared. Jobs had become easier to find and pay-packets were just beginning to fatten. Ordinary working people were daring to look beyond merely subsisting as they had had to for the past seven or so years. My father's death, on New Year's Eve, 1938, had forced me to leave school and find employment. With the school's assistance, I had found a decent job with Firestone Tire and Rubber, a vast improvement over my initial low-paying labourer's position in a textile mill. My prospects were much better and, as I was my mother's sole support, the higher wages were, I confess, the job's most appealing aspect.

My athletic abilities in school had kindled my hopes of using them as a ladder to success. Even though I had had to put school behind me, I had not given up entirely on this idea. I played in the city leagues, wherever I could get on a team, becoming a junior player in the Ontario Rugby Football League. Then I was invited to attend the next Senior Football training camp of the Hamilton Tigers. The Tigers played in the Canadian Football League, known as the Big Four, comprising teams from Hamilton, Toronto, Montreal, and Ottawa. In the meantime, though, my older brother had been mobilized into a military artillery unit and my uncle, a veteran of W.W.I, was talking of re-enlisting. The draw was becoming irresistible.

I was young, single, physically fit and, seemingly, academically qualified for air crew training in the RCAF. When my uncle assured me that my mother would qualify as my dependent, and thus be taken care of, my mind was made up. I would say good bye to football and apply for air crew training.

When I arrived at the RCAF Recruiting Unit on James Street, I had no idea what I was getting into, or how to go about it. I knew nothing about the RCAF, the different air crew trades, or the length or content of the training programme. I didn't know you enrolled as an aircraftsman second class, the bottom of the ladder, and that you graduated as a sergeant. As a matter of fact, I was well into my training before I realized that some graduates could be commissioned, let alone become sergeants! As one can easily imagine, I was obviously so green that the recruiting officer must have been overjoyed to land a fresh recruit who wasn't expecting to become a pilot! During my interview he evaluated my academic record, my general proficiency, and my aptitude for mathematics. He concluded with the comment that he felt I was most suited for training as an observer and that, subject to my passing the medical, this would be his recommendation. I didn't know what an observer was but, if he thought that was what I should be, then so be it.

And so, on such ethereal grounds are some of life's most important decisions made. Whether that recruiting officer was unusually omniscient or whether he was simply filling his quota for the various air crew trades, I will never know. But, from that moment on, in spite of my ignorance, my mind was made up. If I was going to be anything in the Air Force, I was going to be an observer. Even at the close of Initial Training at the Eglinton Hunt Club in Toronto, when the selections for training as pilots, observers, wireless operators, and gunners were being made, the prospect of not being selected for observer training disturbed me so much that I asked my flight commander to intercede on my behalf if necessary. When I look back, such naiveté seems incredible, especially considering that most of the candidates would have given their eyeteeth to be selected for pilot training.

My call-up came on July 2, 1940. A group of us from Hamilton and the surrounding areas were sworn in and immediately bussed from the James St. South Recruiting Office to the James St. North Railway Station. It was my first train ride ever. We were going to Toronto, just fifty miles away. On arrival, we were quickly transferred to the No. 1 Manning Depot on the grounds of what had been the site of the Canadian National Exhibition. There, on the shore of Lake Ontario, we joined hundreds of other recruits for our indoctrination into the RCAF.

We were barracked in the empty expanse of the area that normally would have housed the farm animals brought for exhibition, the cattle runs I guess. We slept in double bunks in orderly rows, paraded in the animal show ring that we called the Bull Pen, and ate in a large canteen on bare trestle tables. Our caterer was a private contractor whose experience must have been in feeding penitentiary inmates, captive audiences you could say. Quantity was never in question, but quality was simply non-existent. More food was dumped into the trash barrels than was consumed. Sometimes the food never reached the tables; it went from the handlers to the trays and from the trays directly into the trash. Many of the recruits, restricted to barracks throughout almost the entire three weeks of Manning Depot, survived on sandwiches and snacks they purchased from the Salvation Army kiosk in the Bull Pen gallery.

Because the BCATP was in its early stage, there was a shortage of uniforms. All of us experienced some difficulty finding all the items of clothing, in the correct sizes. Without a complete uniform, we were not permitted to go beyond the gate of the depot. Some enterprising members of the depot staff, who had been there longer and had been able to fully equip themselves, made regular pocket money renting out individual items of clothing to desperate recruits willing to pay for a chance to get out for a few hours in the evening. It wasn't until our class of recruits was being posted from Manning Depot to Initial Training School that we were finally kitted. Even then, many of us had to accept incorrectly-sized items.

Nevertheless, at Manning Depot we had been provided with sufficient articles of work dress or uniform to permit us to carry out route marches in the locality. With the wonderful summer weather, these marches became some of our most enjoyable times; opportunities to escape the confines of the depot and to participate in some pleasantly enthusiastic group activity. Singing the many popular, and often bowdlerized, versions of marching songs, and marching proudly in time with the music along the suburban streets of Toronto provided us with our first public demonstrations of pride in what we were doing. "Tall oaks from little acorns grow . . ." Those early route marches from Manning, and later from Initial Training School, began the long process of building both individual and unit pride and morale so vital to the development of good airmen.

If there were shortages because of the rapid expansion in the ranks of the BCATP, they certainly didn't apply to the medical services. We seemed to be getting inoculations at every turn in Manning Depot, sometimes quite literally so. On one occasion particularly, we were told to bare both arms. As we stepped individually into the doctor's sanctum, we were jabbed first in one arm and, while thus distracted, jabbed in the other by someone else. New recruits vigorously rubbing, flexing or swinging one arm or both in pain were regular evening sights.

Manning Depot was a place and time of new experiences. Some were startling, some shocking, but they were made more bearable by the fact that they were shared by us all. What was even more conducive to the cohesion of our disparate group of young recruits from every corner of the country was that we were in this together for the same two fundamental reasons — to fight for our country and to fly.

Our transfer to Initial Training School No. 1 (ITS), on the site of the former Eglinton Hunt Club in Toronto, brought with it immense improvements in our living conditions. We were, however, still sleeping in animal stables! This

AC2 Watts and Aunt on visit home from Manning Depot.

time they were converted horse stalls, albeit those of a renowned Hunt Club. Much higher class, you had to admit. Our mess tables now had white tablecloths and the food was not only edible, it was excellent.

If anything, however, the pressure on us increased. We were now accepted air crew candidates and it was up to us to meet the challenge, to earn our wings, and finally to crew the aircraft which would defend our country. We competed endlessly in our assigned flights, to be the best on parade, to have the shiniest brass and shoes, to be the smartest in our dress and deportment, to have the cleanest, most orderly barrack with the most highly polished floor, and to be the best in academics. We drilled in squads, we drilled in flights, we drilled in squadrons and even in wings. We practised our leadership and we exercised to exhaustion. And this was in addition to a full and exacting academic programme.

*Showing off newly issued flying kit on visit home
from A.O.S. Malton.*

It was in every individual case, I believe, a time of unprecedented demand for continued achievement of excellence in measures beyond our previous dreams. It was totally absorbing and yet fantastically exhilarating. If we were successful, at the end of the programme we would be selected for further training as pilots, observers, wireless operators or air gunners, and sent off in those groupings to our next training units. In my case, it was to No. 1 Air Observers School at Malton, Ontario, a few miles closer to home.

If it had even entered my mind that AOS would turn out to be a relief from the demands of ITS, the work load, the pressures, and the demands of AOS would have quickly dispelled that idea. Though drill and exercise continued to take up much of our time, the academic programme assumed an even greater role in our lives. Ground School brought with it a curriculum containing numerous completely unfamiliar subjects in addition to those we did expect such as air navigation, meteorology, maps and charts, magnetism and wireless. Before any of us could move into the final phase, that of actual flying training, this first phase of Ground School had to be successfully completed. For most of us, this would be our first ever flight, yet, when that day arrived, we would be expected to perform as working members of the crew.

In the flying programme, each of us took turns in the crew as either first or second navigator. The second navigator always had the unenviable task of manually winding up the undercarriage after take-off, some one hundred and twenty turns of the crank. This would often induce the inexperienced airman to vomit because of the cramped position, the heat of the prolonged effort, and the unfamiliar nauseating smell and motion of the aircraft.

We crewed up on the Avro Ansons which had been provided by the RAF for training purposes, and which were piloted by civilians, some Canadian and some American. The base itself was run by a civilian organization, Dominion Skyways (Training) Ltd., which had presumably been formed for the purpose of overcoming the shortage in service personnel in that early stage of the BCATP. As second or first navigators, we flew on numerous exercises to practise the lessons we had learned in Ground School. Between flights, we carried out simulated exercises. The combination sharpened our embryonic skills as navigators, taught us more advanced techniques, and developed our speed and confidence in these newly acquired abilities. Accuracy was the watchword, and we learned the wisdom of doing things properly the first time, even if it seemed to take a little longer. There was never time to repeat. You simply had to be right, and to be sure you were right. Confidence, based on careful and accurate workmanship, was a quality that every navigator required if the chances of survival in wartime operational flying were to be optimized.

Fifth course at Malton A.O.S.

After AOS, we moved to Bombing and Gunnery School No. 1, this time at Jarvis, Ontario, and again, not far from home. There, Ground School courses introduced us to more unfamiliar subjects such as armaments — guns, shells, bombs, bomb-sights — air gunnery, aerial bombing, photography and more wireless. We flew bombing and air gunnery flights in Fairey Battles, single-engined, Rolls Royce powered, wartime operational aircraft from the RAF Air Order of Battle. The bomb-sight in this aircraft lowered into bombing position through an open bomb panel in the floor of the nose. A gas-operated Vickers .303 machine gun was mounted on a heavy metal track on the top of the fuselage behind the pilot where there was also an open cockpit in which the observer/gunner stood while manoeuvring the gun on its track to bring it to bear on the target. Fortunately for the trainees, and their pilots, the designers had included two essential safety features. One was a ring, solidly bolted to the floor of the open cockpit, to which the gunner could fasten the safety strap from the crotch of his parachute harness so he could concentrate on his target and not on trying not to fall out of the aircraft during manoeuvres. The second was the interrupters on the gun track itself. These prevented the excited gunner from shooting off his own tail.

It was Christmas by the time we completed Ground School and the required number of bombing and gunnery exercises. We had registered sufficient accuracy in our high and low level bombing missions and put enough shots into towed targets to satisfy the staff and our instructors. Another parade, but this time with special reason to be proud. The commanding officer, G/C P. Gibb, a peacetime member of the RCAF, pinned on our observer wing and handed us our sergeant stripes. We were qualified air crew. But, before being posted overseas, we had yet another training course to face. At Rivers, Manitoba, we were to take the newly introduced Astro Navigation Course.

We spent New Year's on the train heading for Brandon, the railway station closest to Rivers. It was a most pleasant interlude, with comfortable berths and marvellous meals in the expertly staffed dining car. But it was abruptly terminated when we de-trained at an open siding in bitterly cold, freezing weather and piled into an open truck for the drive to camp. Memories of the sheltered comforts of the Trans-Canadian evaporated quickly as we huddled down together against the slicing, frigid wind.

Astro School turned out to be a monumental challenge for all of us. The extreme cold was a severe physical test and the higher mathematics we needed to learn, to understand and apply astronomical observations was a psychological bombshell. Only weeks before, most of us had known absolutely nothing of the complexities and techniques involved in flying. Suddenly we were delving into spherical trigonometry and the planisphere, learning about the heavenly bodies, their relative positions vis-à-vis Earth, their predictability and how to use a sextant to obtain their altitude from our horizon and then how to use the appropriate air almanac and star tables to convert this altitude observation into a position line on a navigation chart!

The very concept was a novelty to all of us. The methodology was exact and complex, and it was all too easy to err in the calculations that had to be made in extracting the correct data, for the exact time of the observation, from the almanac and the proper star table. It was a system fraught with hazards for amateurs such as ourselves. And yet, rapidity was essential, dictated as it was by the speed of the aircraft. Astro navigation aboard ship is one thing; on an aircraft in flight, it is quite another. Our lessons in accuracy and self-confidence were reinforced.

We practised taking sextant shots at night, dashing out from the warm vestibule of the barrack block to locate a star or the moon before adjusting the sextant for the shot, then back into the warmth to adjust the sextant and back out again to take the shot and note the exact time of the observation. Back in the vestibule, we recorded the heavenly body, the observed altitude, and the exact time before setting up the sextant for a repeat on another star, carefully pre-selected to ensure that the resulting position lines would cross at a sufficient angle to create a fix on the site of the Rivers aerodrome on the local map. We kept logs of the number of observations and the results obtained as a means of establishing some of the justification for our subsequent qualification.

Taking similar shots in the Avro Anson, which we nicknamed the Flying Greenhouse, was much worse. It was so cold in the aircraft at altitude that we had to keep the sextant batteries inside our flying suits, under our armpits, to stop them from freezing between shots. Even with this, you could watch the light that illuminated the bubble in the sextant slowly fade to a useless glimmer during no more than two of the two-minute shots we had to take to average out for an accurate sighting measurement.

In the closing days of the course, some of our members had been singled out and told to report to the Station HQ. There, an Eaton's representative took our measurements and orders for officers' uniforms, assuring us that the order would not be binding, but conditional on our being selected for promotion to commissioned rank on completion of training. This was the first I had heard of such a possibility, but the selections had presumably been made on the recommendations of the staff. It was quite a pleasant shock to be included. Even if it guaranteed nothing, it seemed to indicate the success of my efforts.

In spite of the Prairie winter, the complexities of astro navigation and spherical trigonometry, a forced landing in a snow-covered field and a two-week quarantine for scarlet fever, we qualified. For the first time since our arrival, we passed again through the gate of Rivers Airport, leaving the same way we had come six weeks earlier. It had been a real sweat, and not because of the weather. We drove directly to the siding, boarded the train, and began our trip back east for home and embarkation leave. It was not from lack of respect for the OC of the school or his dedicated staff that we were so happy to see the last of Rivers, and the Prairies for that matter; our hopes and our sights were set, for overseas.

During my leave in Hamilton, I received a large parcel from Eaton's containing the complete uniform kit of a RCAF pilot officer observer. By the end of the leave, however, I had heard no news of any promotion. So, after being convinced to at least try it on for a photograph at the Harkness Studio, I sadly repacked the uniform and returned it to Eaton's. As a sergeant still, I travelled to the embarkation depot in Debert, Nova Scotia, savouring that fleeting taste of glory.

The airfield at Debert was still under construction when we arrived and we had to be accommodated in the hangars with a growing number of other BCATP graduates also awaiting transfer overseas. The period of waiting was trying. We had all said our goodbyes to family and friends and uppermost in our minds was the desire to finally set off for Europe. There were no facilities in Debert to ease the boredom, no community nearby where all those young, exuberant men could burn off their excess energies. We went on long route marches over country roads and entertained ourselves listening to Mary Martin's rendition of "My Heart Belongs to Daddy" on the nick-

Harkness studio portrait.

Trying out pilot officers uniform before returning it to Eaton's.

elodeon at a lunch counter not far from the airfield's boundary. Some of us enjoyed a very pleasant break from Debert when our names were called out on parade one morning. We were advised that our files had been mislaid in Ottawa, but had since been found, and we had been promoted to commission rank, rather than sergeant, on completion of training! Without further delay, we were to travel to Halifax on a 48-hour pass to outfit ourselves with pilot officers' uniforms.

Shortly after our return to Debert as fully fledged P/Os, a number of the commissioned observers, including myself, were assigned to the Atlantic Ferry Organization (ATFERO), in Dorval, Quebec, to assist in ferrying American-built aircraft to Britain. I expected to navigate an aircraft across the Atlantic instead of going by sea. It would be a one-way journey serving two purposes: one, to get an aircraft delivered to Britain and two, to get another trained airman overseas.

Our stay at the Queens Hotel in Montreal was pleasantly prolonged by the absence of any aircraft for ferrying. We were at liberty to enjoy the sights and sounds of the city at the government's expense. Evelyn, a lovely girl from the Maritimes, and songs like "Amopolo" still fill dream-like memories of those days. But we were at war, and good things had to end. We were finally called into Capt D.C.T. Bennett's office in Dorval.

Capt Bennett had been the main organizer of ATFERO and was the head of the Dorval office and the North American end of this unusual arrangement between Britain and the USA. When we walked into his office, we were confronted with a scene right out of W.W.I and the "Dawn Patrol." Capt Bennett had a handful of straws. Those of us who drew the ten short ones were to entrain immediately for Halifax and join a convoy for Britain.

Included in the group in Bennett's office were four of us from the same course, Ron Scott, Bruce Servos, Jack Lister, and myself. Although we had not known each other previously, we had become quite close and very supportive, a sort of Four Musketeers, throughout our training in the BCATP. This was to be a parting of the ways. Jack and I drew short straws and joined the other eight bound for the convoy to Britain. There would be no trans-Atlantic flight for us.

That time there were no delays in Halifax. We were ferried almost immediately across the harbour and into Bedford Basin where an impressively large convoy had been assembled. All the ships were freighters or tankers, except one. It was by far the largest among them and therefore, the most imposing in our eyes. It was to that ship we were ferried! As we boarded, it became obvious that we were to sail under the flag of the Royal Navy. All the crew and officers were in navy uniform. It was a daunting prospect for us, as inexperienced officers, to realize we were faced not only with the responsibility of our draft of 385 NCOs and airmen, but also with maintaining protocol in the midst of these experienced navy officers. We had never seen an Officers' Mess, not even an air force one, never mind sharing one with such a seasoned, competent group. For me at least, it was going to be a case of keeping a watchful eye and treading lightly, a case of following suit and, hopefully, sparing myself public embarrassment. All these thoughts mingled simultaneously with my excitement.

Without exception, all the ships in the basin lay low in the water, obviously heavily laden. Among them were tankers with American-built light bombers lashed to their decks. The sight could not help but impress our innocence and, as we steamed out, most of us stood on the upper decks, over the guns of the Aurania, and looked down over our convoy. We were in the middle, in the most protected position. The cargoes of high-octane fuel, aircraft, food, and other seemingly vital supplies must have been rated secondary to the shipload of trained airmen. This was a lesson which was brought home to me not long after when, in Bomber Command, I had the misfortune to come down in the sea and lose the flight commander's aircraft in the process.

Chapter VII

Before the war, HMS *Aurania* had been a passenger/freighter but, on her induction into war service, she became known as an armed merchant cruiser. Though she was capable of a speed in the order of eighteen knots, the fact that she was now in a convoy of older, slower freighters forced her to sail at only eight knots. The *Aurania* had a deck gun both fore and aft and her deck was loaded with depth charges she could drop from the stern. Except for a small stern gun on a few of the freighters, this constituted the complete defence of the convoy. In light of our later experience, the convoy proved to be, in reality, utterly defenceless. On that morning, though, to our uninitiated eyes, the entire picture was one of warlike readiness and capability. We were, to say the least, very impressed as we sailed away from land toward a distant and empty horizon.

As our world shrank to that of the convoy and as the navy put us through our emergency drills for sea and air attack, we began to grasp the fact that we were finally off to war.

Being responsible for nearly four hundred NCOs and airmen aboard a navy ship in wartime was quite an assignment for ten young, newly commissioned and inexperienced air crew officers. The organization and control of the many details which were involved in the feeding, housing and administration of such a large group in such confined quarters, and under such strict regulations, were demanding and unrelenting. Yet it all seemed to function smoothly and efficiently, probably due more to the willingness and cooperation of the men themselves, along with the understanding and sympathy of the navy personnel, than to our skills or effectiveness.

Days slipped by and routines became automatic. We appeared to be sailing in a random fashion, sometimes in warmer waters, sometimes in colder, on a seemingly unpredictable basis. On one of the pleasantly sunny days, we organized an air force vs navy sports meet. There were numerous events among which was a boxing competition. We were most fortunate in having an Australian officer with us who had been a successful light-heavyweight amateur boxer. He put on a fine exhibition with one of the navy boxers who, unfortunately, had to retire in the third round with a sprained thumb. I say unfortunately, not because the match ended with the opponent's injury, but because it meant it was my turn a little earlier than I was prepared for. I had been coerced into entering a bout in the one hundred and seventy pound class, and had drawn a navy stoker as my opponent! I recall what a mannerly exhibition it was, for all of a round and a half. At that point, for some inexplicable reason I dropped my guard. The stoker didn't hesitate. Like a flash, he hit me flush on the chin with a real haymaker. For an instant I went blank and my knees sagged; I was close to being kayoed. But instead of collapsing, I felt a surge of anger and the heady carelessness of adrenalin. I charged into the attack, throwing caution to the wind and gentlemanly conduct with it, determined to repay my adversary in full. Between rounds two and three, I remember one of my course mates, a fellow by the name of Nugent, from Toronto, telling me to ease up, that it was only an exhibition. My buddy, Jack Lister, who was also acting as my second, told Nugent to cut the crap. He urged me to keep it up and get, "Stuck into the bastard." Luckily, my anger, which was really at myself for having been foolish enough to get tagged, began to subside and the stoker and I were able to start the third round in a more sporting manner and end the bout in a draw.

WHOOoo-WHOOoo-WHOOoo! If you have never heard, or felt, the eerie wailing of a shipboard emergency alarm, you should be grateful. Even the deepest of sleepers tumbled out of his double-decker bunk, startled by that dreaded sound. Fourteen days out of Halifax, on the Atlantic crossing to Britain, we were still a ponderously slow, heavily laden, unescorted convoy. In mild panic and great haste, we pulled greatcoats and life jackets straight over whatever we were or were not wearing and stuffed our pockets with emergency supplies such as chocolate bars, candies, and flashlights. Some even made sure to grab a sealed can of Players cigarette's which were so popular with the navy. We scrambled out of the cabins into the passageways and, following the established drill routes, we hurried to our assigned stations on deck.

Our boat stations awaited us, shrouded in a cold grey dawn. As the officers took charge of the arriving airmen, counting noses to make sure everyone was accounted for, it was all too apparent that the normal atmosphere, aboard ship and throughout the convoy, had changed drastically. The methodical, slow-paced naval routine aboard the *Aurania* and the staid orderliness of the other thirty-eight ships in the convoy had disappeared. The navy crew of our ship were moving about their assigned duties with disciplined speed and serious mien. Though all the ships were still holding their positions in the sailing formation, hooters everywhere sounded the alarm and I could see the crews on the decks of all the ships, moving about their tasks on the double. The previous serenity of ships at sea had been shattered. On the *Aurania*, the gun crews removed the covers and manned her guns as did the crews of the other freighters which had the little gun mounted on their stern.

So much for the fleeting hope in the back of our minds. This was no drill; it was the real thing and there was absolutely nothing we could do except what was already done, muster and control the airmen in our boat parties, and prepare to abandon ship in an orderly fashion — if that became necessary. It was a terrifying prospect, particularly for those airmen who had never seen a large body of water, never mind an ocean, before embarking on this convoy.

Some of the airmen who belonged at my boat station had been in the lower decks on galley duty when the alarm sounded. One of them, a much older, wiry American from the West — a sort of Gary Cooper type — was holding his hand and was obviously in pain. I asked him what was wrong. He pointed to a young aircraftsman beside him and said in his drawl, "This kid was behind me in the galley when the alarm sounded. He panicked and started screaming. I didn't stop to think, I just spun around and swung at the same time, hitting him on the jaw harder than I have ever hit any man. I think I broke my hand. But the kid here stopped screaming, shook his head and took off for the boat station with me right behind him."

Suddenly, as we stood waiting by our boats, the masthead lookout cried "Submarine, port." Sure enough, between the swell of the waves, we could see a small object on the surface well ahead of the convoy on the port quarter. While we were trying to assimilate this, the same lookout cried again "Submarine, starboard!" We swung our heads around and looked to the other side. Just barely visible was another similar object about the same distance ahead of the convoy. We were clearly in the middle.

What we didn't know was that what seemed like an unpredictable course to us, first southerly, then northerly, away from our direct route, had actually been set in response to radio warnings from Naval HQ about enemy submarine positions. Now, albeit unwittingly, we were sailing right into the jaws of a wolf pack.

One of the subs had caught up with, and sunk, the noisy diesel-engined freighter on the edge of the convoy during the previous night and, correctly anticipating our morning position, had assembled the others. All the available submarines were waiting for us, in two submerged lines, forming a corridor into which we had blindly sailed. The two we sighted were those stationed at the far end of the lines. Presumably they had broken the surface to divert our attention from the trap.

"Torpedo starboard!" "Torpedo port!" the watch called, breaking the knowing silence. Their foaming tracks headed directly for us. But, first one and then the other missed our bow, crossing each other immediately ahead of us. We saw the torpedoes hit and heard and felt the explosions as the tanker on our port side and then the freighter on the starboard were mortally stricken. The tanker, loaded with high - octane fuel and a deck cargo of aircraft, split into two pieces which up-ended and sank out of sight in a matter of terrifyingly short moments. The fuel had been ignited by the explosion and the surface of the water where the tanker had been turned into a writhing sheet of smoke and flame. Three of the crew tried desperately to get aboard a Carley Float that had escaped the sunken deck but were engulfed in the spreading flames as we stood watching, helpless to assist. I don't think there are words that can describe our horror as they disappeared into those flames.

While these events mesmerized us in our inaction, the captain of the *Aurania* was doing his job. The course of the ship was already altered to turn us down the track of the first torpedo and we proceeded no longer at convoy speed, but full ahead. His orders were to save his vital cargo, no matter what the cost and, in turning toward the enemy, he had chosen the defensive tactic that would present the narrowest possible target for his attacker.

Even as the dense black smoke from the burning fuel rolled up around us, we could see the stricken starboard freighter falling behind us. She was listing badly and looked in danger of sinking momentarily. A second freighter which had been further astern in the convoy came alongside her crippled mate to take on survivors before she foundered. But fate was unrelenting and again we could only watch as the succouring ship was herself struck amidships by another torpedo. We saw her boiler blow on impact, and she began to sink immediately while the first ship continued to float, her list increasing precariously.

Alarm hooters were still blaring throughout the convoy as it broke up and began to disperse, ships heading off in every direction, and the smoke gradually obscured much of the area around us. Suddenly and shockingly, the *Aurania* seemed to founder, and then to slowly shudder from bow to stern. We were sure we'd been hit by a torpedo. But there was no order to abandon ship. Instead, there was a rush of activity at the stern. Depth charges began to tumble into the water behind us and explode beneath the surface astern.

It was more of a relief than a pleasure to learn that we had apparently struck a submarine just below the surface and then sailed right over her. In all likelihood, it was the same sub that had fired the first starboard torpedo and was rising for a periscope sighting when we charged into her. I'm sure this must have been a sinking. In another context, it would have given the captain of the *Aurania* considerable satisfaction but, at the time, his overwhelming emotion must have been one of bitterness. He had had to abandon his convoy to save his precious cargo of airmen.

I guess I should have been terrified. The scenario certainly called for it. We were somewhere in the middle of the Atlantic with only cold grey water as far as one could see. The explosions themselves hadn't been so severe as to be shocking, muffled as they were by the water. But the results were devastating. Our ships seemed so weak, pitifully so, utterly defenceless and without any means to escape the terror and destruction surrounding them. The smoke, the fires, the alarm hooters, the sinking ships, and the apparent confusion within what had previously been an orderly and disciplined convoy should have put the fear of death into all of us. I say "should have" because I know that I, at least, was too excited by all the action around us to be afraid. This was the war for which we had been training those past eight months. We may have been spectators, we certainly weren't flying, but this was our initiation. We were part of the war. And we weren't out of danger yet.

We continued at full speed away from the carnage. Nine of our thirty-eight sister ships were lost. Towards evening, we saw some specks on the horizon ahead of us. It wasn't long before they were obviously three destroyers moving at high speed, white water boiling under their bows and long wakes trailing astern. As they neared us, the lead ship began to heel over in a turn to take up position as our escort. There was a blaze of Aldis lamp flashes from our bridge. The destroyer kept turning to complete a full circle and moved back into formation with the other two, racing to reach the site of the slaughter, and what might remain of our convoy. Our captain may have had some satisfaction out of ramming that submarine, but he obviously had no stomach for any further special treatment for himself or for his ship. We pushed on, at high speed and alone. By the next day, we came in sight of Iceland. There, we were off-loaded and left to await further transport.

Iceland was a strange and unexpected place for all of us. In the years just preceding the outbreak of war, Germany had been actively assisting the development of the island. They had encouraged good relations with the islanders by helping them improve their roads and by constructing concrete viaducts to bring the waters from nearby hot springs into the capital, Reykjavik, for use in central heating. In a country with an extremely cold climate and a scarcity of natural fuels, such a development had won great public approval. With the outbreak of hostilities, however, came the dominating presence of the Royal Navy in the Atlantic. The Germans were forced to abandon their efforts in Iceland, and their presence was replaced by that of the British. It is no wonder then, with the little the British could offer in terms of manpower or resources for such philanthropic projects, that there was little welcome, if any, for British troops on the island.

We found ourselves living in Quonset huts in an army camp devoid of any distractions and providing little in the way of comfort. The food was scarcely edible and we had to take vitamin supplements daily to compensate for the lack of fresh vegetables. Whenever we left camp to walk along the roads or visit Reykjavik, it was disconcerting and embarrassing to see the inhabitants deliberately cross to the other side to avoid us. Our only other recreation was a swimming pool we discovered near the camp. Even in that, our first experience was something of a shock. When we dove into the pool, we found that it was filled with waters from the natural hot springs. Reaching the other end in the hot water was far more of an effort than any of us had anticipated. More than one of us had to pull up in the middle, gasping for relief. Fortunately for us, our stay in Iceland was a short one.

Soon we found ourselves aboard an Irish mail packet on a run from Iceland to Gurroch in Scotland. We took up most of the passenger space. The rest was allocated to sailors who had been rescued from ships which had been sunk in the Atlantic. Amongst them were the three lone survivors of the ill-fated battleship, HMS *Hood,* which had just been sunk by the *Bismarck*. One of the three was a midshipman. He had been on duty on the bridge when the ship was blown up by a direct hit to her magazine. The other two were stokers who had been working in the engine room. All of them had somehow been miraculously blown clear of the ship in the explosion. They had survived not only the force of the explosion and the impact of hitting the water, but also their subsequent wait in the frigid ocean until rescuers found them. Their injuries were incapacitating and they were embarked on stretchers for their journey home.

The officers were assigned berths in the packet's cabins. We were overjoyed to be able to take baths in such comfort, even if they were in salt water. None of us questioned this good fortune until we noticed that the passenger sailors, those survivors of previous sinkings, never ventured below for anything but the bare essentials. Night and day, they stayed on deck. Eventually, of course, we questioned them. Their answer was simple. We were within range of the German Luftwaffe, the mail packets were flat-bottomed, not designed for the Atlantic, and they would turn turtle in the event of even a near miss. Although we couldn't convince ourselves to abandon the comforts of our cabins, there were no more leisurely baths and we did seem to put in a lot more deck time after that.

During the crossing, one of our sergeants, Joe Thompson, who was an accomplished golfer from the Hamilton area and quite successful on the American and Canadian circuits, had parleyed his locker room talents and a Crown and Anchor board into a small fortune. He had pocketed all of the money of the many amateur gamblers in the draft, some of whom had even pawned their extra hooks and wings to prolong their run. As Joe made his way down the gangplank, on our arrival in Gurroch, he was heard to say "With all this loot, I intend to satisfy my life's ambition. I am going to play the Old Course at St. Andrews." I hope that he did because I believe he was lost on operations in his first tour.

Chapter VIII

Our arrival in Gurroch was heralded by a scene of frenzied activity. We were hustled from ship to train so quickly that we could scarcely grasp the fact that we had landed safely — twenty-three days and many lives after setting out from Halifax on that ill-fated convoy. Except for an engine change somewhere along the way in the middle of the night, our ride from Gurroch to London was non-stop. We saw little of the countryside through which we travelled, and by morning we were pulling into one of the London stations. From there we were quickly transported to the RAF reception depot in Uxbridge which was, fortuitously, also the terminus of the subway line that ran to Piccadilly Circus. This was a turn of events for which we subsequently gave thanks to the farsighted RAF type who had so wisely selected such a site for a reception depot.

After a number of orientation sessions designed to prepare us, the Colonials, for the culture shock of living in Good Old Blighty, and in wartime at that, we were issued with identity cards, ration cards, and clothing coupons and given a day's leave. Jack Lister and I took off immediately for the Underground (the subway) and Piccadilly Circus. It proved to be no problem, even for greenhorns such as we. No change of trains was required along the way, and the line we were on terminated at the Circus. We came up the stairs from the underground and out into Piccadilly, with the sun shining in our faces and the Regent Palace Hotel — later to be referred to as the Riding Stable by those of us who made London our rest and recreation spot from operations — right in front of us. We walked and walked all through the area, absorbing the sights and sounds of wartime London, hardly able to believe that we were really there.

As Jack and I explored one of the side streets leading back into the Circus, we were startled to hear a voice with a Canadian accent calling our names. We looked around but couldn't see any familiar face. Then we looked up. There, leaning out of a second floor window of a pub across from the side door of the Regent Palace and waving to us, was a RCAF sergeant from our course. He called for us to join him. Elated at finding a familiar face in such unfamiliar territory, we hastened across the road into the pub, the Devonshire Arms, and up the stairs to the saloon bar where our friend awaited us. As it turned out, Sgt J. McDowall had already made the acquaintance of the young woman who served at the bar, and we found ourselves being warmly welcomed. This pub became our rendezvous while we stayed at the reception depot and, subsequently for me, a sort of home away from home during my numerous London leaves from operational duty.

After that first day in town, we had to catch the last train of the night from Piccadilly to Uxbridge. We descended to the first level and bought our tickets in the apparently normal, noisy crowd of travellers. Then we had to take the escalator down to the lower levels where the trains were. We were totally unprepared for what we saw there. The stairs were inhabited by Londoners, young and old, seeking refuge for the night and protection from the bombs which could fall at any time. All the way down the stairs and on every platform, there were people stretched out neatly, chatting with their neighbours, resting quietly or just sleeping. Obviously, many of them were regulars and well-organized for their night in the shelter. There was one family lying on blankets they had brought in a suitcase which then served as a makeshift cradle for their baby who slept peacefully beside them.

As we picked our way among this throng, both of us felt terribly conspicuous in our patently new uniforms, our Canada shoulder flashes and our new, flat, wire-sprung RCAF officers' hats. Yet as we threaded our careful way through these people, individual after individual sat up, or raised his or her head, and said quietly but firmly, "Give it to them, Canada. You'll pay the bastards back for us." We were deeply touched both by the sight of these people who could take their suffering so indomitably and by their faith in us who had, as yet, suffered nothing in this war. All we could do was swallow the lump in our throats and smile back at them, promising ourselves that yes, we would indeed do our damnedest to pay back the Germans, and manyfold at that, if it was in our power.

We were young and we were impressionable, and we hadn't been in Britain for very long. Yet I feel that any Canadian arriving in Britain at that time would have felt as we did, impressed to the point of awe by the uncomplaining, disciplined orderliness of the entire population. They were unified in their devotion to the war effort and in their determination to defeat the Nazis. Strict rationing governed the lives of every citizen, rich or poor, and included almost every material aspect of life; all food, all items of clothing, heating fuel, gasoline, cigarettes, liquor, even matches. Unquestionably, the individual ration, though indescribably small, was adequate provided that the householder was a wise manager, an astute shopper, a friend of the shopkeepers, and blessed with the patience of Job. Endless queues were often fruitless, yet taken with a smile and a touch of humour. They were part of the housewife's daily obligations. Even rationed items were not always available and most of them were limited to a few ounces per person on a daily or weekly basis. One could not be in wartime England without being overwhelmed by admiration for these courageous people who faced an implacable and seemingly superior foe with never a thought for capitulation. There were no displays of excessive patriotism, just a stoic determination to defeat Nazi Germany, regardless of the price to be paid.

Manpower throughout the nation had been mobilized for the war effort, the young and fit going to the forces, the older and the less fit to production. Almost all the males not in uniform had a secondary job in the home guard, the air raid emergency services – or in the garden allotments growing extra vegetables. But the threat of invasion had pushed the labour requirements beyond the capacity of the male population. The women of Britain were being brought out of the home. Many were already in the forces. The navy, army and air force all had women's divisions which were rapidly expanding to relieve more men for combat assignment. A Women's Land Army was being mobilized to move into farming operations which, though so vital to the economy, were losing labourers to the forces. Total mobilization of the female population was actually under consideration. The young and fit, unemployed women would be accorded the option of serving in the forces or the land army, or assignment to a job in the industrial war machine.

The tube ride back to Uxbridge was a solemn one. Both of us had been deeply moved by our experiences, and I for one was convinced that what we were doing was right, moral, and justified. And the sooner we could finish our training the better.

***

Our next visit to London was on a forty-eight hour pass. As might be expected, we made our way back to familiar grounds, Piccadilly Circus and the Devonshire Arms. Just before "Time, gentlemen, please," was sounded to warn the patrons to drink up before the pub closed for the night, Jack and I were given the nod to make our way upstairs to the saloon bar to await closing. When the rest of the patrons had dutifully departed, we found ourselves in a small party of pub staff, a few relatives, and one or two selected friends. It seemed that Mother, who ran the pub, held the occasional after-hours party for the staff and a few friends. Everyone put up ten shillings. Thereafter, drinks and snacks were on the house for as long as the party lasted.

It was a hilarious party, typical of wartime London, with much music, singing and dancing between drinks. The addition of the two newcomers to the group, both named Jack, created a little confusion to begin with. So, Mother decided that Jack Lister was to be Major, and I, Minor. Since I was also a neophyte drinker, there was some discussion as to what Minor should drink. Once again, Mother's opinion prevailed. She decided that my drink should be port and lemon. It had a pleasant taste, so I had no objection. Had I known at the time that it was the favourite drink of the London prostitutes, I might have felt otherwise. I guess there are times when ignorance is bliss; happily this was one.

When the party had run its cheerful course, it became obvious that Jack and I were expected to escort the saloon barmaid and her younger sister home, the barmaid with Jack and the sister with me. It was very late as we walked the girls to their home in the Kensington district. The dark streets were deserted and quiet. At that time the Germans were still bombarding London but, luckily for us, not on that particular night. The results of their bombings, however, were evident in spite of the darkness and the blackout. When we reached the building where the girls lived, we could see that most of the block had been levelled, and only recently. A parachute bomb with a delayed fuse had been dropped during a night attack. The resulting explosion at ground level the next day had simply flattened the entire area around the bomb site.

But none of this succeeded in dampening our spirits even slightly. When we reached the flat, we were expected to stay. There was no need for a second invitation. In no time at all we had paired off and disappeared into separate bedrooms. I have no idea how Jack made out that night, especially if nymphomania ran in that family. But I was far too busy to care. Thank the Good Lord I was young.

Our stay in Uxbridge came to an abrupt end after only a few days. As graduates from the BCATP, we had accumulated very few flying hours. Though we had achieved wings standard, we were not considered ready for operations. To bridge the gap between basic training and operational flying, RAF Training Command had established Operational Training Units (OTUs), manned them with operationally experienced instructors and equipped them with squadron type aircraft. Their role was to take the newly graduated air crew from wings standard to operational level on the aircraft they would be flying in their assigned squadrons. This relieved the operational commands from the training role, leaving them free to concentrate on the sole task of taking the war to the enemy. The U-boat campaign in the Atlantic had caused a slow-down in the flow of newly trained air crew and thus our arrival was an important one. There were spaces in the RAF OTUs waiting to be filled by us. The last of the Four Musketeers, Jack Lister and myself, were broken up. I was posted to a Bomber Command OTU at Abingdon in Oxfordshire, and Jack to an OTU in Coastal. The next time I saw Jack was to be last. He was posted missing on his first tour of operations. Still, there was a small party of us who travelled together that day from Uxbridge to Oxford, and then on to Abingdon. We were all strangers to the country, new to the RAF, green as grass, but anxious to face the challenges that lay ahead.

The train ride from Uxbridge was in itself an experience. Although we were far from home, we were far from being seasoned travellers. Besides, all of the signs had been removed from the roads and, in our case, from the railway stations, to deny the enemy even this bit of intelligence should he invade. Whatever success it might have had on an invader, it certainly had the desired effect on us. We never knew where we were at any given moment of that journey. We had to ask at every stop whether it was Oxford, where we had to change trains and where we had to be quick off the mark to race down to the baggage car to off-load our trunks before the train left again. Because of the manpower shortage, there were no porters to assist passengers and very few officials of any kind. We dreaded the thought of possibly losing our baggage even if we managed to get off at the right station. After what seemed like ages, we reached Abingdon safely, heavy baggage and all.

Just as we stepped out onto the railway platform, we were greeted by the roar of aircraft engines overhead. Looking up and ducking at the same time, we caught sight of a large, black, single-wing, twin-tail and twin-engine aircraft flashing across the narrow space between the platform roofs at quite a low level. We just stood and gawked. Someone in the group muttered, "What kind of an aircraft was that?" Before any of us had time to disclose his ignorance, a clear, piping child's voice said, with a distinctive English accent, "That's a Whitley, Mister." We thanked the little uniformed schoolboy standing alongside us, and at the same time thanked our lucky stars that we had been saved the embarrassment of publicizing our appalling lack of aircraft recognition.

Abingdon turned out to be a pre-war, permanent RAF station, a grass airfield in the lush, English countryside. The buildings were sturdy, grey brick structures laid out along a neat, formal pattern of tarmacked roads. I was assigned a room in one of these buildings that had served as a married quarter before the war and was now converted to officer accommodation for the influx of graduate air crew trainees. Another RCAF observer from western Canada, Bill Arnold, shared this room with me. He was about my own age, fair haired and slight, and he turned out to be a very friendly and compatible room-mate. Another RCAF observer, Jim Davies, was on the same OTU course as Bill and I, but not in the same flight. The familiar and faithful old Ansons would fly us on the first phase of OTU which was basically to familiarize us with flying in wartime Britain. We would be assigned to the larger, black, metal Whitleys for the final phase for operational qualification. In our innocence, the Whitleys loomed large and formidable, seemingly invincible. They were, without a doubt, the biggest and most warlike aircraft any of us had ever seen, and we looked forward, a little apprehensively perhaps, to the time when it would be our turn to be members of a Whitley crew.

One day while I was sorting out my odds and ends, I came across the Canadian change which had been in my pocket when we landed in Gurroch. Among the pieces were seven of the large Canadian beaver nickels. I strung them out on the dresser top in front of me and thought that they could be made into a chain that would fit around my wrist, a sort of identity bracelet, something to remind me of home. On my next visit to Oxford, I called into a jeweller's store and asked if this could be done. The jeweller was an elderly man who solemnly advised me that it was against the law to deface any coin of the realm. After saying this, though, he smiled and said he would see what he could do. With those encouraging words, I left the nickels with him, feeling quite confident that he would be able to do what I wanted. On my following visit, I called on him again and was pleased to find that he was as good as his promise. He had neatly soldered small silver rings to each of the coins and then used similar rings to join them together into a bracelet which fit my wrist perfectly. I put it on my right wrist while I stood in the shop and happily started wearing my personal bit of Canada. It became a kind of talisman that accompanied me throughout my time with the RAF.

My uniform allowance of $200 in Halifax hadn't stretched far enough during that forty-eight hour pass to provide me with a raincoat or a spare pair of black oxfords. Though the weather in England was not cold enough for a greatcoat, it was cold and wet enough to make it distinctly uncomfortable without any topcoat at all. And, in spite of the rainy time of year, umbrellas were taboo for officers in uniform! There was, therefore, a crying need for a raincoat. As soon as my finances permitted, I made a trip into Oxford and visited the Alkit Tailors. I had noticed that many of the RAF officers at OTU were wearing crepe soled black oxfords, commonly called "Brothel Creepers." These seemed a most sensible item in that climate, and they would never require soling or heeling. So, along with my raincoat, I purchased a pair of "Brothel Creepers" and a couple of Van Heusen shirts with separate collars. Although the shirts were well-tailored in excellent Egyptian cotton, their popularity in the RAF had, I am sure, more to do with the fact that one could change collars much more easily, and certainly more economically, than one could change into clean shirts. Spare collars and even spare cuffs simplified the laundry arrangements — shades of Dickens and his frugal Cratchit!

It wasn't very long before my purchases were put to the test. After an afternoon visit to Oxford and tea at the Miter Hotel, I returned to Abingdon on the country bus. Its route didn't actually go into Abingdon, but dropped us at the corner where the Abingdon road left the main road out of Oxford. We had learned to enjoy this walk back to the base through the superb countryside where the roads were lined with magnificent trees and the fields gloriously green and lush, boxed in by unbroken hedge rows. On this day, however, the surrounding beauty was not our preoccupation. By the time the bus dropped us off, the skies had literally opened up. It was raining heavily and incessantly. It would have been useless to try to take shelter under a tree; we would have been stuck there for the night. There was nothing for it but to strike out and head for the base as quickly as we could. Before we were half-way to the station gate, I was sure the rain was getting through my new raincoat. Either that, or it was running down my neck off my hat and soaking my collar and back. The shoes, however, seemed to be standing up to the rain and the pools of water on the road admirably, if you consider that water filling them and squishing out over them was admirable. It was really the water running down my legs into my shoes that was filling them and not the water on the road. They seemed to be perfectly watertight which made them fill up very nicely, thank you.

Chapter IX

The days and the nights at Abingdon were filled with the roar of aircraft engines as the OTU pressed on with the task of turning the freshly graduated air crew into qualified crews for Bomber Command. The constant noise became the norm for all of us. But, one night, Bill and I were suddenly aroused from sleep by the closeness of an engine roar, followed by the terrible rending sound of a crash that seemed to be right outside our bedroom window. Pulling on pants and sweaters, we dashed out to find what was left of one of the Whitleys piled against the married quarters right next to ours. The impact had compressed the front of the aircraft against the brick wall and flames were enveloping the rest of the fuselage even as we ran towards it. Oxygen bottles and .303 ammunition began exploding in all directions. There was no way to reach the crew, the only two Sikh pilots on the course and the RAF NCO wireless operator who was flying with them. From the appearance of the wreckage, it seemed unlikely they could have survived the crash and, if they had, the fire would have killed them for sure. So, Bill and I turned from the wreck and dashed into the building to see if anyone there needed assistance. We remained in the house helping the firemen control the fire and save the house from complete destruction. By the time we were finished, it was daylight. As we came out, we could not draw our eyes away from the sad, pitiful remains of what had been, to our previously naive eyes, a powerful and formidable war machine, now a pile of greyish white ash. It certainly removed any thought we might have had of the Whitley's invincibility.

My first flight from Abingdon was a shock. It was in an Anson with which I was at least familiar but, outside of that, everything else was completely foreign. To begin with, I had been given my first real Mercator's chart on which to plot my navigation. That in itself was strange enough, but, when I looked out of the aircraft after take-off, I was shattered. Back home, built-up areas of housing were relatively infrequent, well-separated and, therefore, easily identifiable. Roads and railways were equally few and far between and, therefore excellent sources of navigational data. In England, at least in the immediate Abingdon area, there was a veritable plethora of villages, towns, roads, and rail lines. It was no longer a case of looking for pinpoints upon which to base your navigation; it was a problem of sorting out the confusing mass of detail which presented itself to the airborne observer. To say that one had to make a major adjustment to flying in England was not simply stating the obvious, but rather being guilty of understating the obvious. We had our wings and had presumably earned them. Ahead of us, however, there remained a lot to learn.

We were still in the Anson phase of our course when we were detailed one morning to fly in a combined army/air force exercise. Our task was to simulate the air support element of a local Army defence force against an invader. We were required to fly at low level on daylight bombing operations using flour-filled bags which we were supposed to drop on the invading Army elements as directed by the ground defence forces. It was a break from the usual OTU routine and particularly enjoyed by the pilots who flew us on our training flights. Most of these men were experienced operational pilots on their non-operational rest tour. Authorized low flying and dropping even simulated bombs on mock ground forces were real breaks from chauffeuring student navigators around the skies of England. The weather was excellent and the prospects for the low-level flights were great.

When I landed after my part in the exercise, I found the flight staff in a tizzy. A report had been received from one of the participating army units that an Anson had crashed. At the time of our landing, the aircraft had not been identified except by type. The flight staff knew it had to be one of ours, but not which one. It was a depressing time for all of us as each craft landed, to be welcomed back and join the growing throng until only one was missing. It was the one in which my room-mate, Bill, was the observer. We learned later in the day that they had been flying a low-level attack on a road junction. They had followed one of the roads from the intersection up a hill, and were unable to avoid a high tension wire which crossed the road at the crest of the hill. They crashed after hitting it and all of the crew were killed on impact.

It was a sad time for the OTU staff as well as the students. The pilot had been a pre-war officer in the RAF with an excellent reputation and a pleasant personality. To make matters worse, his family lived in a nearby village and were well known by the OTU and station personnel. Bill, too, had been well-liked. He was a clean living young Canadian whose presence would be missed by many of our course members, not just by me. I felt it perhaps a little more than the others because he had been a friend and a room-mate too. It was my sad duty to escort Bill's body to the Brookfield Cemetery, south of London, and to be the attending officer at his burial. The official party was otherwise a disinterested group of RAF airmen whose wartime task this appeared to be on a full-time basis. And Brookfield was a very large cemetery with many airmen's graves. The presiding minister was a civilian Methodist, Bill's faith, but he had never known the young man he was burying and his service was devoid of personal feelings. All in all, it was a sombre, drab and sobering experience for me, one which I fervently prayed would not be repeated.

Flying at OTU may have been boring much of the time for the pilots, but the Luftwaffe managed to spice things up for them on numerous occasions by flying night intruder missions over the airfields and the lighted bombing ranges. They were always ready to pick off the unwary. I can recall my first night cross-country when I had no wish to become one of those unwary victims. I had never experienced such blackness. From the moment we took off and left the airfield behind, the blackout was total. It seemed as if the light over my navigational table and those reflecting from the flight instruments were the only specks of light in the universe. It was more like being shot into space than flying.

As we proceeded on course that night, making no visible progress other than the marks I was making on my navigational chart, I was alarmed to see an increasingly reddish glow on the horizon ahead. We seemed to be flying right for it. I was feeling strange enough on this, my first night flight in England. But the thought of flying into what I felt must be a city on fire, and the Luftwaffe who must also be there, just didn't seem wise. It was a dilemma for me. The further we flew on this course, the more apprehensive I became. But I was equally disinclined to sound an alarm when my pilot was operationally experienced and seemingly unconcerned. I just kept checking my navigation, biting my tongue, and keeping my options open. You cannot possibly imagine my relief when the red glow on the horizon became a full, rising moon! I think my relief was as much from having held my tongue as it was from not having to fly through a nest of Luftwaffe. The agony of shame and embarrassment would have been the harder to bear.

While I was still in Abingdon, I received a letter from the younger sister in London. Her words nagged at me incessantly until I could get a weekend pass. She had written only a short letter saying that she *must* see me, but with such urgency that fears of her possibly being pregnant weighed heavily on my mind. It was a very harassed young fellow who made the trip to London and a much relieved one who returned. The urgency had apparently been sexual, not what I had feared. That experience, though decidedly unpleasant for me at the time, was beneficial. I promised myself that there would be no such risks any more, and no more visits.

My stint at OTU came to a successful end in August. I had established a new record in OTU for bombing accuracy, so my attendance there did not pass unrecorded. It might, however, have been made more notable for another reason, and this time one that was more reprehensible. Our graduation happened to coincide with a major party in the Officers' Mess to which all the officers, their wives, and their girlfriends were invited. A bus load of young ladies from the displaced Air Ministry, billeted in Keble College, Oxford, to escape enemy bombings, was transported to the party to improve the male-to-female ratio. My graduation, my posting to 10 Bomber Squadron, the excitement of the party, and the presence of all those unattached young ladies combined to lead me into excess.

I abandoned my usual abstemious behaviour and dove in. By the end of the party, the young woman I had singled out earlier had already left in the bus without me, and I found myself in the Mess Manager's Office at the invitation of the NCO mess staff, male and female. They seemed to be well supplied with liquor and I can recall leaning against the office wall, a glass in hand, feeling quite privileged at being included in this select group. I had no idea how difficult it would be for me to stand up without the support of that wall. Suddenly, someone, probably the orderly officer, poked his head in the door and said, "Break it up. The CO's making the rounds!" My new-found friends, far more aware of the consequences than I, pushed me out of the office into the adjoining billiards room, towards a set of French doors which led into the garden. There, they left me to fend for myself. Without the support of the wall or friendly hands, I was unable to stand. In fact I must have been practically paralysed. I somehow managed to stumble through the French doors and out onto the lawn. I have no recollection of the events which followed, but can safely guess that I staggered and crawled through the garden and down the lane to my quarters, missing the CO by chance and good fortune.

When my batman, a World War I veteran, woke me the next morning with the usual cup of hot tea, he discreetly said nothing as he quietly picked up my muddy, creased uniform from the floor, and disappeared into his workroom to try to restore the uniform and the shoes to some semblance of military smartness. I was too young and fit to suffer from any obvious hangover, but that didn't make the rest of the day, or my final flying exercise, any easier to cope with. As I climbed down from the Whitley that morning, my feet never seemed to quite reach the ground. For the rest of the day, I felt as if there was still one more step down.

I had learned another lesson, and something else which I could profitably swear off for the future.

Chapter X

10 Squadron was in 4 Group of Bomber Command and was based at RAF Leeming in Yorkshire, the county of my forebears. Its aircraft were Armstrong Whitworth Whitley IIs which were powered by Rolls Royce Merlin engines. I had learned that 10 Squadron was more familiarly known as Shiny Ten, that it was a pre-war bomber squadron with an enviable reputation, and that its motto was "Rem Acu Tangere" (meaning?). The Leeming base itself was also pre-war. The design of its grass airfield and imposing brick buildings was the same as at Abingdon and, though the surrounding countryside was just as green, it was not as soft nor as gentle looking. Leeming stood in a rather broad valley, the Vale of York, which ran roughly north and south, with significantly higher land rising from it on both sides. The airfield was about forty-five miles inland from the sea.

I arrived in Leeming on August 30, 1941 and reported directly to the squadron adjutant in the squadron hangar offices. After registering my particulars, he took me in to meet the squadron commander, a W/C Bennett. It was not DCT Bennett of AFTERO, who was to turn up again, later in my life, but an RAF career officer of the same name. From his office I was taken to "B" Flight to which I had been assigned. There I met S/L Webster, the "B" flight commander, another RAF career officer. The timing was convenient, so S/L Webster accompanied me to the Officers' Mess where arrangements were made for a room. Then he took me into the anteroom where a number of men were lounging prior to tea. S/L Webster looked around the room until he spotted a dark-haired young pilot stretched languidly out in one of the standard dark green, padded leather chairs with which RAF Officers' Messes were equipped. When S/L Webster tapped him on the shoulder, the young man started out of his daydreaming and

jumped to his feet. This was my captain, P/O Godfrey. After our intro-ductions, Webster instructed Godfrey to complete my indoctrination as quickly as possible and to let him know when I was ready.

The next day, with Tom Godfrey's assistance, I was fitted and equipped with my parachute and harness and my flying clothes, and was assigned a locker in the flight room. Then I was taken to meet the squadron navigation officer, F/L Bagnald, and was issued a navi-gation kit that included a Mark IX A sextant, a current almanac, star tables, a wrist chronometer, parallel rulers, dividers, a protractor, a course setting computer, and a green satchel to hold them all. By the close of the day, my preparations were complete. The flight com-mander was so advised, and I found myself posted, with Godfrey, on the "B" Flight roster of operational crews. I was finally ready to begin the life for which I had been so strenuously preparing since my enrol-ment fourteen months earlier.

The following morning, September the second, we were assigned an aircraft for a night flying test (NFT) in preparation for a bombing

10 Sqn. aircrew in front of a Whitley. Self sixth from the right of second row.
Tom Godfrey tenth from the right in same row.

sortie. I met the rest of our crew: a Canadian sergeant, Jimmie, the wireless operator; a New Zealand sergeant, the tail gunner; and a Scottish sergeant, the co-pilot. Our captain, P/O Godfrey, was the crew's most experienced member. He was on his fourth trip, but his first as captain of an aircraft. His previous three trips had been as co-pilot with another experienced crew as preparation for his role as captain of his own bomber. The average age of our crew was 20.

So much had happened in the two days since my arrival on the squadron that I must have been saturated with new experiences. I moved in a sort of automated daze as we prepared for our first operation as a crew, and for my first-ever flight over enemy territory. We flew the NFT that morning and found the aircraft to be serviceable. In the afternoon, while the craft was being refuelled and armed, we attended the operational briefing. As a new crew on our first sortie, we were given what was known as a Nursery Target, one which was within reasonable range, on or near the coast, and which required only a brief penetration of enemy defences. It seemed a reasonable and sensible method of breaking in a new crew to actual combat conditions with minimal risk yet not wasteful of ammunition or fuel. Our target that night was the port facilities of Ostend.

The briefing team included the squadron commander, the station intelligence officer, F/L Shepherd, the station navigation officer, F/L Buchan, the station meteorological officer and our squadron bombing and gunnery leaders. As a crew, we sat and listened in silent concentration to the target location and intelligence, the route there and back, the estimated locations of enemy defences along our routes, the timing of the attack, the forecast wind speeds and directions at various altitudes and the cloud conditions en route to and in the target area. We didn't dare miss a single word. When the question period came, we hadn't a single question among us. We broke up after the briefing and the observers gathered in the navigation plotting room for the detailed task of making their flight plans.

It was there the observers prepared their navigation charts, marked the target, laid out the route, measured the tracks and distances, and calculated the flight plan based on the meteorological forecast. There were remarkably few navigational aids available to observers in those days to supplement the dead reckoning (DR) form of navigation. Black-outs over both friendly and enemy territories made visual observations rare, unpredictable and therefore unreliable for planning purposes. Astronomical sights were more often than not precluded by weather and limited by operational conditions over enemy territory even if the weather was amenable. And though I was familiar with the use of radio bearings, the same blackouts that denied us visual sightings also applied to radio transmissions. During hostilities, radio signals were silenced to prevent the enemy from using them as navigational aids. It was, of course, a double-edged sword; denying them to the enemy denied them to us, even in our own territory. To be of practical value, radio bearings have to be obtained from a known, precise location before they can be translated to a map or chart reference. A bearing of unknown origin was of little value, unless, in desperation, you wished to home in on it, regardless of where it led you.

With these thoughts in mind, I was, therefore, at a loss to understand what the other observers were doing as they passed a stiff sheet of perspex from one to the other, using it in turn to mark their navigation charts. I was the only newcomer in the group and it was fortunate for me that the squadron navigation officer was there to notice my consternation. He explained that the perspex sheet was a master locator sheet which, when placed on the correct latitude and longitude intersection of our Mercator plotting chart, pinpointed the locations of three transmitters in each of the three groups of radio beacons located in England. Each group of transmitters broadcast a signal on the same frequency, but only one at a time, on an unpredictable rotational basis for short intervals. With the fixed position of each site pre-plotted and a destructible (edible) flimsy sheet showing which station in each of the three groups was transmitting at any particular time during the flight, it was theoretically possible to convert any of the loop bearings you might receive from them into accurate bearings. Thus, if atmospherics and the radio receiver in the aircraft co-operated, it would be possible to fix the position of your aircraft by a combination of intersecting position lines obtained from the loop bearings. In actual fact, however, as I was to find out for myself, the reliable range of these loop bearings rarely extended beyond the British shores, and even then, only at the best of times. Accurate loop bearings were in direct disproportion to the range of the bearing and, over enemy territory, were simply not available.

With that very valuable assist from the squadron navigation officer, it was not long before my log and chart were ready. The track to and from the target was plotted, the courses and magnetic variations measured, ground speeds and timings calculated, and the transmitter sights plotted. My flight plan for the trip to Ostend was completed as carefully as my training and skill could accomplish. I route-marked the topographical maps and placed them in chronological order just in case visual observation became possible at some stage in the flight. I had studied the large-scale, specially coloured map of the target and memorized it for the bombing run. Later on, when we were in the aircraft, it would be placed alongside the bomb-sight where I could see it during the bombing run and direct the pilot to the desired aiming point. My preparations seemed to be complete. It was time to return to the mess for a rest before our pre-operational meal and final flight preparations.

Throughout our entire training as observers, the need for accuracy had been pounded into us. Time after time, our instructors had utilized every opportunity to impress this upon us, pointing out how our life and those of our fellow crew members would depend on the accuracy of our navigation. Accuracy and reliability had become my guiding principles. The time had come to put those principles and myself to the test. Would I be able to get us to Ostend? Would I locate and bomb the aiming point? The thought of penetrating enemy air space and the prospect of encountering enemy defences created no feeling of concern in me at all. First I had to find the place. The rest would take care of itself with no worry on my part.

Those pre-operational and post-operational meals became very much of a pattern in Bomber Command as well as being somewhat of a privilege. In the tightly-rationed wartime economy, food had assumed a place of considerable importance in everyone's mind. Eggs were a rationed rarity and yet the practice of providing a fried egg meal for every air crew member before and after each operation was religiously preserved throughout the war. In fact, it was so much a part of the pattern to which the crews became accustomed that it became a ritual. To have broken with this pattern might have had serious repercussions because of the superstitious and fatalistic attitude which seemed to become an integral part of each airman's character the longer he survived in that lonely and costly form of warfare. It was at the post-operational meals, in the early morning hours when you were tired, if not emotionally exhausted, when your defences were eroded, that the absence of those who failed to return was talked about. Only briefly, even then, and never again.

After Tom and I had eaten at my first of those meals, we walked to the hangar where we joined up with the rest of the crew and put on our white roll-necked flying sweaters, long, white wool stockings and flying boots. Next, we had to pull on our parachute harness, which contained a Mae West, and zip up. I gathered my parachute pack, my sextant and my navigation bag, and off we went in the lorry to the dispersal point where our aircraft and ground crew waited. The pilots did a quick external visual check while the rest of us clambered into the craft to verify our own equipment such as the radio, the astrograph, the bomb-sight, the gun turrets etc. Since the aircraft had been compass-swung without a bomb load, there was always a possibility that the bombs could make a difference in the measured compass deviation. Therefore, once the engines had been started, and before it was time to taxi out for take-off, I de-planed and set up a hand-held compass while Tom manoeuvred the aircraft onto the outbound headings of our flight plan. I took the readings on each of the planned flight headings to compare with the compass correction card for any changes in deviation which might have been introduced by the bomb load. Then I scampered back into the aircraft and we taxied out for take-off.

Down the flare path we lumbered. As the tail lifted, we began to swing from the effect of propeller torque at full power. Things began to look a bit dicey. But, with some judicious rudder application and a lot of muscle, Tom had the swing corrected before it became really hazardous. Although it was only a minor lesson, I decided that, for future take-offs, it would be wise for me to keep my attention on the navigation table until we had cleared the ground; I felt it would be considerably less wearing on my nerves. As was the general practice in those days, we made a climbing circuit of the airfield before setting course. At last we were on our way, ten bombers of which one would be lost that night, climbing through the darkness towards Ostend.

As I mentioned earlier, the Whitley was a pre-war RAF bomber. It was originally powered by two air-cooled engines which had been replaced in the later Mark II version by the more powerful Rolls Royce Merlin, liquid-cooled, engines. At that same time, an astrodome had been incorporated into the fuselage above the observer's plotting table. The aircraft was long and slender, somewhat box-like in form, without much taper from its nose to the large, sturdy twin rudders of its tail. The main spar of the single wing ran across the fuselage behind the crew compartment like a huge, boxed girder over which we had to climb to reach the emergency hatch, the flare chute and the tail turret. The hydraulically-powered tail turret mounted four belt-fed Browning .303 machine guns. Above the bombing panel, in the nose of the aircraft, was the front turret which was also hydraulically powered, but mounted only one drum-fed, gas-driven, Vickers .303 machine gun. Each drum contained fifty cartridges and had to be changed by hand.

To all appearances, the take-off of the Whitley defied logic. It looked like a bloodhound on the trail, tail up and nose down sniffing the ground. Take-off speed was eighty-four miles per hour and initial climbing speed to altitude with a bomb load was only ten miles per hour faster. Cruising speed, if and when you reached operational altitude, was one hundred and ten. Many crews were beginning to operate at higher and higher altitudes, so oxygen was available at each crew station. But we found the gear to be cumbersome and restrictive, and the additional altitude further complicated pinpointing and identifying the target. So, we persisted in operating within the ten thousand foot ceiling and thus avoided using the oxygen equipment. For all its awkward appearance, the Whitley carried a maximum four thousand pound bomb load and, even fully loaded, could fly for eleven plus hours.

The feelings I had on that first flight into enemy territory left no room for fear. My excitement was intense, but my greatest concern was for my personal objective — that of navigating to and bombing the assigned target. I was so absorbed with the many details of the task at hand that the fear of encountering enemy action simply never entered my consciousness. It was therefore with nothing but feelings of exultation and relief, as I lay in the nose of the aircraft looking down through the bombing panel at Ostend, that I could say, "Target ahead. Open bomb doors. Left. Left. Steady," while the docks slid smoothly down the drift wires of the bombsight. Then again, "Steady, steady." When the aiming point reached the release spots on the drift wires, I pressed the bomb release, "Bombs away!" and, after checking that all the bombs had gone, I heard my own voice say "Close bomb doors, turn on course for home."

The play of the searchlights and the colourful hosing of light and medium anti-aircraft fire as they searched for us in the night sky had been registering in my subconscious during the run on the target, but they hadn't seemed threatening, even when the traces of the shells appeared to be curling over our wing tips. Once we were on the course for home though, the flak did seem to become more of a threat and a good cause to worry. However, just as had been planned in this Nursery Target assignment, our exposure to enemy fire had not been prolonged. We could settle onto our course for home with happy hearts knowing we had found and bombed the primary objective.

Although we didn't realize it then, this was to be our one and only Nursery Target. The pressure of the bomber offensive, and perhaps the success of our effort at Ostend, had moved us out of the "Nursery" class into the main force.

Chapter XI

Because of the high standard of navigation training being provided in Canada, and particularly because of the Astro Navigation Course we had been fortunate enough to receive, the RCAF observers were in popular demand among the RAF crews. This, and the fact that I was the only RCAF officer at Leeming, may have helped to account for my sudden propulsion into operations and to our permanent crew status in the squadron Order of Battle. When I looked back, it seemed incredible that I was crewed up and operating on what turned out to be a regular basis within three days of reporting to the squadron.

In the following few days we had the time to consolidate our new crew status and rehearse our emergency crew drills. On September 6th, we were alerted for a NFT and advised that we would be on operations that night. This time it wasn't so strange; we had been through it once before! The target was a synthetic rubber factory located in Germany at a place called Huls. According to the briefing, it was a strategic target upon which a very high priority had been placed. The task, however, was not a simple one. Huls was a very small community and the plant was not within the town itself, but in a nearby rural location. It was well-camouflaged and not close to any significant body of water which might have made visual identification a little easier in the faint light of a clear night. It was also well within the borders of Germany, which would make navigation more difficult because of the imprecise meteorological information available from within that country. We would also be subjected to enemy defences for a much longer period. This would be a severe test of the Bomber Command crews and their observers who would have to navigate perfectly and aim the bombs at the right target.

I was keyed up to a high pitch during that briefing. The squadron commander and the intelligence officer impressed upon us the importance of the target and the factory's vital role in Germany's war effort. The very idea of participating so directly, and possibly so effectively, in the war against Germany was exciting and stimulating. It was a bit like being put into the starting line-up of an important game for the first time, an honour and a pleasure yes, but also an imposing responsibility. We had been trained and equipped at great expense and effort; it was time to repay some of that investment.

We took off that night, again with that threat of an uncontrolled swing as full power was applied. This time, I kept my head down and my full attention on my navigation plot. Once airborne, we made our circuit over the airfield and set course into the night, for Germany and Huls. I worked hard and steadily, using all of the limited means available to keep us on course for that important factory secreted deep within the darkened German landscape. The weather cooperated and I was able to incorporate some astro observations in my navigation. As we came off the North Sea into Germany, I felt confident that we were right on track for Huls. There was little of an identifiable nature to be seen on the dark earth beneath us. Ten minutes before our estimated time over target, I crawled forward to the bombing panel in the nose to set up the bomb-sight and, letting my eyes adjust to the darkness and night vision, I began studying the ground for any recognizable feature.

When we reached our time over target, there was not a break in the dark mass beneath. The area seemed to be wooded, but the indistinct shape gave no clue to its location. I was able to pick up, dimly, what appeared to be a railway line and to follow it to a small marshalling yard not far away. This correlated reasonably well with the target map on which a similar line served the factory we were looking for. I was convinced we were in the target area, so we carried out a square search using the railway for our point of reference. We wanted so badly to see that factory. But no matter how hard we looked, no matter how long we stared down into the blackness, we could see nothing else. At the end of the time I had allowed for searching, we were no further ahead, other than being convinced that we would never see the target. Where I felt sure the factory must be was just an impenetrable void. I agonized over our inability to identify the target visually, but we had to break off the search if we were to preserve enough fuel for the return flight. We flew back to the railway line as I reset the bomb-sight and made our attack on the marshalling yard. It seemed reasonable to assume that we would cause more damage to their production system by disabling their transportation than by dropping our bombs blindly in what we thought was the general area of the factory. We made a good run, dropped our bombs with the usual patter, and watched them explode right on target in the marshalling yard.

On our return flight, we were more absorbed in rehashing our decision to attack the marshalling yard than in our journey through German air defences. We were a worried crew all the way home and not at all happy with our failure to attack the primary target. My navigation home helped to reassure me that we had been in the target area. This raised my spirits somewhat until we reached the debriefing room later that night. We could not help but overhear some of the reports of earlier crews which reflected a far more successful and more colourful operation than we had to report. It was even worse when we awakened later in the day to news reports of a highly effective air attack on the Huls factory. Crews were quoted as seeing brilliantly-coloured explosions and columns of smoke rising thousands of feet in the air. Tom and I felt like crawling under the mess furniture. If all that had taken place at Huls, where in heaven had we been? If we were no longer certain of where we might have been, we felt quite sure about where we would be, shortly — on the carpet in front of the CO!

When we finally reported to the squadron offices that afternoon, nothing was said about the attack on Huls. Certainly not by us. Later in the day though, all air crews were ordered to report to the station theatre immediately. Though there was a lot of chatter, everyone was at a loss to understand why we had been assembled. There was plenty of speculation as one might imagine. Suddenly, all the rustling and talking ceased. We were called to attention for the station commander, G/C Staton, an impressive and highly decorated fighter pilot of World War I, who had also flown Whitleys over Germany in the first raids of World War II. The CO was a big man, known as Bull rather than Bill Staton, and as he climbed onto the stage he was obviously incensed. In terse and bitter tones he told us that the Photo Reconnaissance Unit (PRU) aircraft had been out at first light to photograph the results of the attack on Huls. Copies of their photos had been sent to every station in Bomber Command. The reason for his anger became all too evident when the photographs were distributed to us. They showed the factory clearly. No damage at all had been done to it. In fact, not a single bomb crater could be seen in any of the photos. Eighty-six aircraft had attacked that night, seven had been lost, and all to no purpose.

Our failure to destroy or even damage the Huls factory was bad enough, but the glowing reports which had been made by some of the crews, and which had been joyfully reported by the press that very morning, were acutely embarrassing for those at the highest levels. It was a shockingly rude exposure of the ineffectiveness of Bomber Command. The air crews, and in particular those who had taken part in the Huls raid, were dismayed. They could not credit what the photographs irrefutably proved. It was a very quiet and chagrined group of airmen who sat in the theatre that afternoon after their CO stomped angrily off the stage.

One must appreciate that, at that time, Bomber Command was technologically a crude weapon. It was in a rudimentary stage of development, still utilizing weaponry and techniques from the First World War. It was also a relatively small force in size and numbers for the task which was being laid upon it. Fifty bombers carrying approximately two tons of bombs each, directed at a single target, was considered a major attack for the command. For the individual crews, each mission consisted of almost insurmountable tasks, without taking into account the enemy's defences: first, to navigate at night to targets deep within the European land mass over blacked-out alien territory in unpredictable weather conditions; second, to locate and visually identify the specific assigned target; third, to drop the bombs accurately while under attack by enemy defences; and finally, to bring their aircraft and crew safely back to base. If the meteorological forecast was grossly in error, and one must recall that weather reporting stations were few and far between and virtually non-existent within Europe itself, then even this small force could be dissipated over a large area wide of the target itself. The attack on Huls was a clear demonstration of the difficulties facing Bomber Command. If these problems could not be overcome, they would, at best, result in a reduction of the priority accorded to this singularly offensive weapon. At worst, they might even ground the command. Although we at the squadron level were in no position to appreciate the political gravity of the situation created by the debacle at Huls, we were certainly able to appreciate the violent temper it had provoked in our CO.

Despite the discomfiture of the crews sitting around us, and the disgrace which had befallen our command, my crew and I could not help feeling relieved. We had been vindicated in a way and some of our confidence was restored. So, it wasn't an entirely downcast squadron of airmen who left the theatre that day. At least one crew had glimpsed a silver lining in that horribly dark cloud that hung over Bomber Command.

Because of inclement weather at base or over target areas, we had a few days respite. There was still plenty to keep a new crew busy. We needed repeated and persistent drills to eliminate our lack of familiarity with equipment and procedures. If and when required, these would make the difference between life and death or between a bed back in the mess and a bunk in a POW camp. We spent as much time together as a crew as possible and, since Tom and I were the only officers in our crew, we were together almost all of the time. It didn't take long for us to develop a close comradeship and an instinctive rapport. From the very beginning of our relationship, we were a good crew and shared the same determination to achieve high standards. We trusted each other to do his part regardless of the risks.

On the 11th of September we flew another NFT to prepare for a raid. This time the target was Warnemunde, a port on the Baltic not far from Rostok. The route provided a long leg over the North Sea and thus, a good base for navigating the relatively shallow penetration of the European land mass. Major changes in meteorological conditions occurred most frequently at the coast, so the deeper the penetration inland, the greater the risk of navigational inaccuracy. With Warne-munde, we would be running much less chance of erratic navigation within the attack force and stood to increase our accuracy and concentration. Because of the proximity of the coastline to our target, we would have more opportunities for pinpoints in the immediate vicinity, provided, of course, there were breaks in the cloud cover when we arrived.

Like most of the thirty-two Whitleys that night, we had no difficulty reaching the target area. We were fortunate enough to avoid most of the heavily defended areas on route by staying to the north of the track and remaining over water as much as possible. To deliver our attack though, we had no alternative but to fly through the belts of searchlights and anti-aircraft defences which surrounded the port. At our height, the anti-aircraft firing was intense and once again vividly colourful. The streams of light and medium flak gushed up around us. You see the tracers reach up for you, curl off at the peak of their trajectory and fall back in a seemingly harmless sort of fireworks display. Harmless, that is, if you weren't in their way. We had seen the evidence of this "harmless" stuff in one of the maintenance hangars where the squadron commander's Whitley was being repaired after a raid. There were more than fifty separate holes in the fuselage and tail! Fortunately, nothing vital had been hit by any of the shells. If a little worse for the wear, at least they had made it home. On the Warnemunde attack, one of the Whitleys wasn't so lucky; it didn't come back.

It was on the next trip, on the 29th, that we began to build a reputation. The need for prompt intelligence and an accurate assessment of attacks was the primary reason for the debriefing of crews immediately on their return from an operation. These debriefings were done individually, crew by crew, by an officer of the station intelligence staff. Though these officers were becoming quite adept at their job, they badly needed confirmed data to rationalize the differing reports being obtained verbally from the individual crews. On this particular night, our aircraft had been fitted with a camera specially rigged for night aerial photography and with a stock of photo flashes. I had been briefed on the operation of the camera which was controlled from the bombing position and on the use of the flashes which would have to be launched from the flare chute aft in the fuselage, near the escape hatch. The object was to photograph the target during the attack, ideally while the bombs were exploding. During the day, I worked out a procedure with the wireless operator who would be otherwise unoccupied during the bombing run. He would be positioned at the flare chute with a flash in hand, ready to pull the safety pin of the flash and launch it on my command, a calculated number of seconds after I had dropped the bombs. The exact number of seconds would depend on our height over the target when the bombs were released.

Our objective was Stettin, an inland port on the German-Polish border. It was an important raid for those days, comprising one hundred and thirty-nine aircraft of which sixteen were the new four-engined bombers. It was also a long trip and difficult for the navigators since it required deep penetration into Europe, far from any coastal pinpoints. Again, though, by using a northerly track over the long North Sea leg, navigation was easier and we avoided enemy defences. It took us close to five hours to reach the target area which left us with a strictly limited time in which to search. In what little light there was, the water reflections seemed to confirm our DR position. I had been at my bombing station long enough to set up the sight and adjust my eyes to the darkness. With everything ready, I steered Tom onto the attack heading towards what I could dimly perceive to be dock installations. After "Bombs away," I held Tom steady on the attack heading, timed myself for the fall of the bombs, and called for the photoflash to be dropped. There were further seconds of straight and level flight as the bombs completed their descent and as the flash exploded into light a safe distance below us. I triggered the camera for a second time, closing the lens on whatever picture we had taken. Like a scalded cat, or more appropriately, a lumbering elephant, we finally broke away from what seemed like an interminably long, straight, and level flight over the target. The defences had not appeared to be that violent, but the longer we held our aircraft straight and level, the more threatening the searchlights and flak became. The urge to break into evasive action had been strong. The flight back was a long, lonely, nerve-tingling trip which terminated ten hours and twenty minutes after take-off. During that return leg, we had plenty of time to wonder at the wisdom of bringing back a photograph which would prove beyond a doubt whether or not we had successfully reached and attacked Stettin.

By the time we shut down our engines at dispersal, members of the photo section were already waiting for us along with the aircraft ground servicing crew. Even as we climbed down through the hatch and gave our "Aircraft serviceable" report to the flight sergeant, the photo technicians were removing the film from the camera. We changed out of our flight gear to go to debriefing; they rushed to develop the film.

During the debriefing, we mentioned our attempt at photography. The intelligence officer immediately called the photo section who confirmed that they had a photo under development and requested us to wait to see the results. He might have something else to discuss with us before closing his report.

Although we did not wait long, the other crews finished and left for the mess before we were joined by the rest of the intelligence staff on duty that night. All of them were excited at the prospect of some hard evidence to back up the verbal reports. Meanwhile, we were beginning to feel more than a little apprehensive at just how important that photo might or might not be. If it was good, it would serve admirably to confirm and corroborate the squadron's operational reports. It could also serve to confirm the opposite. The group was in high spirits, laughing, chatting, smoking; I was beginning to feel the pressure. Hard evidence it might be, but of what? And the burden of proving what we had or had not done that night seemed to fall squarely on my shoulders, on only my fourth sortie with the squadron. My confidence in my navigation had been growing, but would it stand up to this latest test?

When the door of the debriefing room finally opened and the sergeant from the photo section entered, the tension was palpable. One look at his face, though, and we all relaxed. He was grinning from ear to ear as he placed the still-damp print on the table in front of us. There, near the centre of the photo, were a number of fuel storage tanks and other details which could be clearly identified. There were no dock installations though, and no bomb bursts visible. We must have banked slightly or started our turn a little early in the explosion of the photo flash. There was no doubt, however, that we had indeed attacked Stettin and dropped our bombs on the target area. We were a highly elated crew as we left for the mess, and an equally elated group of intelligence officers stayed behind to complete their reports. They had more confidence that morning than they had felt for some time, especially since the debacle at Huls. Our spirits might have been dampened if we had known then that eight of our bombers had been lost, half of them our own Whitleys.

Although we had no inkling of it, nor would it have made any difference had we known, the reputation of our crew was now firmly established within the intelligence staff if not within the squadron. The frankness of our report on the Huls attack had established our honesty and integrity. Now our proven success at Stettin had established our perseverance and technical skill. Although the success of Bomber Command in later years still depended on crew integrity and perseverance in the face of increasing enemy resistance, there is no question that any success in those early raids hinged almost entirely upon the individual crew skills, their initiative and tenacity, and, in particular, on the skill of the observer. His ability in primitive conditions to navigate to the target area, visually locate, identify, and bomb accurately, and then navigate the aircraft safely back to base, was vital. In light of the rudimentary aids which were available to him, this would have been a daunting challenge had it not been for the foolhardy youthfulness of those who had to face it and take it in stride.

Chapter XII

It was at about this time that we were issued RAF battledress. We no longer had to fly in our tailored uniforms! This was a considerable relief to the pocketbook, particularly for a young RCAF pilot officer who was drawing the same low rate of pay as the RAF. The fabric of the battledress was much coarser than that of the tailored barathea uniform and a little less comfortable for that reason. However, it was much harder-wearing and styled for greater comfort both working and flying. Not the least of its attractions was the fact that it was a free issue from stores. Since it was a break in tradition, the battledress was received into the force with the expected reservations, and restrictions on its use were quite arbitrary in the early days. If an officer was not required for flying duty, he had to change from battledress into uniform after tea break. Only officers on night duty were permitted to dine in battledress and this rule was strictly enforced by all the senior and duty officers from the station commander down.

Our Mess was staffed by airmen who, except for some of the senior NCOs, were wartime recruits. One of the dining room attendants was obviously a homosexual though this in no way affected the conduct of his du-

In newly issued battle dress at Leeming.

ties. He was, in fact, an exemplary member of the mess staff. At this particular time, the bombing leader on the squadron was a RAF officer of apparently good family, but whose style of living was somewhat debauched. His nickname was "Steve the Stoat," in reference to his arduous pursuit of the female species. One Sunday morning, Clancy, the attendant, was standing behind the hot table serving the officers as they made their selections. He kept his head well down, not looking up as the officers trooped by him. Steve the Stoat, who probably had some prior knowledge, would not let this pass unnoticed. He told Clancy to lift his head while he was serving him. As soon as Clancy did so, the reason for his unusual behaviour became all too apparent. He had two splendid black eyes. Steve immediately broke into laughter and brayed, "Oh, no, Clancy, picked yourself a tartar this time did you?" Not to be outdone or publicly humiliated, Clancy drew himself up to the maximum of his short stature and retorted in his clear lisping tones, "People who live in glass houses shouldn't throw stones . . . Sir."

Although we had no WAAF contingent on our base at this stage of the war, we did have two female officers in the intelligence section. They seemed to be respected by their section. Of course, as the only two attractive young women on the base, they were extremely popular with the air crew, and particularly with some of the Canadian NCOs. Whether it was justified, or simply a matter of wishful thinking, I will never know, but the squadron members referred to these young ladies as "SEMO" and "MOPA," the intelligence acronyms for targets defined as "Some Enemy Military Objective," and "Military Objective Previously Attacked." Such witticisms abound in wartime, frequently satirical but often times brutally honest.

Life on squadron was primarily male-dominated: self-centred, instinctively protective, with the crew supplanting the family. Life was passing by so quickly for so many of the flyers that there was no time for subterfuge, and little if any time for compassion or concern for others. It was a time for donning the armour of untouchability: the ability to witness death and disaster around about you without letting it get to you. It was a time for developing the additional armour of invincibility and immortality: the knowledge that, no matter how many other crews might be lost, yours would be the exception. In such an atmosphere, the thought that one might be less than justified in pinning labels on people had no chance of being conceived, let alone surviving one's conscience. We weren't malicious; we just didn't have room in our psyche for the niceties of life.

On squadron, operational life became quickly, if not immediately, totally absorbing. There was, of course, time to write home, but somehow even this contact with the "other" life seemed fleeting and tenuous. It failed to break into our obsession with duty. The only thing that mattered was the war and, if one were to be brutally frank, just one's own part in that war — the bombing of enemy targets. It was never referred to in those words by the airmen, and it seldom reflected any personal vendettas. You just went on operations, or Ops as they said in Bomber Command. When the US Army Air Corps became involved, they used the term missions. But the RAF expression seemed to me to impart the more correct meaning. The attitude of the RAF bomber crews was more analogous to surgery and operations than to religion and missions. Ours was an intense and dedicated application of skill and technique rather than an emotional or psychological issue. There was also a certain remoteness in the dedication of an airman, perhaps an instinctive safeguard against personal involvement in the mass slaughter which he might be perpetrating. However, the weakness in the surgical analogy was a vital one: the airman who failed in the application of his skills and technique didn't lose a patient, he lost his own life.

The airman's world was the airfield from which he flew. At times, this shrank even further to the compartment of your aircraft as the black of the night swallowed you and as the chart upon which you laboured became the centre of your focus and the very reason for your being. Life on squadron was very much like being a member of a club, and a very exclusive one at that. Only those who shared the experience could be members. There was, therefore, no need to talk about the experiences. Since they were mutually shared, conversation, though spirited at times, was non-involved and mainly technical, if flying was talked about at all. Sentiment was denied, and a shell of protective indifference slowly developed around the individual's emotional core. This armour became more vital to the survival of operational air crew than any protective armour in his aircraft. The insidious and deleterious effects of the loss of squadron mates, night after night, had to be resisted. The only way to accomplish this was to refuse to become emotionally involved with anyone. Such a philosophy may seem unduly harsh and perhaps even unattainable. It was, however, the philosophy of survival and it seemed to be instinctive in the young veterans of Bomber Command.

For some, this protective insulation became strongly cynical in nature. It was occasionally brutally displayed by a few veteran members of the squadron callously greeting a suspect newcomer with "Welcome. Enjoy it while you can. You won't last long," particularly if he had arrived after serving in some training unit where he gained time and rank under less trying circumstances. Such attitudes were sometimes spurred by bitterness when NCOs, who had been flying operationally for some time, saw the newcomers arrive with commissioned rank and seniority but no operational experience. These occasions were relatively rare and universally unpopular. But unfortunately, the odds were more often than not in favour of such a black forecast. It made welcomes like these very demoralizing when they were allowed to proliferate.

As happens in all such exclusive activities, the operational air crew developed a jargon of its own. You know already that a bombing raid was an "operation." An early return was an "abort." A crash was a "prang" while a crash landing in the water was "dunking in the drink." To be killed was to "go for a Burton," so named for the first RAF casualty of the war. A colourful and successful raid was a "wizard prang." An operation which was relatively easy, or one which might be sarcastically referred to as such *after* it had been carried out, was a "piece of cake." "Stooging" described the time spent searching for visual identification of the target. It was surprising how much action could be so succinctly described within the club without having to resort to any emotional or descriptive language. It probably reflected the airman's sense of exclusivity, his remoteness from the rest of society, and his armour against emotional inroads.

One could always pick out the observers in the mess without even looking at their brevet. It was customary for everyone in the mess to listen to the daily BBC news broadcast at 1300 hours. For the observers, this was even more of a ritual than for any other officer. As the pips of the time signal sounded on the air just before the news, you would see all of the observers shoot back their cuffs to count off the seconds to the start of the long dash which signified precisely 1300. This provided them with a daily check of their chronometers to ensure accuracy in the timing of any astro observations they might have to make. To me, those pips were as important as the V for Victory signal of the BBC was to occupied Europe. To this day, I can never hear the time signal without instinctively shooting back my cuff to check my watch.

Chapter XIII

On the 1st of October, our crew was one of thirty-one Whitleys and Wellingtons briefed for an attack on Stuttgart, a large city in south-west Germany, well inside the European land mass. The route took us from Yorkshire diagonally across the North Sea, through the heavy coastal defences, over occupied Europe, and into Germany. We were engaged by searchlights for prolonged periods and subjected to heavy anti-aircraft fire as we penetrated the static defence belts which lay between us and the target. Whether their marksmanship was sharper or our evasive actions weren't as effective, is hard to say. We were hit a number of times, but never, it seemed, in a crippling spot.

Navigation had been fairly straightforward until we reached the defence belts. It was a moonless night and we were sandwiched between layers of broken cloud. To penetrate these defences, we had to fly irregular patterns for long intervals to prevent accurate predictions of our flight path. We varied height, speed, and heading on a frequent but what we hoped was an unpredictable basis. Our aim was to break up the concentrations of searchlights and anti-aircraft fire which might be targeted on us and to make it more difficult for the ground radars to guide any night-fighters to an intercept. This kind of flying, at which we were by no means expert, was a necessary evil in that it added yet another element of uncertainty to the already difficult task of navigation within enemy territory. The further we had to penetrate after crossing the enemy coast, the greater the risk of straying from the desired track and the less the chance of finding the target.

When we finally arrived in the area of Stuttgart, at least according to my navigation, we could see nothing in the blackness beneath. Nor could we see any activity which would have indicated a target under attack. We conducted a systematic and prolonged square search, without success. There was simply no target to be seen and therefore no target to be attacked. So, in accordance with standing orders, and in spite of the fact we were in enemy territory, we did not drop our bombs blindly. We turned and headed for home. Our return flight had to be calculated, theoretically anyway, from Stuttgart, despite the fact that we had been unable to locate it. I was able to shoot a few quick astro sights on Polaris on the way back, which should have provided us with at least a latitude check. The results of these shots, however, seemed erratic when compared with my dead reckoning. These results might have been expected in the operational conditions in which the shots were taken. Regardless of these inhibiting aspects, they did seem to indicate a more southerly position than should have been the case. With the number of variables involved and the fact that we had begun our return flight from a questionable location, this evidence was still very little to work with. At least I could make an allowance for a probable southerly error while preparing myself for adjustments when further evidence might become available.

It was a worrying time and was made more so by the helplessness of not being able to do anything about it. When we finally reached the enemy coast and obtained some visual sightings, we knew we were far to the south of track. The wind must have strengthened and veered drastically after we crossed into Europe. Throughout the flight over enemy territory, when we were unable to obtain any current navigational data, I had been using an adjusted forecast wind direction and velocity based on data we received earlier, over England and the North Sea. This had obviously been in error and we had flown steadily further and further south of track on the way to and from the target and even on our square search.

As soon as we had, supposedly, reached Stuttgart, I had calculated the maximum time available for searching before we would have to break off for home. Because of the trouble we encountered in the target search, we had, in fact, stretched our time beyond this safe margin before abandoning the operation. When we found ourselves so far south of track and behind in our expected time for reaching the enemy coast, we realized that there was a distinct chance of running out of fuel. We set course with a sinking feeling of uncertainty and a heavy uneasiness in the pits of our stomachs. But there was no question in our minds; we preferred to take our chances with the overwater flight than risk the certainty of capture if we crash-landed or bailed out in occupied Europe.

As we headed out to sea, there was not much we could do other than jettison our bomb load and fly the aircraft as economically as possible, gradually losing whatever height we could afford to lose in order to gain a few extra miles per hour in air speed. It was still night. It was dark and lonely as we watched the trackless face of the sea. We saw the occasional glimmer of light on the eastern horizon; nothing else disturbed the blackness. As the fuel gauges crept inexorably down towards the empty mark, so the cold surging of the sea crept into our imaginations. In the oncoming dawn, our hopes were raised by the sight of a line along the horizon ahead. Was it land? Those hopes were quickly dashed as the dim line of low cloud formed and dispersed on the approaching sea. Finally, with the fuel gauges signalling empty, there was nowhere to look but at the dark grey water running in heavy swells just under us. There was no more height to spare, no fuel, no land, no time. We prepared for the dunking.

Sgt Watt, the co-pilot, went back to the crash position in the fuselage along with the rest of the crew while I stayed up front with Tom. He tightened his seat harness and I lay on the floor beside him, feet first with my head against a bulkhead. The wireless operator and the tail gunner were with the co-pilot, their backs against the main spar. Aft of where the crew were, the side door in the fuselage had been jettisoned to ensure they could escape once we landed in the water. The tail gunner had the packaged dinghy across his lap, ready to be tossed out of the hatch as soon as the aircraft was down. It looked as if our crew emergency drill was going to be put to the test, and soon!

The communications equipment in the Whitley was on a par with the navigation equipment, if not of a lower standard. Voice communication with the ground was provided by a set called the TR 9, a high-frequency set which had so little range that you knew, if your base heard you and you heard their reply, you were practically on top of them. Its range limitation was a sort of navigational aid. If you were returning to base at night and above cloud, you knew you were within the aerodrome circuit if you made voice contact. However, since we had no blind approach or blind landing system at our base and since we were given no training in any such system, it had become an unwritten law on squadron that you never broke cloud over land on your return unless you were certain you were over the base. With hills on both sides of the valley in which Leeming was situated, a blind descent through cloud cover was just too risky. On every operation, it was recommended that you make your descent through cloud while you were still over the sea. That way you were always certain of ground level. Over land, those clouds too often proved to have solid cores.

For longer-range communications we had a medium-frequency radio with a transmitter key for morse code. With the trailing antenna extended, the wireless operator could reach stations in England at a much longer range. Unfortunately, the dependability of this set left much to be desired and many of the operators frustrated. As it so happened, on our flight to Stuttgart, the operator had spent much of his time with the guts of this set in his lap. Long-range communication and loop bearings had been impossible. Jimmie had sweated over the set with increasing anxiety as our chances of dunking became more and more probable. He had, however, succeeded in putting it back together and getting it to work in time to send out a burst of SOS signals before locking the key down and taking up his crash position.

There was sufficient light for us to see the surface of the water and to determine the direction in which the seas were running. We still had power, and Tom made his approach along the line of the swell, just above stalling speed, with the nose slightly higher than for a normal landing. I braced myself. When the impact came, it was hard and sudden. In spite of my prone position, I must have jammed my head against the bulkhead support, straining my neck and momentarily dazing myself. My next conscious effort was of struggling to get up off the floor where the water was already beginning to cover me. Tom was slumped forward in his seat over the control column. His seat harness had snapped on impact and he had struck and cut his forehead on the instrument panel in front of him. Fortunately, the harness had absorbed most of the shock before it broke. He was not completely knocked out. I shook him and shouted for him to get out of the escape hatch over his head. He seemed to rouse himself and began to climb out of his seat. With a little assistance, he made it up through the hatch and out onto the top of the fuselage.

In his dazed condition, Tom had heard me call him to get out, but had thought I was already out and calling him from up top. When he made it out and stepped onto the fuselage, he expected to see me there. Still dazed, he turned to look for me but stepped in the wrong direction right off the aircraft and into the water between the engine nacelle and the fuselage. The cold shocked him into full consciousness for the first time since he had landed the aircraft. By the time I climbed out of the hatch, Tom was floundering in the water, trying to climb back onto the wing.

To climb out of the water onto a smooth, wet, metal wing was a physical impossibility. So I went down onto the wing and gave him a hand. We then scrambled back onto the top and started to walk back towards the side escape hatch to check on the rest of the crew. As we walked, the water rose. Before we reached the hatch, the water was over our boots. We didn't have to step off the fuselage to get into the water, the aircraft literally sank beneath us. I was wearing my suede, fleece-lined, zippered flying boots. When the aircraft sank, my boots simply peeled off and sank with it. I had been using my Canadian, Boy Scout-type flashlight and had slipped it into my boot with the lamp still on when I helped Tom. It was eerie watching the light in my boot sink slowly out of sight in the cold, dark water.

As Tom and I submerged, the flotation gear in our Irwin parachute harness kept us from going completely under. We looked around in the half light and saw the three heads of our crew mates. But, just as we caught sight of them, one head disappeared beneath the surface in a floundering, splashing fashion. As quickly as we could in our cumbersome gear, we made for the spot where that head had disappeared. Hindered as we were by the flotation gear and our clothing, we could only make slow progress. Before we could reach the spot, the head broke the surface and went down again. We were still frantically trying to reach him when he broke the surface one more time. This time, we were close enough to grab for him, but found he was able, on this occasion, to remain afloat on his own. It was our tail gunner. He had been braced in the crash position with the dinghy in his lap, ready to throw it out as soon as we landed. When he saw the water lapping at the edge of the open escape hatch, he thought we had come down. However, at that stage in our crash-landing, we were at water level with the nose still up and just about ready to stall. No sooner did he rise to his feet than the nose dropped and we hit the sea. It was somewhat comparable to hitting a brick wall! The tail gunner was tossed up the fuselage like a rag doll, the dinghy still locked in his arms. He struggled to his feet again and rather than throw the dinghy out of the hatch, he decided to throw himself out with the dinghy in his embrace.

This was actually quite sensible on his part since the dinghy was attached to the aircraft by a lanyard which was, in turn, attached to the trigger of the gas cylinder inside that was supposed to inflate the dinghy. Tossing the dinghy out of the aircraft would have applied sufficient tension to the lanyard to trigger inflation; jumping out with it should have applied that much more tension and ensured inflation. In our case that was not to be. When the tail gunner jumped, he went far enough to reach the end of the lanyard which stretched out between him and the aircraft, tautly, right between his legs. It just about castrated him, but the lanyard failed to trigger the cylinder. Fortunately for all of us, he had had his knife at hand and his wits about him. He was able to cut the lanyard before the dinghy could be dragged down by the aircraft. In all this quick thinking, however, he had forgotten to inflate his own flotation gear. As a result, he had very nearly drowned saving the rest of us. It was only as he was going down for the third time that he realized his error and pulled the toggle of his Mae West.

Chapter XIV

So there we were, in the cold, final hours of the night, floundering around in the even colder waters of the sea. The still neatly-packaged bundle of the orange dinghy bobbed among us as we tried to get a grip on ourselves and on the dinghy at the same time. It was terribly awkward struggling in the water with that dinghy, our hands getting colder and clumsier by the moment. The lacings seemed to be inflexible and impenetrable. Finally, I managed to get my fingers far enough through the lacings to reach the cylinder and activate the trigger. We listened in nervous anxiety to the hiss of the gas and watched the cumbersome but welcome unfolding of our life raft. But our feelings of relief were almost as quickly severely dampened, if I can use such an expression in our already soaked state, when we saw that the dinghy had inflated all right but upside down.

Surviving the crash itself and the long drawn-out sequence of events that had followed were having their effects. We were beginning to suffer from nervous fatigue, probably accelerated by the numbing cold of the water. With a united and, what seemed to us a final effort, we succeeded in righting the raft. We were shivering and limp, our energy exhausted, and we couldn't climb into the dinghy. None of us had noticed that, when we righted it, the ropes around the rim had become entangled. Each of us tried to climb into the dinghy, only to find that the clips of our parachute harness caught in the ropes in such a way that we could not raise our bodies high enough to get over the swell of the tubular sides. In our exhausted state, this obstacle threatened to finish us. Before it was too late, however, common sense came to the rescue. Since none of us could climb into the dinghy alone, we decided to all help push the first man in so he could help pull in the next. Tom climbed as far as he could on his own, then three of us held him up while the fourth disengaged the harness clips of his parachute from the entangling ropes. Then we all got behind him and boosted him the rest of the way. After that, it was only a matter of minutes before we had the next one on his way and each of us followed in turn. It was a very exhausted and slightly desperate crew of airmen who finally huddled together in that little round, orange island of security on the dark and heaving sea.

The rise and fall of the swell slopped water rhythmically from end to end of the dinghy. Each of us was soaked through and through, yet it seemed that, every time your part of the dinghy dipped, the cold water sloshed up your legs and back as if you were being dunked all over again. By this time, the crack on the head and the whiplash effect on my neck took over. I began to feel nauseous and dizzy. Tom decided to give me a dose of brandy from the dinghy's emergency pack. Although it didn't have the effect Tom had intended, it certainly decided the issue for me. I immediately threw up, fortunately over the side, and began to feel better right away.

Before abandoning the aircraft, I had stuffed my log and chart inside my battledress tunic so that my trip could be re-plotted on our return to base to determine whether we had reached Stuttgart, or, if not, then where we had been. Where we were at this point, except for the obvious, no one knew. But there was nothing we could do about it anyway, other than wait. We bailed the dinghy out as much as we could and watched daylight creep over the seascape. It was overcast and rather dull, but the visibility was good enough for us to see that there was nothing in any direction to break the horizon between sea and sky.

We knew that Air Sea Search and Rescue should have been alerted and should be looking for us . . . if our SOS had been received. There was no way of knowing for sure if it had been heard, but we could see no reason why not. But, had they been able to obtain cross bearings on our signal? Or a good bearing and distance? Would it be accurate enough to lead them to our location? It was virtually impossible not to think about the technique involved, and not to speculate on our chances of being picked up. And yet, there was no logical way to rate our prospects. It was more a matter of fatalism and faith. Though we remained optimistic, I think we all realized how slim our chances were, particularly as we looked around us at the breadth of the rolling sea and accepted the insignificance of our position, a tiny dot in a vast emptiness. I also knew only too well the difficulty of obtaining a fix from a single radio bearing and the accuracy which might be achieved in such circumstances. At best, there would be a large area to be searched. And if there was a search, would we be within its boundaries?

For more than three hours there was no other sight or sound. There was, however, no reason yet to become despondent. Then, at the extreme range of our vision, we saw what we felt could only be a ship, just a spot on the horizon. As we excitedly strained our eyes, willing the speck to become clearer, wanting our prayers to be answered, it slowly grew larger. It was a ship! And it seemed to be heading our way. We were almost hysterical with joy. We stood up as much as we dared, waving and shouting to attract their attention, long before we could possibly be seen or heard. But it wasn't a time for logic or common sense. We were simply beside ourselves with joy at the prospect of being rescued. We were already hoarse from shouting when, to our horror, the ship began to turn and head back the way it had come.

There is no way I can describe the terrible emptiness this apparent desertion created in us, coming as it did on the very heels of the joyous hysteria we had been feeling. Our saviour had been so near. Now we felt forsaken, shocked, and desolate. The Fates seemed indeed against us. First, the failure of the dinghy to open automatically, then the upside-down inflation and our subsequent difficulties getting in. To top that, the flares from the emergency pack failed to ignite when we tried to hail the ship and, worst of all, we were being abandoned.

Our dismay, however shattering it was, didn't last long. As we tearfully watched, first in hope and then in horror, our hopes were born again. The ship kept turning. It went right around in a circle and was heading back towards us. We were too emotionally drained by this time to stand or wave. We just sat and watched in silence as the ship drew closer and closer, until finally, it hove to alongside us. It was a

Royal Navy minesweeper. This time it was the minesweeper's crew who lined her rails, jubilantly waving and shouting.

We were quickly hoisted up onto the deck, one at a time, and our dinghy was brought up and lashed down. We were, of course, overjoyed at being rescued, but still so emotionally drained that we must have seemed like sleepwalkers. Not so the crew of that mine sweeper! This had been their seventh participation in a sea search for downed airmen, and their only success. Their pleasure at finding and rescuing a crew was heartwarming. As it turned out, we had been floating in a mine field beyond the area which they had been assigned to search. They had been looking for some time and had reached the extremity of their area and the edge of the minefield. It was their turning to go back that we had witnessed with such dismay. As the ship was swinging around, the captain, a young RNR lieutenant, was sweeping the horizon with his binoculars. Just as the stern came around, he had caught the merest glimpse, a flicker really, of something against the horizon. Whatever it was had risen simultaneously with the ship on the swell. He realized that it could well have been a floating mine, but it had been their only sighting up until then. In spite of the risk, and although he knew it was a slim possibility, he had ordered the ship to complete its turn back to the direction in which he had seen that brief flicker. It didn't take them long to confirm that what was on the surface was indeed a dinghy.

The crew couldn't have treated us with greater care and concern had we been royalty. We were hustled below deck, made to strip off our wet battledress, and provided with fresh, dry clothes from the escape kits which all the ships carried for survivors at sea. They plied us with hot food and drinks and put us into comfortable bunks to sleep while the ship sailed for port. A very happy crew and a much relieved group of tired airmen headed for home.

By the time we docked at Southampton and were admitted to the navy hospital, we had adjusted to the realities of being back and alive. Except for our tail gunner who was justifiably worried about his bruised and swollen testicles, we were uninjured. We were trouble-free except for the fact that it was the deputy flight commander's aircraft we had ditched in the drink, and we were accountable for its loss. As the two commissioned officers of the crew, Tom and I felt this accountability assume larger and larger proportions the nearer we came to returning to base. I still had my log and chart, but they were nothing but a soggy mass of paper with absolutely no more use or value.

We were discharged from hospital in forty-eight hours with clean bills of health, and set off immediately by train for our base. Our battledress had been dried and pressed so we were able to travel in uniform, minus our caps since we never took them on operations anyway. The hospital had let us keep the rescue clothing the mine sweeper crew had given us — grey sweaters, wool slacks, and cloth slippers.

Our reception back at base both surprised and relieved us. We were welcomed like celebrities. When we began to apologize for losing the aircraft, the squadron commander impressed upon us that he could replace an aircraft in a matter of days, or even hours, but the

Before and after our dunking.

replacement of trained and experienced crews took years. Even the deputy flight commander made light of the loss of his aircraft and joined in the party spirit. Following our debriefing, we were photographed outside Station HQ in our rescue garb — the "Before" — and then in our uniforms — the "After." We were then granted a seven-day survivor's leave, which I intended to spend in London.

Before we left, we were pleased to hear that, because of our report about the failure of our dinghy to inflate, an inspection had been made of all squadron aircraft. They discovered that, in every case, the lanyard had been knotted on the wrong side of an eyelet through which it passed under the outer cover of the dinghy before it reached the gas cylinder trigger. Not one of them would have opened automatically since the knot prevented the lanyard from sliding through the eyelet and pulling on the trigger. Corrective measures were taken immediately. It is conceivable that the ramifications of this incident were felt throughout Bomber Command, and equally conceivable that the loss of our aircraft may have been instrumental in the saving of many other airmen's lives.

Chapter XV

Bomber Command crews were normally given a week's leave every three months for rest and recreation. It certainly wasn't for moral purposes, at least as far as the overseas personnel were concerned. For the RAF members, it was an opportunity to visit home and loved ones. For the foreigners, it was mainly a chance to visit London and enjoy the many pleasures of that historic city. In my own case, it was a most welcome change of pace. After my celibate, non-drinking concentration on squadron life, it was party time in London with old and or new friends, as the case may be. The money I saved between leaves seemed to be just enough to finance my adventures.

The survivor's leave, however, was my first from the squadron, and it set the pattern for those to follow. When I reached London, I headed straight for the West End and Piccadilly Circus, where I registered at the Regent Palace. It was only a short distance from there to the same pub where Jack and I had been made so welcome on our earlier trips from Uxbridge. The friendly barmaid had left by this time, so I was not tempted in my resolve to stay away from the sex-hungry younger sister. However, as was so often the case in Piccadilly Circus, I happily ran across some one I knew, my same old friend from Hamilton, Jack Lister. Our meeting was purely accidental and both of us were solo at the time. We joined forces once again and enjoyed London's delights together, much more than either of us could have on our own . . . Major and Minor one more time.

When he heard that I was on bombers, and on survivor's leave after the dunking, Jack was a little bitter. He seemed to feel that he, not his young friend, should have the apparently more dangerous assignment and berated the fact that he had been assigned to the safer

Coastal Command. But things are not always as they seem. For, as it turned out, that was the last time I was to see him. I learned much later that Jack had lost his life, along with all of his crew, in the frustrating attack on the battleships *Scharnhorst* and *Gneisnau* as they made their way from Brest through the Channel to a safe harbour. The irony of his disillusionment was lost on both of us at the time, for we were each to be involved in that fray when Fighter, Coastal, and Bomber Commands combined to try to prevent the escape of those dangerous ships. We failed, and the friend with the safer assignment didn't come home.

On our return to base, the crew and I had to be re-equipped. All of our flying gear had been lost in the ditching. Without any conscious intent, I kept my white flying sweater even though it was noticeably stained from the yellow dye which is used to enlarge the field of colour around a floating dinghy. The battledress was much less stained and had survived immersion quite well. As time passed and I became more operationally experienced, these items of dress assumed a sort of good luck significance and a touch of superstitious importance. Had I been ordered then to replace them or had they been lost in the ditching, I feel sure it would have caused me no concern. But, as it was, I was allowed to keep them and they became a part of the ritualistic and symbolic superstition to which most wartime airmen were prey.

For some unknown reason, I persisted in not wearing my identity discs, but I was never without my bracelet of Canadian nickels. Those seven coins became another unconscious but immutable habit of this superstitious airman. They may also have been an implicit but tangible link between a youngster and his far-away home.

In those early days, with no WAAFs on the station, it had become an operational ritual before take-off for the air crew to relieve themselves on the tail wheel of their aircraft. A sort of last minute, nervous pee before setting off for enemy territory. This practice was so widespread that the RAF had to issue an official order banning the practice. The deleterious effect on the life of the tail wheel tires was becoming too severe for the practice to be condoned any longer, regardless of the short-term effect the ban might have had on the morale of superstitious air crew. Peeing on the grass was not the same thing at all.

Shortly after returning to base from leave, I received a letter telling me that I had become a member of the Winged Goldfish Club, organized by the directors of the company which manufactured the dinghies for the RAF. Because of the scarcity of metal for anything but armaments, the directors had contributed their evening dress suits to be cut up into small patches upon which were embroidered a silk winged goldfish over a blue wave. This token, an identification card, and a letter of explanation were sent to each airman whose life had been saved through the use of a dinghy. It was obviously a very restricted club, but not one to which any airman particularly aspired to belong. Those who qualified for membership were simply grateful to have survived, our crew included.

Winged Goldfish emblem.

For a while, we used to take a supply of empty beer bottles along with us on operations. We stored them near the flare chute and dropped them when we were heavily engaged by searchlights and flak. It was something positive to do when you felt otherwise so powerless; it was definitely against orders to drop your bombs on such occasions, no matter how tempting it was to take out some enemy defences. The piercing shriek the bottles made as they fell must have sounded like heavy bombs coming down. In any case, it *seemed* to disturb the concentration of the ground defences, at least for a short time, and it gave us a psychological boost as well. After all, we were emulating our esteemed leader, Churchill, who was reputed to have said in an aside to his famous "We shall fight on the beaches . . . " speech, "And we will hit them over the head with beer bottles, which is all we really have!" Later, we substituted four-pound incendiaries. We had to tape the spring arming mechanism to handle them and we notched one edge of the octagonal-shaped cylinder that housed the bomb. This way they not only shrieked as they fell, they also provided us the added prospect of starting fires wherever they landed. Such crude measures would have little real effect on organized ground defences, and certainly not for long if at all. But it made us feel better than when we were being shot at with impunity.

On October 20, we took to the air again, one of forty-seven Whitleys, Wellingtons, and Hampdens, for an attack on the harbour of Wilhemshaven on the North Sea coast of Germany. It was tucked inside a fairly deep bay that provided a good ground base for heavy defences against almost any direction of attack. However, the coast line would also furnish us with good pinpoints for an accurate bombing run, if the visibility was good. In addition, if we attacked from the seaward approach, the depth of defences we would have to penetrate would not be great. The prospect of a successful raid appeared to be in our favour, and our hopes were high in spite of some trepidation at the thought of attacking such a major target.

Navigation was no problem for me that night. I didn't have to contend with a deep penetration of the European land mass with its drastic changes in meteorological conditions. The weather, though, was typical of October, masses of cloud covering a great deal of the sky. I was confident of our position but, when we reached Wilhemshaven, it was under solid cloud cover. We could see where the tops of the clouds were, but we had no idea how low the cloud base might be. At that time, policy in Bomber Command was firm; our attacks were confined to military targets which were known military objectives or targets which had been previously attacked by the command. We would have to descend below the cloud in an attempt to make a visual identification at what seemed to us unacceptable odds — dropping the bombs blindly through the clouds in the hopes of hitting the harbour was no good. Not too far away, however, we could discern what looked like breaks in the cloud cover. As we flew toward the breaks, I was still in the bombing position and began to see patches of ground. Suddenly, I was able to identify Wesermunde and pick out the docks there. Once again, we decided to attack the recognizable objective rather than carry out a blind drop or bring home the bombs.

Because of the weather, the enemy had opted to keep their defences quiet in order not to give away their location or identify themselves as a target. We were, therefore, able to complete a very satisfying and accurate bomb run on Wesermunde and to escape without encountering serious resistance. It was a very gratifying return to operations after our survivor's leave.

As the only squadron on a pre-war station, we enjoyed facilities which were almost up to peacetime standards. Even as a pilot officer, I had a single room in the main mess, with hot and cold running water and the shared services of a batman. The latter assured me a morning call and a hot cup of tea to ease the awakening. Only the few senior officers' suites had their own bath and toilet, but there were enough common facilities to avoid crowding. Just about this time, however, we found our comfortable lifestyle disrupted. The Luftwaffe attacks on airfields had struck in our group. One of our sister squadrons on Whitleys, 77 Squadron, had been forced to vacate their base in order to continue flying while repairs were made. In my case, this had a dual effect. First, I found myself sharing my room with an RAF observer by the name of P/O Dickenson. He had been in the first group of RAF observer trainees to come to Canada for their training and had joined in the course behind us at AOS in Malton. Second, I became re-acquainted with Capt D.C.T. Bennett of AT-FERO, now a W/C and OC of 77 Squadron. In the succeeding months, our two squadrons were to become fiercely competitive.

On October 23, we flew a major attack of 114 aircraft against the naval base at Kiel. For our crew, this was the most heavily defended target we had attacked to date. We again used the long North Sea crossing for navigation and to keep us north of the Dutch islands and Cuxhaven where defences were heavily concentrated. We were to cross the peninsula of Schleswig Holstein to the north of Kiel which was situated on the Eastern shore serving the Baltic. This route minimized the defences which we would have to penetrate, gave us two coastlines to add to our opportunities for pinpointing, and permitted us to attack the dockyards from the sea rather than from over the city.

All the way across we had clear upper skies and I obtained numerous astro observations to assist us in maintaining the desired track and timing. In spite of the broken cloud which had formed beneath us when we reached the peninsula, we were able to confirm our navigation and our course for the target. We arrived over Kiel on ETA and flew through the searchlights and the flak a number of times, crisscrossing the target, hoping for a break in the clouds and a clear sight of the docks. Our efforts were in vain. Visual identification was impossible. Further to the east we could see the coastline clearly. As we headed for this break in the cloud cover, I picked out Neustadt and was able to identify buildings that could only have been military barracks. We could spare no more time for searching, so we proceeded to attack Neustadt instead, using the military installations as our aiming point, and saw our string of bombs bursting on target.

Although I was not aware of it, my log and chart of that nine-hour flight to Kiel was submitted to Bomber Command by the station navigation officer, F/L Buchan, for consideration as the command trip of the month. Whether any other trips of mine had been submitted, I never knew. The only reason I found out about this one was that command accepted it and published it in the command report which was distributed to all Bomber Command Stations. On this particular occasion, because one of their own was being honoured, it was posted on the notice boards of the Officers' and NCOs' Messes for all to see. I had happily found that I could work just as precisely and neatly under operational conditions as was my habit on the ground. My logs and charts always looked as if they had been recopied on return to base. Thus, when the trip to Kiel was reproduced by photocopy in the command report, it was regarded a little sceptically by some and, in particular, by members of 77 Squadron including W/C Bennett. I should have said earlier that Bennett was one of the most outstanding air navigators in the world. Unfortunately, I did not know him well and was unable to appreciate his cutting sense of humour. I naively took his remarks at the notice board as reflecting squadron jealousy rather than the witty sarcasm intended. This incident created in me a somewhat antagonistic attitude towards, and a poor opinion of, this remarkable man which was to persist for some time. It was not until much later, through personal experience, that I learned better. It was a juvenile reaction on my part at the time, but one that perhaps youth and inexperience might excuse.

One hundred and fifteen aircraft took off in bright moonlight for Hamburg on October 26th. It was our biggest objective to date and was considered by some veterans to be the most vigorously defended target in Germany. The city had been attacked before and would be again, in spite of the dreaded reputation it was rightfully earning among the crews of Bomber Command. To reach this major port, you had to penetrate heavy coastal and port defences, thick bands of searchlights and concentrated nests of anti-aircraft guns. Similar ground defences had been set up along the banks of the Elbe River, which was more like an estuary extending from Hamburg to the North Sea.

We had never seen such concentrations of searchlights. Some of the aircraft became so hopelessly engaged by the searchlights that they lost too much height trying to break free, and had to seek the doubtful security of escape at ground level. Those that survived to reach the river then had to face a veritable hell-on-earth as they fought to stay below the arcs of the anti-aircraft guns along both shores while trying to avoid the hidden obstacles of the river course through blinding searchlight beams. All in the otherwise black night. Not many succeeded. Those who did paid a high price in casualties and aircraft damage.

One of the crews that made that hazardous low-level journey had a Canadian observer on board who had been on course with me. They were actually on their bombing run when searchlight and anti-aircraft concentrations became so intense, and their evasive action so violent, that they fell out of control. The observer had been in the nose during the run when he saw a bright light in front of him. He took it to be a nightfighter equipped with a searchlight in a head-on attack. "Fighter. Fighter," he called, as he struggled up into the front turret. It was, in reality, a ground-based searchlight. They were literally pointed down the searchlight beam, diving at full throttle. No pilot could have recovered from that dive. It was certain death when suddenly, and unbelievably, they felt a powerful braking effect in their dive. They slowed so much that the pilot was able to regain control, lose whatever little altitude was left, find the river ahead of them and stagger out to sea through that hellfire of flak and searchlights. It was not until they safely landed back at base and inspected the aircraft that they discovered the extent of their good fortune and the reason for their miraculous escape from that deadly dive. There was a clean cut through the horizontal strut of the big twin rudder of the Whitley, right through to the main spar. In the cut was what remained of a balloon cable. They had hit the cable at such an angle in their dive that it had slowed them before it snapped and before it could cut through the spar of the rudder!

During this period of operations, our pilots still had no blind-approach training and there were no bases with an airport blind-approach system. We continued to break cloud over the sea on return from operations. As it so happened, one of the squadron aircraft arrived over base according to their navigation, but above the clouds. Completely contrary to standard procedure, they began circling and descending through the cloud cover. Each crew member was alerted to watch for any sign of land. The observer, who happened to be a Canadian NCO, was standing with his head in the astro dome as his best place for observation. As they descended, one must assume that nobody saw anything. The next thing the observer knew was when he picked himself up off the ground, shaken and dazed, blood trickling down from a cut in his forehead. Staggering about in the dark, he bumped into someone else. It was the wireless operator, equally dazed and stumbling around. The observer had been launched through the perspex dome which cut him and the wireless operator, who had been sending a message to base, had been popped out through the side of the fuselage as it split. The rest of the crew were dead, crushed beyond recognition when the Whitley smashed into the crown of a hill. I cannot recall what happened subsequently to the wireless operator, but I do know the observer was crewed up again after hospitalization and was shot down over Germany later in his tour. He spent the remainder of the war in a POW camp.

There was something of a contradiction in the conditions which governed the early tactics of Bomber Command. In order to keep losses within a survivable limit for a prolonged campaign, the RAF had been forced to operate at night. Yet, the effectiveness of bomber attacks depended heavily upon accurate navigation and visual identification, both of which were rendered exceedingly difficult under night conditions. Thus, in 1940-41, moonlight was a decided asset. It provided night coverage with the added benefit of enough light to reflect off water, rail, and road surfaces and to distinguish between built-up and wooded areas. We looked forward to the nights of the full "Bomber Moon" for our most effective attacks. Later in the war, it was to become the "Hunter's Moon," when vastly improved ground and aircraft radars made it a circus for the nightfighters.

On October 31, we were included in a force of 123 aircraft once again headed for Hamburg. That time, however, when we arrived the city lay under thick cloud cover. The more we searched, the more evident it became that we would not see the target through the cloud so we directed our search to the north where prospects looked better. The further north we flew towards Kiel and Denmark, the thinner the cloud became. Fortunately, just before we reached the border, beyond which there was no suitable target, we located and identified Flensburg. With no time to lose, we made our attack and dropped the bombs on the docks there, taking a photograph of the bombing before setting course for home.

The second Hamburg raid took us forty minutes longer to complete than the first, presumably because of our prolonged search for a suitable target. But we were most fortunate that night because the defences had kept silent beneath the cloud and those at Flensburg had been only a pale version of what could have assailed us from Hamburg. All in all, though our crew had not been successful in finding our primary target, we had still delivered an effective attack on the enemy and we had not had to endure the searchlights and flak of Hamburg a second time. Not all the others were so lucky. Four of our Whitleys were lost in that operation.

Chapter XVI

Occasionally we were able to get an evening away from base, and how we looked forward to them. Our favourite place was Harrogate, a spa town about 30 miles away. If we were successful in arranging private transport — Angus Buchan had a personal car and once in a while enough petrol — we would stop in Ripon for a meal. There was a cafe which could be depended on for some restricted item such as a chop or an egg for the young airmen passing through. Otherwise, we were restricted to a station bus when, and if, such a luxury could be provided on a squadron stand-down.

On one of my early visits, Steve the Stoat introduced me to the Carlton Club where one was permitted to drink, as a club member, at much more convenient hours and long after the pubs had closed. But, it wasn't the drinking hours that attracted me. It was the young lady, perhaps girl is the better description, who was serving at the bar that drew my attention. We were introduced that same evening; her name was June and she was very attractive. It didn't take long to discover that she was only serving that evening to help out her mother who owned the club. We seemed to be instantly and mutually attracted. I was determined to see more of her, as much as time would permit. From then on, I spent all the free time I could in her company. The club became a home away from home and I was welcomed there whenever I could get away from base.

June and I grew very close. Some of our favourite ports of call on our evenings in Harrogate were the Hotel Majestic, the Queens Hotel, and the Prospect Bar, but we seldom ate out. The best meals in all of Harrogate were those served by June's mother at the club or, later on, at the private hotel which her mother subsequently bought and ran until the end of the war. When we were going some place special, June would occasionally borrow her mother's small Ford. It always amused me to watch her lift up the hood when we parked and remove the distributor cap to immobilize the car. This was all in accordance with regulations aimed at denying the threatening invasion forces any local transport. She would deposit the rotor in her handbag for the evening and replace it in the distributor for our return trip. This businesslike procedure seemed most incongruous in one so young and so feminine.

In spite of her youth, however, June was far more worldly than I. The elder of two sisters, she had matured quickly following the divorce of her parents and her mother's subsequent ownership and management of the club. Her mother was a very astute, entrepreneurial type, but she did lean heavily on June for moral and physical support.

Since I was primarily a non-drinker, it was not much of a measure to say that June handled her liquor better than I. She could work behind the bar and enjoy being in front of it with equal aplomb and a cool head. I can re-member walking home in the blackout, after an evening at the Queens or the Prospect when it wasn't my head but my bladder which showed up my weakness. I suffered agonies until I realized, and appreciated, the practical attitude English girls adopted on such occasions. What a relief it was to learn of their understanding of men's inability to hold their beer for long!

But that also brings to mind one time when an Englishman's under-standing proved to be less sympathetic. It was on one of those bus trips to Harrogate. Angus had come along on this particular outing. I had vis-ited with June and her family while the others went on a pub crawl. We all met at 2300 hours in the town square where the return bus was to pick us up. It was a dark night with the usual stringent blackout prevail-ing. As one might expect after making the round of the pubs, Angus found himself badly in need of bladder relief while we waited for the bus to appear. With the surrounding blacked-out conditions, he felt no concern as he searched for a convenient clump of bushes and pro-ceeded to ease his discomfort. Either by sheer chance or having been drawn to the scene by the gushing sound, a RAF service policeman caught Angus in the act in the beam of his torch. Although it was hard for us to believe, the SP took Angus' name, rank, and number to charge him with conduct unbecoming an officer! It was touch and go for a while as to whether that would be the only charge as Angus' Scottish pride and temper were put to the test. Fortunately, cooler heads prevailed, but poor Angus found himself paraded before the station commander the following morning on the charge made by that SP through the area provost marshal. It was a relief for all of us to find that the CO was far more sympathetic to the demands of nature than the police.

Winter was a trying time for Bomber Command. The pressure to maintain the offensive was always there, but the weather rarely cooperated. There were many days when the squadrons had to stand by for operations, briefed and ready to go, only to be stood down because the conditions over the base or the continent prevented flying. Such cancellations were wearing and frustrating for both the ground and air crews. There was always the compulsion to get on with the job, which, for the air crews at least, was tempered by the knowledge of the added hazards created by the winter extremes. Not the least of these was that of encountering heavy icing over the North Sea while the already burdened aircraft was struggling to climb to operational altitude. There is nothing so frightening nor so sobering to an airman than facing the furies of nature. The power of man and his machines pales to insignificance before that of Nature when it is turned against him.

One day in November, when we had been going through such a period of frustration, we were relieved to be given a clear stand down by the early afternoon. Someone immediately started to arrange for a bus to take a group into the nearby town of North Allerton where there was a nice pub and restaurant called the Red Lion. It seemed to me that Angus was the principal organizer and I was asked if I wished to go along. I happily agreed and found myself one of a bus load of squadron air crew heading out for drinks and dinner. It wasn't until we were all seated at the dinner table and they began to sing, "For he's a jolly good fellow" and "Happy Birthday," that the penny dropped. It was November 10, my twenty-first birthday! I had forgotten entirely about it and would not have remembered the event until some time later when it would have been too late to celebrate. I must confess that I was deeply moved by the thoughtfulness of my squadron friends who had organized it and all of those who attended. We had a hilarious party and

I was, quite literally, poured into the bus for the ride back to base. It may not have been your usual twenty-first birthday party, but it was a most notable and happy one in the circumstances.

On another occasion, when the squadron had been standing by for operations, word came through from Group HQ that the operation had been cancelled and we were stood down. Because of the inclement weather that had been plaguing us for days, the feeling of relief was widespread. It called for a night out. Buses were authorized, loaded, and bound for Harrogate in short order. On that particular night, I was already on a forty-eight hour pass in Harrogate attending a dinner dance at the Majestic with June and her mother. As the evening wore on, we could easily distinguish many of my squadron mates among the patrons, including the squadron commander, my flight commander, and the adjutant. I mention them in particular because of their involvement in the events which followed.

Just before midnight, there was a sudden change in the atmosphere of the room and a ripple of movement that grew into a wave of people moving out. Word had just reached the hotel that the air crews of 10 Squadron were being recalled on an immediate basis. SPs were scouring the town, gathering them from house, pub, and hotel. While the crowd sorted itself out on the dance floor, there was a bit of a turmoil in the middle. There, we could see my CO, flight commander, and adjutant on their hands and knees, scrabbling around at people's feet in what seemed a most drunken and disorderly fashion. It turned out to be not as bad as it had seemed at first. They were unquestionably all a little the worse for the wear, but they were quite seriously searching for a small bridge which had fallen out of the CO's mouth when word of the recall came!

Before long the buses were loaded and each took off with its quota of revellers. It was inevitable that word of the state of the Squadron personnel reached base before they did. As each bus unloaded its cargo at the briefing room, the medical officer was there to greet the crews with a large dose of his patented, sobering potion. Apparently it was a disgusting concoction, but no one objected in the hope that it would be as effective as its taste was deplorable.

The briefing was completed in record time and would have been comic if it had not involved the life and death of those young men. For the few among them who had not been imbibing that night, it must have been horrifying. What followed was even worse. By the time they were ready for take-off, it was snowing. The weather was such that, once they were airborne, they would not be able to land back at base even in an emergency. The first aircraft to take off swung a little and wrote off the first three flares on one side of the runway. The second finished off a few more. The third swung completely around, straightened out, and then rumbled down the runway to disappear into the snowy night. By the time all the aircraft had taken off, there were no flares left at all on one side of the runway. Their target that night was an airfield in Norway. To have been ordered in such conditions, the attack must have been part of a combined operation. With the weather and the confusion, it was difficult to say what results were achieved. Only one of our aircraft made it back to base that night, but at least no one was lost.

Before we were able to get in another operation, the squadron was stood down. All of the qualified crews were posted to the Heavy Conversion Unit (HCU) at Linton, Yorkshire, for training on the Handley Page Halifaxes. The Halifax was a bomber built in wartime, powered by four Rolls Royce Merlins, and capable of flying faster and higher than the old pre-war Whitleys. It was designed to handle three times the load we had been carrying on our Whitley flights into Germany. Bomber Command had been slowly building up its numbers and was increasing its bomb capacity significantly. The first of the new "heavies" (the Stirling, the Halifax, and the Lancaster) were already flying, and we had been selected to join them.

The HCU was commanded by one of Bomber Command's most experienced and most outstanding pilots, W/C "Willie" Tait. He was a truly remarkable and unusual man and had established an enviable reputation for coolness, skill, and daring in the two tours of operations he had already completed. And yet, he preserved an exuberance for the task at hand as well as a quiet, shy and almost self-effacing resourcefulness that inspired those around him. With such a man at the helm, the Con Unit ran like a clock, the key to which was the efficiency of the ground crews who responded to his appreciative leadership with perhaps even more alacrity than did the air crew.

Our Whitley crew had to be expanded by two, a flight engineer and a mid-upper gunner. In addition to Tom and myself, our crew now consisted of Jimmie, our Canadian wireless operator, Count, our Canadian tail gunner, and Rupert, our English flight engineer. These were the regular members. The mid-upper gunner and the co-pilot, when we had one, were provided from the squadron pool of air crew who were not yet assigned on a regular crew basis.

Before the end of the year, we were back at Leeming with our very own Halifax, "O" for Orange, assigned to us. While we had been at the Con Unit, 77 Squadron had remained at Leeming and had continued to operate in their Whitleys. We must have been insufferable when we returned with our Halifaxes, feeling as we did so much superior to anyone still flying the old Whitleys. It certainly eliminated any feeling of competitiveness; they just weren't in our class any more!

10 Sqn aircrews in front of Halifax. Tom and I are in first seated row, tenth and eleventh from left. CO is W/C Tuck in center of same row.

"O" for Orange Ground and Aircrew.

Our crew and aircraft.

Chapter XVII

The Story of "0"

On January 5th, 1942, we were briefed for our first Halifax operation — an attack on Brest. The primary targets were the dock area and the battleships Scharnhorst and Gneisnau which had been harboured there since taking refuge from the Home Fleet in March of '41. There must have been signs of renewed activity on the ships because Bomber Command was directed to launch 154 aircraft in a major attack to be divided equally between the docks and the ships.

In spite of the usual hazards and poor visibility associated with winter flying in Europe, we were relieved to find that Brest was under broken cloud. In the face of intense anti-aircraft fire and heavy concentrations of searchlights, we were able to make a good bombing run with the target remaining visible in the drift lines of the sight throughout the run. Our stick of bombs fell accurately in the dock area which housed the battleships. As we turned away and set course for home, we were highly pleased with "O" and with our first operation in her. It was an auspicious start for a new era in our operational tour.

Two nights later we were briefed for another raid in occupied France, again in support of the war in the Atlantic. This time, a small force of only 27 aircraft was to attack St. Nazaire on the Bay of Biscay, where the submarine pens were the primary target. We carried a load of 1000 lb armour-piercing bombs which had to be dropped from high altitude in order to reach the terminal velocity required to penetrate the heavy concrete roofs of the sub pens. Again, Fortune smiled upon us. The sky was clear enough for me to identify the target visually and to make a good steady run. The bombs fell directly on the target, but we were unable to see their effect. This was possibly due to the darkness and our altitude or the penetration required and the delay involved. Even without this firsthand evidence, we still headed home with a sense of well-being and a reasonable hope that we had done something effective against the U-Boat menace. After the experience of my own ill-fated Atlantic convoy, this was a goal that was particularly close to my heart.

Late in the morning of February 12, we received a sudden alert for immediate action. The Scharnhorst and the Gneisnau had survived. They were escaping through the English Channel under the cover of low cloud, rain and fog! Our earlier attack on Brest had failed to prevent this and, somehow, despite the threat they represented and the attention paid to them, the ships and their escorting force of destroyers and E-Boats had slipped undetected out of Brest. The convoy was on its way to a safer German port but was within the confines of the Channel. We were to launch a maximum daylight offensive against them. There was very little time left in which to organize the attack in the remaining daylight before they could reach the safety of a well-defended port or disappear under cover of darkness. Some of our aircraft required air testing before they could be fuelled and armed with armour-piercing bombs. And the observers had to be ready to carry out pinpoint accuracy bombing on moving targets.

All of our observers had theoretical knowledge of bombing a moving target, but none had practical experience. Since I had only recently completed the Bombing Leader's Course at RAF Manby, I was detailed to take all of the observers to the Air Ministry Bombing Trainer (AMBT) on the base and put them through a series of refresher drills. While we were thus engaged, the rest of the crews were brushing up on fighter defence tactics and completing the air tests. This would be the first daylight operation for just about all of us. Most of the flying would be over friendly territory, but there was no doubt that the enemy would be expecting our attack and no doubt about the kind of reception they would be prepared to give us.

My crew had been taken over by the squadron commander, W/C "Friar" Tuck, for this operation. While I was in the AMBT, he arranged an air test for "O" with the rest of my crew. What followed was tragic. Our drills in AMBT were suddenly interrupted by the sounds of air-craft engines at full throttle and the terrible sounds of a crash. We rushed out only to witness a horrible sight at the intersection of the main runways. One Halifax had crashed on top of another. Smoke and glycol fumes were billowing all around the wreckage. Service-men ran from all directions to the site and crew members were tum-bling out of the carcasses of the two aircraft. From the smashed cockpit window of the Halifax underneath, one arm dangled limply. An NCO crew member of the upper Halifax jumped down onto the wing of the other to render assistance. He leaned over the cockpit and reached in to help the pilot, but instead reeled back and stumbled off the wing onto the ground. Sgt Tripp, one of our experienced Canadian pilots, had had the top of his head severed by the flashing propeller of the aircraft above. The NCO stood retching in shock on the side of the runway; only minutes before, Tripp had been a friend. The wireless op-erator in the same aircraft was sliced in two by those deadly propellers but, by some miracle, everyone else escaped serious injury.

The tragedy notwithstanding, operations had to continue. My crew and "O," however, were no longer part of the raid. They had been the ones who crashed on top, with the squadron commander at the con-trols. I watched as the rest of the squadron took off that afternoon for the attack on the *Scharnhorst* and the *Gneisnau*. The weather over the Channel remained foul, protecting the battleships, and the opera-tion was a dismal failure. There was absolutely no chance for the high-level attack required by the armour-piercing bombs. Later on, we heard about the courageous low-level assaults made by light bombers and torpedo bombers in the face of intense and accurate anti-aircraft fire and fighter defences. But anything hitting the ships bounced off the heavily armoured hulls like peas off an elephant's back. It was a desperate attempt in which many lives were fruitlessly lost. All in all, it was a day of disheartening tragedies.

It was on this trip, however, that one of our crews succeeded in shooting down an attacking Messerschmidt. Sgt Porrit, the gunner who made the kill, was a Canadian and this had a profound effect on our tail gunner, Sgt Falkoski, the "Count." He was so envious that he began to pray that we would meet a fighter just so he could shoot it down. Jimmie, although also Canadian, was not so bloodthirsty. Or perhaps he didn't have as much confidence in Count as Count had in himself. At any rate, he implored Tom and me to stop Count from praying for such an event. No doubt it was the irreverence of youth speaking, but we told Count that we had no objection, providing he made good on his promise to shoot it down. Jimmie was unhappy with our reaction and swore that he would go to church every Sunday to pray in opposition to Count. Though we didn't realize it at the time, this was the first indication that Jimmie was beginning to have a problem. Not long after this, his brother was posted missing from a neighbouring bomber squadron and Jimmie grew steadily more introverted. His work in the air, however, showed no deterioration and caused us no immediate concern.

Once again we were briefed to attack the Scharnhorst and the Gneisnau. This time, they had taken refuge in Kiel after escaping from Brest. It was in late February, and the sea crossing was made extremely hazardous that night by heavy cloud and severe icing. We blessed the good fortune which had seen us convert from the old Whitleys to the Halifaxes; to make a safe crossing, we had to climb above the cloud quickly enough to avoid the icing. And if any of our aircraft suffered damage in the attack, the return flight would be even more risky than usual.

We managed to get above the cloud and obtained some good astro sights that helped us stay on track. By the time we reached the target area, the wintry night was actually in our favour, making it easy to pinpoint our position on the coast. There was good moonlight and the ice and snow on the ground improved definition to such an extent that we didn't have to hang around and make a square search. We made our bombing run through the heavy concentration of flak and searchlights that surrounded the floating dock which was our primary target and dropped our bombs in a string along it. The Germans quite obviously resented our renewed attack on their ships and put up a most vigorous defence. The anti-aircraft barrage was impressive, if not awe-inspiring. Of our forty-nine bomber force, three were either shot down over Kiel or succumbed to the deadly icing on the return.

During those last raids, we had been trying to achieve line-overlap photo coverage of the attacks. Rupert, our flight engineer, stationed himself at the flare chute to throw out three photo flashes on my command, hopefully timed to explode just prior to, at the same time as, and just after the explosion of the bombs on the target. It meant that we had to continue our straight and level bombing run after the release and until the explosion of the bombs. No evasive action could be taken to alter our course or we wouldn't catch the sequence. Theoretically this was quite feasible, even though we had not yet succeeded. But the ferocity and accuracy of the defences at Kiel didn't seem suited to this prolonged non-evasive flight. Amidst the probing searchlights and the bursts of heavy flak, wisdom prevailed. Or was it a more primordial instinct? Whatever, a single photo had to suffice that night. Our experiments could wait for another time, another target.

Perhaps unconsciously, the pressure had been building up, at least a little, because we really got a kick out of the next operation. Up to then, the British policy had been to restrict the activities of our aircraft over occupied territory to invasion ports and military bases, and in daylight, to specific targets in the communications field. Bomber Command had never been permitted to attack an industrial objective at night. However, the persistent use of factories in the occupied countries for German war production brought about a change in this policy. On March 3, 235 crews were briefed for a major attack on the Renault factory in Baillancourt, just on the outskirts of Paris. I think our pleasurable anticipation came from the fact that this was not only an important target but also one that promised more satisfaction and less risk than usual.

The weather was excellent. Visibility was ideal. We identified the target easily and from a sufficient distance to provide a perfect bombing run. That night we were carrying eight 1000 lb bombs as we descended to 1000 feet for the run. The factory was so close we could see the activity around the buildings. The factory structure ran smoothly down the drift wires of the sight, much more quickly than usual at that low altitude. I pressed the tit and, as we roared over the top of the main building, I could feel each of the eight blasts individually, as they exploded beneath us, right in the centre of the structure. I had been following my usual bombing patter and had said, "Bombs gone," when I released them and proceeded automatically to check that all the bombs had been released. Before I could finish and call for the bomb doors to be closed, Tom said, "You don't have to check. I have eight bruises on my backside!" Count was calling ecstatically from the tail turret, "I can see them exploding. Right on the factory. It's terrific. I can pinpoint them exactly on the target photograph. Boy, I've never seen anything like this before." The overall attack had been planned for three waves, the most experienced crews in the leading wave. We must have been in the very forefront of the attack, since the factory had been completely undisturbed while we made our approach. By the time we left, it was in ruins. The concentration and accuracy of this operation was unprecedented. For the crews who participated, it was like a day out of school, a welcome break from the hot bed of the German air defences. One solitary crew was lost.

Climbing over main spar of Halifax after N.F.T.

Three veteran Canadians of 10 Sqn.

Chapter XVIII

A few days later, we were drawn out of the hangar offices by the agonized sound of Merlins pushed to full throttle, at low level, and very close by. One of our new crews had jumped at the chance to get a little extra flying time, and had volunteered to test fly a recently-repaired, flak-damaged Halifax. We could see the aircraft clearly as it flew alongside the aerodrome trying to complete a circuit for landing. Though its engines were at full power, it just kept losing height. Hypnotized and horrified, we knew a crash was inevitable as we watched it skim closer and closer to the ground. A rush of people and vehicles headed across the airfield, dreading what was about to happen. The Halifax never managed to pull up in the slightest; it simply surged on at full throttle until there was no more air between it and the ground. There was a terrible, rending crash as it struck just below our line of vision. When we reached the farmer's field on the edge of the aerodrome, there was nothing to be seen but a jumble of twisted metal and the tail section of an aircraft sticking up out of the mess.

While we were running to the site of the wreckage, the turret in the relatively undamaged tail section rotated until the turret doors were clear. The gunner fell out of the turret, onto the ground, unhurt, to be welcomed by a couple of farm workers climbing out of a nearby ditch and cursing, in their broad Yorkshire accents, all these crazy fliers. That they and the gunner had survived was nothing short of a miracle. Unfortunately, the rest of the crew was not so lucky. What remained of them was beyond recognition.

An investigation was launched. Apparently, when the tail section, which had been damaged by flak in an earlier raid, was repaired, the controls of the aileron trim tabs were reversed on reassembly. The inexperienced pilot had taken off with the trim set for climb and had found that the aircraft would not. The more trim he applied, the harder it must have been for him to overcome the reverse effect the trim was having. Not realizing this, he had continued to apply full power and maximum trim in a manful attempt to complete the circuit and bring his aircraft and his crew in for a safe landing, but to no avail. He had run out of space and time, and crashed while still under full power and maximum trim.

February was a fateful month. We, too, had been damaged by flak during an attack on Kiel and had been forced to land at an alternative base. But at least we were home. While we were there waiting for repairs, I received an urgent signal ordering me to return to Leeming immediately. The rest of the crew was to come with the aircraft when it was serviceable. No hint of the reason for my hasty recall was given in the message, but I wasted no time. I took the first available train, which required a couple of transfers en route, wearing my battledress, white sweater and flying boots, but no hat. With me, I carried my navigation bag containing my log and chart of the trip we had just completed, my Mae West and my parachute harness. Though my unusual appearance among civilians caused more than one head to turn, the only concern that preoccupied me was why the hasty recall. When I finally arrived at Leeming, I was much relieved to learn that it was to attend a high priority and highly classified course. It was my introduction to a revolutionary new piece of navigational equipment called GEE, related to radar. While I was away on the familiarization course, the sets were to be installed in the squadron aircraft.

It was only a matter of days before I had completed the course and returned to Leeming, where I was assigned the training of the rest of the observers. They had not only to learn how to use GEE, but had to believe they could trust their lives to this new aid. It gave me a terrific kick to fly with each crew in turn as their observer took them faultlessly through a cross-country and not only back to base, but right down the main runway, while completely screened from any ground observations. Crew scepticism of this little piece of "black magic" disappeared forever as the observers repeated this standard of pinpoint navigation, day and night, fair weather and foul, without visible contact with the ground. The dread of returning to base in cloud was erased.

Although the range of GEE did not extend far into the Continent, it did guarantee accurate navigation on departure from England and improved prospects for accuracy over Europe. And, just as importantly, it assured our precision once we re-entered GEE range on our return. Following the introduction of the four-engined heavies, this was the first of the technological advances which Bomber Command needed so badly in order to become an effective strategic offensive weapon.

As the squadron navigation officer and bombing leader, I was responsible for the standard of navigation and bombing in my squadron. We made a practice of reviewing each log and chart the morning after each operation. These were conducted by any of the senior observers who had not been in the operation under review and their objectives were twofold: primarily to ensure that proper procedures were being followed and the required standards of navigation maintained and secondly to provide an additional check on the probability of each crew having attacked the primary target.

One particular morning, as I was organizing a review, one of the pilots who had been on the previous night's operation came into my office. It was surprising to see him at that early hour, but it was evident he was deeply disturbed. Although his observer had an excellent reputation, the pilot was so concerned about his experience the previous night that he had risen early enough to come to my office and complain. He wanted a satisfactory explanation or replacement of his observer.

From the pilot's account, it seemed that the trip had progressed quite normally until they were over enemy territory. They had been on their final course to the target for some time but, according to the observer's estimate, still had more than an hour to go. By then, the pilot could see searchlights and anti-aircraft activity just ahead. Quite clearly, there was a full-scale attack taking place and they were going to fly right over it if they held their course. The pilot had questioned his observer about his ETA, pointing out the attack immediately ahead. As they flew alongside the activity, he felt certain that something was wrong with his observer and that they had arrived at their target in spite of the observer's adamant stand about his ETA of one more hour. Overriding his observer, the pilot informed him that they would join the attack in progress and they made their bombing run without further comment.

It was easy enough to picture the strained atmosphere in that aircraft as they turned for home after the attack. The morale of a good operational crew is a delicate and friable matter. Trust and mutual confidence are vital elements when the skill and ingenuity of enemy defences are pitted against you, and when any mistake, carelessness, oversight, or lack of technical proficiency by any member of the crew at a critical moment can mean disaster or death for all. To make matters worse for the observer in question, on the way home it became increasingly evident to all the crew that they had indeed attacked the right target. The pilot's concern was understandable. They would not have had much of a chance of surviving had they pressed on for another hour, alone, into Germany. A single invader in the enemy sky would have been a sitting duck for the nightfighter forces.

Placatory words would have been wasted on the irate pilot, so I searched his observer's log and chart, and began a careful re-plot of their flight from base to target. As it turned out, the answer was astonishingly simple. I worked from log to chart, following the time sequence of events, checking the accuracy of the calculations and the plotting of each change in height, speed, course, and track of their flight. I came upon a log entry which skipped an entire hour of flight time! For some reason, the observer had made two entries in his log which were almost an exact hour apart, but had not plotted on his chart any record of flight progress for that hour. As far as his chart showed, that hour did not exist. Hence his conviction that they were still one hour from their target.

What this discovery meant, we could only surmise, but the previous good reputation of the observer demanded a logical explanation. We presumed that the hour gap in flight recording had coincided with an accidental stoppage of the observer's oxygen supply. A pinched tube would certainly have sufficed. The characteristics of hypoxia are most insidious; you surrender to the narcotic effect of oxygen starvation without knowing it and you awake, if the supply is restored in time, without any recollection at all of anything untoward having happened to you. The period during which you were hypoxic is a complete blank. You don't even know you had a memory lapse. In this particular case, we surmised that the observer had succumbed after making an entry in his log and his chart and had revived an hour later without realizing that he had been unconscious. When he next turned to his log and chart, the hour difference between his watch and his last entry failed to alert him because of the nearly exact hour involved. It was not only understandable, it was also pardonable. The error had only become apparent because we re-plotted his work in the quiet and security of my office knowing beforehand that a mistake had been made. To have uncovered it in flight, while navigating on operation, would have been miraculous once the illusion had taken effect.

Hazards of the air war weren't confined to the chances of falling prey to enemy action. You could fight the enemy, physically and technologically, to minimize his chances of success; that was part of the game. You could also struggle to overcome the mechanical failures which might beset your machine. But just as important as the crews who flew the aircraft were the ground crews who serviced them. It was their baby you took into battle, their sweat and dedication that gave you a machine which would serve you well — take you to the front and, God willing, bring you home. As much as we were, by our knowledge of flying, the custodians of our fate, so were the ground crews by their knowledge of the machine.

But the most implacable foe of the airman was, and still is, the weather. The best efforts of man and machine are nullified when bad weather prevents take-off or, worse still, landing, or hides the target. But when you face the fury of Nature in the form of icing or severe turbulence and instability in towering thunderstorm clouds, you know only too well that you are badly outmatched. To keep a heavily-loaded bomber climbing on course in the dark of night through dense cloud as the ice accumulates and rattles off the propellers onto the fuselage is a grim, humourless struggle. The only hope seems to be in silent prayer. You are uncertain as to the tops of the cloud and you wonder if the ice accretion, slowly and steadily destroying your ability to maintain the rate of climb, will achieve its goal before you can break out of that deadly cloud. You know that the bitterly cold North Sea and almost certain death wait below should you fall out of control, overloaded with ice. You debate the wisdom of descending to escape, but you have no more knowledge of the conditions ahead, above, or below. And you know that your chances of reaching the target at low altitude and alone are dismal. Of course, you can abort and return to base through the weather conditions you have just experienced. The alternatives reduce themselves simply to two: either you keep climbing in the hope you will break out in time, or you give up and go home. In every case of its kind, the choice of the bomber crews, though individually made and without benefit of any intercommunication, was almost unanimously to press on. The cost of such dedication was exceedingly high on numerous occasions. It was, however, a price which had to be paid and it demonstrated the level of dedication and will power which was essential to success in this form of warfare. Self-discipline and unwavering loyalty formed the pith of every crew in Bomber Command. Success had no cost too great.

Chapter XIX

In spite of my being in the air force, my activities seemed to bring me frequently into contact with the German navy. First, there had been my grim introduction to the real war when our convoy fell victim to the submarine wolf pack, followed by the fringe association with the survivors of the *Hood* in their action with the *Bismarck*. Then, there was the fruitless and tragic sortie against the *Scharnhorst* and the *Gneisnau* on their escape from Brest and the subsequent attacks on Kiel and St. Nazaire. The next was to involve yet another of the mighty German warships.

W/C Bennett had been transferred from 77 Squadron to take over 10 Squadron following the collision of the two Halifaxes on the runways in February. The accident hadn't been entirely the fault of the squadron commander, and he had been a very personable and popular officer. Those particular circumstances made a difficult task even harder for a man such as Bennett whose cold, intellectual grasp of technical expertise far exceeded his personability. His qualifications in every air crew specialty were exceptional and his standards were set at nothing but the highest. No flight leader, be he pilot, observer, wireless operator, engineer, or gunner, was free from his personal, technical supervision. As his navigation officer, I felt particularly susceptible to his scrutiny. After all, navigation was his specialty above all else.

I can recall two occasions when I had the temerity to oppose his intrusion into my area of responsibility. One had to do with his suggestion that we change the Mk IXA averaging sextant we were using to the earlier Mk VIII single shot version. I resisted the suggested change and, when I persisted, he challenged me to prove my point by having a competition with him to establish which sextant was the more accurate. My reply was that any competition between us would hardly be a fair test of the sextants, he being a professional, and I a rank amateur. It's possible he was just testing me, or he accepted my arguments in support of the better "amateur's" sextant because he made no further effort to enforce the changeover. Later on, however, when I refused to name poorer navigators in the squadron so that he could replace them with navigators he would select from 77 Squadron, he lost his patience and simply made his own choices. Although there was considerable resentment, particularly among crews involved in the changes, for me at least there was a brighter side. Bennett included his own navigator in those he transferred from 77 Squadron and I was henceforth relieved of any requirement to fly with him. I went back to flying with my own crew, something which soon proved to be more than just enjoyable.

Late in March, all the squadron air crew members were ordered to report to the station theatre. Because this was unusual, many of us found ourselves remembering the Huls affair, and it was a noisy, curious crowd that assembled, waiting to hear what was in the wind. There was a good deal of chatter and the usual humorous and raucous remarks circulated as we speculated aloud on the possible reasons for this assembly. Then the room became still. We stood at attention, in silence as the station commander entered, accompanied by Air Vice Marshal Carr, the AOC of our Bomber Command Group, 4. The silence was ominous, heavy with anticipation.

The way the AOC asked us to be seated was serious, his voice overshadowed by thought. What was coming next? Fortunately, he was not one to stall and as soon as everyone was seated he said, "Gentlemen, I know how proud you are of the reputation your squadron has earned. It is because of that excellent reputation and the high standards which you have achieved that 10 Squadron has been selected for a special and possibly vital assignment. I must emphasize, however, that the hazards of this operation are such that it will be on a "volunteer" basis only." He paused at this point and looked about the room, giving us a few moments to absorb the import of what he had just said. Then he added, "Any crew member who wishes to withdraw has that opportunity now, before I say any more."

No matter what any of us had speculated, I am sure that no one had contemplated a suicide raid. There was a quiet shuffling of feet and craning of necks as various crew captains made eye contact with their mates, receiving a smile here, a thumbs up there. Signs of agreement spread throughout the room as crews mentally came together in acceptance of the commitment which was being laid upon them. After a short pause, during which it became evident that no one was leaving, the AOC spoke again. He was visibly moved by this show of solidarity and, perforce, kept his remarks brief. "Gentlemen," he said, "you do me proud. Security in this matter is paramount. We will not be able to use every crew in the squadron, so we cannot tell you more until we have made the crew selections. Even then, the information you receive will be only for those who are selected. Until that time, I want to thank all of you. And may God bless you." We dispersed. This time speculation was quiet as individual crews gathered to discuss their prospects of being selected and wonder what the target might be.

It was soon apparent that only the most experienced of our crews had been chosen, regardless of rank or responsibility. It also meant that every flight leader from the squadron commander down was involved. We learned that the weapon we were to use didn't even exist; it was being developed and built under the personal guidance of the admiral in charge of explosives at the admiralty. This information raised the prospect of mines being involved and led to a new round of speculation. Subsequently, we learned that the size of the weapon we would be carrying would prevent us from closing our bomb doors in flight. But what was more disconcerting was the discovery that we would have to drop whatever it was from very low level without knowing whether it would blow us out of the sky on detonation! Time was running out apparently, when we were finally advised that one of the weapons was being delivered in time for us to flight test it.

We prepared two of our squadron Halifaxes, "O" and another belonging to one of our more experienced RAF NCO pilots, Sgt Wyatt. We were detailed to fly to Filey Bay on the coast of Yorkshire where there was a firing range. There, we were supposed to drop the weapon from a height of exactly 150 feet above the sea. Our task was to fly alongside Wyatt's aircraft and photograph the results. The weapon resembled a gigantic football. It weighed more than 1000 lbs and half of it hung out the bomb doors, below the fuselage. It didn't seem as if there would be any difficulty in following them and taking pictures of its fall.

Our two aircraft made the bombing run together and I began taking photographs as soon as they called "Bombs away," wondering at the same time if I was going to witness and record their demise in a monstrous spout of water. But nothing happened! The great metal ball still hung in their bomb bay. We made another run. Again, the same thing. That damned great ball refused to fall and hung there obscene and mocking. As we circled for a third run, we heard Wyatt say, "To hell with it. If it hasn't gone by now, it isn't going to go, at least not with me flying it." With that, he turned for home with us tagging along behind and, perhaps, equally relieved by the lack of results. It would have been sickening to watch them die in the experiment. When we reached base, we allowed the other aircraft to precede us, figuring that the sooner it was on the ground, the happier the crew would be. We were absolutely horrified when he touched down. The weapon fell out of the bomb bay and began rolling in pursuit of them down the runway!

Fortunately, the weapon had been designed not to explode on impact but under some thirty feet of water. It was detonated by a hydrostatic fuse which, in this instance, had been driven into the centre of the mine when it hit the ground. The scene from our perspective was Mack Sennett all the way, particularly after the nerve-wracking frustration of the abortive tests. But there was nothing comic about it for Wyatt and his crew. As soon as they had touched down, albeit a little hard, the tail gunner had called on the intercom, "Hey, Skipper, did we lose our tail wheel?" Wyatt had replied, more than a little caustically at this implied criticism of his landing, "No, of course we haven't you bloody clod." At which the gunner quickly came back with, "Well, something's chasing us." Wyatt realized immediately what had happened and, though he could not get airborne again at that stage, he pushed the throttles wide open to speed up his taxiing and keep ahead of the mine until he could finally turn off to greater safety. Although the flight test had not worked out quite as planned, it did seem fairly certain that the mine would not explode on impact with the water and that our chances of dropping it safely at low level were fairly good.

More and more incidental information had been coming our way, but we were still ignorant of our target. It was almost the end of the month when the selected crews were assembled and briefed on our objective. We were to attack the German battleship *Tirpitz*. It was moored in the Aaltern Fiord, near Trondheim, Norway, where it had been under repair. Reports had been received that she was nearing readiness for action. The prospect of the *Tirpitz* on the loose in the Atlantic or on the northern flank was a dreaded one. It was essential that she be sunk if possible, or at least rendered inoperative, at any cost. The Home Fleet, so necessary for other duties, was being wasted by its obligation to stand by in case the *Tirpitz* broke out. The importance of the operation was impressed upon us by the presence of the AOC at the briefing and the personal messages he brought from the Prime Minister and from our C in C, A/M Harris.

From excellent photographs and small-scale maps of the site, we were able to visualize our task quite clearly. The Aaltern Fiord was situated at the inner, eastern end of the much larger Trondheim Fiord on whose southern shore was the town of Trondheim. The berth of the *Tirpitz* placed the ship against the northern shore, almost completely sheltered by an overhanging cliffside. Just over a mile from her, the eastern end of the Aaltern terminated in cliffs that rose abruptly to about 1500 feet. The four oversized footballs that each of us would carry would have to be aimed under the stern of the ship, her most vulnerable area. Since the mast height of the *Tirpitz* was 150 feet, that was the height at which we were to attack.

We were briefed to enter and fly down the Trondheim Fiord at 4000 feet, then dive to 150 feet, and enter the Aaltern at 225 knots for the attack. This was supposed to assist us in making the steep pull-up over the face of the cliff at the far end. It would be a hectic few minutes of violent activity in very confined quarters and under trying conditions. Accuracy was vital, even inches could mean the difference between success and failure, life and death. If all went as planned, we would fly the route to the target and make our attacks individually in bright moonlight. We would have to leave from Lossiemouth, an advanced base in Scotland, whence the trek was almost entirely over water. Because of the lack of navigational aids, the flight to and from the target would be primarily a problem only for the observers. Though the route was essentially undefended, it would be a very grim prospect for any aircraft returning in a damaged condition.

On the 29th, we took off from Leeming with our weapons on board and flew out to sea, then northward along the coastline toward Lossiemouth. Even that part of the operation was not without excitement. Our flight path that morning took us by one of the in-shore convoys that regularly plied those waters. Though we were well clear of the ships, flying parallel to them in broad daylight and in our easily identifiable, black, four-engined bombers, their escorting mine sweepers and gun ships opened up on us with very accurate light anti-aircraft fire. We veered quickly away, giving them a much wider berth, but not before we had sustained some minor flak damage!

When we reached Lossiemouth, one of our pilots, trying to gain the maximum landing run for his heavily-laden aircraft, put his wheels into the ditch at the edge. The aircraft skidded literally on its belly and its balls all the way across. Fortunately, the airfield was grass, but the aircraft kept on sliding until the nose finally rested against the wall of a hangar. It was another of those Mack Sennett scenes. From the air, we could see the crew spewing out of the escape hatches, running for safety, while the aircraft was still sliding. The last man to leave was the pilot, from the hatch above his head. His speed afoot made up for his later start and we saw him overtake some of the slower escapees in their race away from the exposed monster balls.

The following day we made our sortie. We reached the general area without incident, but the weather was hopeless. No attack was possible. It was such an abortive attempt that we probably didn't even sacrifice our security. To avoid a repeat of this kind of wasted effort, a Blenheim daylight bomber from 2 Group was assigned to carry out daily reconnaissance of the Northern area. It was flown by a Canadian in the RAF, then W/C "Mike" Pollard, with an RAF observer, F/L Hindle, who had been on the bombing leaders course at RAF Manby with me.

33rd bombing leaders course at R.A.F. Manby.

We were committed; there was no turning back. For almost a month we waited at Lossiemouth, getting to know more about the area and the friendly people who lived there. Finally, the alert was given. The forecast was good and the daylight reconnaissance confirmed the conditions. And the Bomber's Moon was out. On the evening of April 27, we took off and set course for Norway.

Night flying was normal for our bombers, but we were operating from a strange airfield, in a different sector of the sky. The flight over those cold, dark waters seemed longer and lonelier than before. It would be about four hours before we made landfall, with nothing positive to confirm our navigation along the way. Search and rescue facilities were just about non-existent and the water temperature would make death quick and certain for any who were so unfortunate as to have to ditch or bail out. Despite the absence of enemy defences, the flight out was not particularly comforting.

Right on ETA we made our landfall on the lonely, rugged coast of Norway, on track for the entry to Trondheim Fiord. It was both a relief and a boost to our morale to look down upon that austerely beautiful coastline where we could see clearly defined and easily identified islands and fiords in the contrasting snow and water. We set our heading into the main fiord, knowing that we were right on the button and on our way to meet the *Tirpitz*.

It was awe-inspiring: snowy mountains, steep cliffs sheering up from dark water and the bright light of the moon emphasizing the stark black and white contrasts. Everything around us seemed still and quiet. It was almost as if we were flying into a massive cathedral. We flew down that majestic fiord at our planned 4000 feet, no sign of life to be seen even though we knew that the town of Trondheim lay quiet and invisible on the starboard as we penetrated deeper and deeper. There had to be Germans down there, we knew, just as there had to be a *Tirpitz* lying ahead of us, like a stick of dynamite waiting to explode in our faces.

We began our dive to 150 feet and entered the Aaltern Fiord at the required speed of 225 knots. As we passed its sharp, leading edge, I punched my stopwatch and picked up the small hand-held bomb-sight with which we had been equipped for the operation. At that very moment, we flew into a smoke screen that was so dense it seemed impenetrable. It was like flying in cotton wool. There was no sense of motion, no spatial relativity. We knew we were thundering alongside a solid wall of rocky cliffs, practically brushing it with our wing tips and speeding towards an even higher, but equally solid cliff not far ahead. And we were blind. Somewhere, in this ghastly smoke lay the mighty battleship whose masts we might even touch. There was no thinning of the smoke, not even a breath and we had reached the end of our timed run. The *Tirpitz* had to be dead ahead or even under us. I pressed the bomb release. We pulled up at full throttle, hoping against hope that we had not miscalculated, not overshot the seconds we needed to clear the bloody great cliff we knew was there but couldn't see. None of us wanted to end up like flies splattered on a wall.

I know that I held my breath as the extra power surged into the Merlins and the revs picked up. There was nothing to guide us but the sound of the aircraft, the feeling as she angled upwards and her propellers bit more aggressively into that thick grey smoke. Everything looked the same above, below, beside, and "O" seemed to hang in limbo. It could have been an eternity before we finally broke clear of that smoky quicksand into the crystalline air of the winter night. Then we could see. Beneath and behind us, the whole Aaltern fiord was covered by a thick, opaque layer of smoke. The Germans had obviously been able to get sufficient warning of our attack to fire up their chemical smoke generators which must have ringed the fiord. They had succeeded in covering the battleship before the first attacker reached her. It was so successful that they had confidently held their fire to prevent it from providing any guidance to us. We had, therefore, at least been spared the ordeal of the hail of flak we had anticipated. We were considerably relieved to be flying home without casualty or damage.

It was almost dawn when we landed back at Lossiemouth. The gathering in the debriefing room was growing large as the last crews arrived to add their reports of attacks through the smoke. The rum, which had been liberally added to the usual mugs of hot tea for the returning air crew, was beginning to increase the high spirits of the relieved men. By the time the last of the crews arrived, the debriefing had an air of celebration. It was the AOC, who had flown to Lossiemouth specially to attend, who burst the bubble. Standing on a chair, he called for silence. When he had our attention, he said, "Gentlemen, I know that everyone has done his best tonight, but your best was not enough. We have no assurance that the *Tirpitz* has been put out of action. The enemy is now alerted to our intentions and we can take no more chances. I want all of you to return to your beds . . . now. Get some sleep. You will attack the *Tirpitz* again tonight. Sleep well."

It was anticlimactic. The hustle and bustle of joyful exuberance dissipated as if by magic. A lot of tired, thoughtful, and rumpled airmen filed out of the debriefing room that early morning. The cold they felt wasn't attributable solely to the temperature of the Scottish morning as they trickled into breakfast and then into bed. The knowledge that they would be off again in a matter of hours to confront the *Tirpitz* in its narrow fiord gave no warmth to ward off the chill of dawn.

There was no air of eagerness in the crew room that evening of the 28th as the men began preparations for their third attempt on the Tirpitz. The novelty and exhilaration of having been specially selected for such a vital and difficult target had evaporated over the long duration and repeated exposures. Grim determination to see the job through and pride in having been recognized as an elite squadron had become the primary motivators. All of us had paid the price for our experience. We all knew what was likely to be ahead of us this time. It could be the last blow many of us would strike against the enemy, but we were adamant. We would get the *Tirpitz*. And the Germans were probably just as determined to defend her. Though each of us knew that some among us would make the ultimate sacrifice, not one believed it would be his fate. Such is the faith of the young and, often, the source of their courage. Even so, it was a somewhat sombre group of airmen who set off once again for Norway and the jewel of the German Navy.

The hours of flight over the sea were a repeat of the previous night and my thoughts and activities were fully occupied by the task of navigating us to that fiord. Once again, we made landfall on schedule. The air over the Trondheim Fiord was clear and cold, visibility was excellent, and the mountains stood in the same black and white relief under the bright moon. This time the feeling was more foreboding than religious as we began our run to the Aaltern Fiord and its waiting cliffs. We were surprised at the town of Trondheim to see a searchlight reaching for us across the water. It caught us, but at our relatively low altitude we felt we were probably out of the slant range of any anti-aircraft guns which might have been sited there. We weren't unduly concerned, and we weren't being shot at. Suddenly, the mid-upper gunner shouted on the intercom, "Fighter. Fighter. In the beam on the starboard!" This came as a real shock, a totally unexpected turn of events. It was enough to raise the hairs on the back of your neck. Any moment I expected to hear those cannon shells hammering into the fuselage.

Everything seemed to happen at once. Jimmie, our wireless operator, began screaming on the intercom, "Get me out of here! Tom! Get me out of here!" If the sighting of the fighter hadn't already raised your hackles, those hysterical screams certainly would have. Since I was the closest to Jimmie, I reached over and pulled out his intercom plug. He could scream all he liked, no one would hear him now. We were almost at the approach to the Aaltern by then, so I directed Tom to make his dive immediately while I guided him toward the entrance of the fiord. As we entered, however, the need for guidance became minimal. Ahead of us was a cauldron of anti-aircraft fire. Across and down into the fiord from the surrounding cliff walls, light anti-aircraft guns were firing continuously. Tracers laced the air from side to side and shells were striking the opposing cliff faces and the water too. In the centre of all this fury lay the *Tirpitz* firing the guns of all her anti-aircraft batteries into the sky above her.

The criss-crossing tracers from the shore guns and the fire from the ship made the air space over the *Tirpitz* a maw of molten metal which appeared to be absolutely impenetrable. Talk about the Charge of the Light Brigade! No one in his right mind would fly through that barrage. Certainly no German nightfighter. I took Tom through the molten hell, over the *Tirpitz,* and out again over the cliff wall at the end. The fighter broke off when he saw us head for the flak and made no attempt to follow us into the Aaltern Fiord. But, I had not been able to make a satisfactory bombing run so had not dropped the mines as we cleared the top of the battleship. We would have to go around again and make a second diving approach. Hopefully, the fighter would not be there to distract us.

As on the previous night, we must have been the first aircraft to arrive at the target when we ran in to shake off that fighter. We had been able to see the entire length of the *Tirpitz* clearly even though they had stretched canvasses on frames at the bow and the stern to disguise her outline. As we climbed out of that first run and began to make our turn, the others were starting their bombing runs. We saw one Halifax rear up out of that hellfire of flak to escape the cliff wall. It was engulfed in flames, obviously crippled. Its flying speed carried the craft up in a high arc before it plummeted back in a blazing stall. We didn't see anyone escape. Everything was happening too fast now for cogent observation. When we made our second run through the fiord and the flak, the picture had changed. We ran along the edge of the walls, exactly at mast height, and began the drop of our four mines in a short string aimed at the stern of the *Tirpitz*. As we pulled up, we could see the explosions of our weapons. One and two were clean spumes of water, three was dirty, and four was slightly delayed. Presumably it had bounced off the cliff wall or rolled off the deck of the ship, but it was dirty as well. The canvas camouflage at the stern was almost totally destroyed and though she appeared clear at the bow, the ship's stern was awash. We were so excited at what we could see and the apparent success of our own attack, that we paid little heed to the hail of fire through which we were flying or the damage we were absorbing. Our stomachs sank as we pulled clear of the cliff and the flak. Only then did we begin to think about our chances of making it back. We had probably been the first on target when we made our initial run and it seemed we were the last to attack when we made the second.

The damage we received was apparently only superficial and, miraculously, no one in the crew had been injured in either of our runs through the flak. It looked as if we would be able to make it back to Lossiemouth and we began to think about the report we would make. We were exuberant about the success of the attack and our escape unscathed. Our joy was tempered though by the knowledge that others had not been so fortunate. We wondered just how many had been lost.

Our dawn debriefing was not a joyful occasion. It looked as if we had failed to sink the *Tirpitz,* though we were personally convinced that she had been put out of action. Hopefully, for the price we paid, she would be unserviceable for a long time. Our CO, W/C Bennett, and almost all of our flight leaders had been lost. Nearly half of the force we sent did not return. Of the half that did survive, there were severe casualties and some of the aircraft had been so badly damaged they had been forced to land on the first island they could reach on the way home. Not one of the remaining aircraft had made it through that cauldron of fire without sustaining damage. The few who made it back to Lossiemouth told their story quietly, hung about until it was certain that no more survivors would make it, and then sadly made their way to bed. The excitement was over, the adrenalin long since exhausted. All emotion had drained away. What remained were weary bodies, shells that needed time to rest and to recoup.

Those of us who were serviceable flew back to Leeming and the squadron members we had left behind. The next morning, Tom and I were walking down the flight line when a saloon car drove up behind us and stopped by our side. It was our AOC, A/V/M Carr. He had driven from Group HQ looking for us so he could debrief us again in person. It had been determined from all the crew reports that we had indeed been the last to attack and, therefore, the last to have seen the *Tirpitz* that night. He wanted to hear our report again and to clarify some of the points he had in mind to assist him in assessing the probability and the extent of the damage to the battleship. This assessment must have been vital to the decision which had to be made about what might still have to be done to keep the *Tirpitz* from escaping into open seas.

Shortly thereafter, the squadron received the following message from A/M Harris. "The courage and determination shown by your crews in the attacks on the *Tirpitz* were indeed worthy of immediate and outstanding success. Moreover, undismayed by their first experience of the full fury of the defences, they returned with undiminished ardour to the charge. Never was more asked, and never was more given of outstanding devotion to duty. We shall, I hope, yet find that their efforts have not been in vain, but be that as it may, your crews have set an example unsurpassed in the annals of British arms." Had our success been more readily apparent, had those weapons we carried been capable of sinking that mighty battleship, who knows what would have followed. As it turned out, the *Tirpitz* remained in the fiord for many months after our attack, presumably under repair again, before further efforts had to be made to keep her out of action. As long as she remained a threat, the power of the Royal Navy's Home Fleet was vitiated.

Not long after our return to Leeming, Tom and I were both awarded the Distinguished Flying Cross for our attacks on the *Tirpitz*.

Chapter XX

There was no delay in our returning to normal operational duty. Within a couple of days, we were back in the pack, in a force of eighty-one attacking Hamburg. Once again, the weather favoured the enemy — and I thought God was supposed to be on our side. It was an unpleasant North Sea crossing and, when we arrived, clouds covered the entire target area. Visual identification was impossible. In spite of our reluctance, we were forced to drop blindly through the clouds, relying on my navigation that indicated we were over Hamburg. Of the five bombers lost that night, three were Halifaxes. It seemed a high price to pay for what was more than likely a wasted effort.

By that time, we had given up tossing the empty beer bottles and the four-pound incendiaries from the flare chute. Sound no longer played any part in the German air defences. The advent of radar had made it the intelligence source for all elements of their defence system: the searchlights, the anti-aircraft guns, and the dreaded night-fighters. One might say that the fun was going out of the game. Not that it was ever amusing; there were just some more lighthearted aspects in the lack of sophistication at the beginning. Even they had gone. The war was becoming much more technical and much more costly in terms of both men and materials.

Unknown to us, the English had successfully conducted experiments to fool radar with specially sized strips of reflective metal foil. These had been done in the greatest of secrecy because of the threat it would pose to our own defences should the Germans have learned about them in time to use them against us. A countermeasure had to be developed concurrently. At last it was found and, instead of beer bottles and incendiaries, we began tossing out of our flare chutes bundles of "window," the code name for those strips. We dropped them at predetermined intervals when we were within the German air defence system. They would trigger innumerable false echoes on the ground radar screens which would either jam them or at least cover the legitimate radar responses to our aircraft. It was just one more device in the constant struggle for supremacy between offence and defence in the air war, an ongoing see-saw which had been waged since the beginning and would be until the very end. This battle of technologies was conducted on our side by those we called the "boffins," of whom we could all be proud and whose ingenuity and creativity were unique and vital contributions to our survival.

My schoolboy enthusiasm may have been wearing a bit thin by that time. But my level of performance had become an integral part of me, and I was able to press on with undiminished dedication. The fact that I had become a veteran had crept up on me and never really registered. Maybe it was because those who survived along with me had become my only companions. And they were evolving in the same pattern as I. The squadron had become home, its members my family. It made a tight little community in the turmoil of war, independent of and isolated from the rest of society by the absorbing and unique demands imposed upon us by our part in the war. Every thought and every effort were directed to one goal — completing the next operation successfully. No one ever planned further ahead than that. It was simplistic perhaps, but it was a philosophy that was both practical and satisfying. I don't think I ever consciously contemplated the completion of a tour. Just as when I joined the RCAF, I had not known that you graduated as a sergeant, never mind a commissioned officer; when I joined the squadron, I had no idea that a tour of operations consisted of thirty trips and few completed more than one. In neither case, therefore, was it a goal to be achieved or a disappointment if I fell short. This ingenuousness made life in the service much easier for me; all I had to do was my best, come what may.

The weather remained foul for some time. It was the 19th of May before we were called upon to mount another attack. Then it was 197 bombers against Mannheim. The sea crossing was uneventful, but the clouds grew progressively thicker the closer we got to the continent. By the time we reached Mannheim, the cloud conditions hadn't improved. It wasn't until we had searched the area for some time that we were lucky enough to identify the target and make a good bombing run. Their defences were determined and persistent, but not as heavy as we had expected. The cloud prevented the attack from being concentrated, but the trail of fire and smoke indicated that considerable damage had been inflicted by the time the raid was over.

Though we had certainly not been suffering from boredom, we were soon to be electrified by the news that our next operation was to be the largest bomber attack ever launched. We were to participate in the first 1000-bomber raid of the war! The target was to be Cologne, in the centre of the Ruhr, the most industrialized and the most heavily defended area in Germany. Many raids had previously been carried out against targets in the Ruhr, but few had been effective because of local visibility difficulties and the concentration of defences surrounding that vital area.

New tactics were to be tested in this raid, tactics that would concentrate this massive force in time and space over Cologne, in a density never before attained. It was hoped that this would bring about certain benefits: first, to overload the ground defences and prevent their concentrating on any individual attacker; and, second, to overload the fire and rescue services by providing no interlude in the attack for organized succour. If successful, this raid could become a turning point in Bomber Command's offensive.

In the original planning of the attack, our crew was the only one in 4 Group authorized to carry a camera to record the raid in progress. However, later in the day, this order was rescinded and all aircraft were so authorized. Presumably, it had been a concern about the number of photoflashes being dropped over the target which had limited the number of cameras being carried. Fortunately, wiser heads prevailed. As it turned out, we had engine failure before reaching the continent and had to abort the operation. Had it been a simple failure, we might have been able to continue. But the rod which controlled the pitch on one of the propeller blades broke. This allowed the one blade to turn to a flat pitch, keeping it out of synchronization whether we feathered the engine or not. The vibration quickly became severe and uncontrollable. We had no alternative but to get down as fast as we could.

We were thus denied the pleasure of helping to make history that night, for the attack did indeed prove that concentration of numbers in time and space could overwhelm even a highly organized and disciplined ground defence, at least temporarily. It was also clear that the sustained concentration of the attack had created an unprecedented level of havoc on the ground. The experiment was a remarkable success. Suddenly, there was renewed hope that the loss rate in Bomber Command, which had been climbing steadily to unacceptable levels, might be reduced. Calculated on a purely mathematical basis, no one would survive to complete one tour of thirty operations at the current loss rates. Of course, in practice, it didn't work out quite that way because the higher losses occurred persistently in the less experienced crews. So, at least a few of the old sweats would always make it. It was simply that, the higher the loss statistics rose, the fewer of even the veterans would survive.

It had taken extraordinary measures for Bomber Command to assemble the mass of aircraft required to attack Cologne that 30th night of May. Some 1092 bombers took off, including all the "heavies," supported by the remaining Wellingtons, Whitleys, and Hampdens. They even pressed aircraft from the operational training units, crewed by instructors and students, into the foray. It was an effort that could never be sustained on a continuing basis. However, because of the significant reduction in the loss rate incurred in the Cologne raid — 41 of the 1047 which actually attacked — it was possible to mount a second 1000-bomber raid on the following night, before the assembled crews and aircraft had to return to their normal duties.

Prior to the 1000-bomber raid on Cologne, attacks on the Ruhr had been essentially ineffective and very costly in terms of men and aircraft losses. Though it rated highly with the strategists because of the heavy industrial targets located there, it was not a favourite of the bomber crews. In their usual satirical fashion, they called the Ruhr

"Happy Valley." As though to prove their point, either in experiment or in strategy, the target selected for the second "raid of the 1000" was again in the Ruhr, the city of Essen.

Fortune smiled on us at last. The weather forecast was ideal, and "O" was serviceable. The moon was bright, the sky clear. Only a ground haze made the target difficult to see for those in the leading wave. But the intensity of the attack increased by the minute as the fires started by the early arrivals lit the way for those who followed. Before long, the whole city seemed to be reduced to flames and billowing smoke. The searchlights were hopelessly erratic, the flak so intermittent as to be much less effective. In fact, there seemed to be greater danger of collision among the bombers or of being bombed from above, than of being shot down by the enemy! When we turned away from Essen, we were astonished to look back for mile after mile and see the fires still burning brightly. It was another successful assault on the heart of German industry. I felt sure that more damage had been inflicted by these two raids than by all the previous attacks on the Ruhr put together.

The results pointed not only to tactics which promised a survivable loss rate for our bombers — 31 out of 1060 over Essen — but also to destructive forces well beyond the simple increase in bomb loads delivered. We were achieving a multiplier effect in the combination of incendiaries and high explosives in prolonged concentration. This phenomenon later came to be known as a "fire storm" when the technique was refined and applied intentionally.

The path to the future was clear, but Bomber Command wasn't yet ready to exploit it fully. In the meantime, the war against Germany had to be fought within the limits of the available means. It was early summer. The nights were shorter. The targets had to be at closer range and the number of bombers on each operation reverted to their previous totals.

Two nights later, we attacked Bremen. In spite of the fact that only 170 bombers participated, we had considerable success in damaging the U-Boat yards. After another two nights' respite, we returned to Essen with a moderate sized force of 180. This concentration on the

Ruhr was having its effect, not only in the havoc being wreaked, but also on the effort which the Germans were forced to expend on their defences. The flak and searchlight concentrations were the most intense we had ever experienced over a German target. Their numbers had increased and their level of skill seemed to have improved just as noticeably. If this could be taken as any indication of the success of our efforts, then they must have been hurting badly. Again, we found the target without great difficulty and we could see good concentrations of fires and explosions within the city confines as we flew overhead. Recovery work from the earlier 1000-bomber raid must have been seriously disrupted by our second raid.

With the smaller attack force, however, and the reinforced defences, our losses were much more severe. We were back to those unacceptable rates again. On the Bremen operation, we lost 11, and at Essen, 12. This was a loss rate of 7 per cent. The majority of them had been shot down by the radar-controlled nightfighters whose effectiveness was enhanced by the smaller forces involved and the resultant ability of the ground radars to concentrate more often on individual bombers in the stream.

Tom, who had flown as a co-pilot before becoming the captain of our crew, was screened from operations following the second Essen raid and was posted to a Heavy Conversion Unit in 4 Group as an instructor. I was recommended to Group HQ for appointment as captain of the aircraft. It was a considerable honour when the AOC approved my appointment, as I was one of only a very few observers to be so appointed in the entire command. On Tom's departure, therefore, the squadron commander gave me my choice of the available pilots to complete my crew. Sgt Gibbons, an Australian pilot, had been flying with us recently as a second pilot. He was among those available. Since this was a matter of importance to all members of the crew, I took the opportunity to discuss the choice with them. It was unanimous; we agreed that it would be preferable to have Sgt Gibbons rather than a stranger. He was already familiar with each of us and with our attitudes and personalities, and we felt he would fit in without creating any disturbing influences.

Just about then, we were elated to hear that W/C Bennett had survived the explosion of his aircraft as it climbed out of the fiord away from the Tirpitz. He and his co-pilot had bailed out and had escaped on foot through the snowy mountains to Sweden. Following internment, he was released and secretly flown back to England where he was awarded the Distinguished Service Order and granted his request to resume command of 10 Squadron. We were unhappy about losing the admirable and popular "Willie" Tait who had been posted in to replace Bennett. But Bennett had also risen immeasurably in our esteem because of his display of fortitude, courage, and intelligence in his escape, and because of his express wish to resume command of the squadron. Loyalty begets loyalty. In spite of the loss of a most likeable and respected commander in Tait, we welcomed our former commander back to the fold.

On the 16th of June, in a force of 106 heavies, we were committed to resume the attack on the Ruhr. The target was Essen again. Bomber Command was determined to maximize the damage done to this important industrial region and to undermine morale even further by rendering their restoration efforts to naught. This was our first sortie with the sergeant at the controls. It wasn't an auspicious beginning. Over the North Sea, we developed engine trouble and couldn't maintain height with the load we were carrying. We had to jettison our bomb load in order to stay aloft and then return to base — a complete abort. The attack turned out to be ineffective. Only a few bombers were able to identify the primary target; the remainder dropped their bombs on alternatives. Once again though, the strongly-reinforced defences made the approaches to the target area a grim battle ground. The nightfighters were much in evidence and quickly proving to be the enemy's most effective weapon. Our loss rate on this raid crept up to 8 per cent, which only served to increase our sense of relative ineffectiveness.

On the 19th and 20th, we participated in medium-sized attacks of 194 and 185 heavies respectively, on Emden. In spite of the heavy flak and searchlight concentrations, we were able to drop our bombs on the primary target both nights, but the effects seemed scattered and sporadic. The results were unlikely to have been as damaging as we would have wished. The nightfighters were very active again and able to work their way well into the bomber stream. On both nights, the incendiary tracers from their cannon fire that cut through the dark sky were dancing balls of fire that either whipped by or struck you.

We were lucky on the 20th. The corkscrew evasive action was taken just at the right moment of the fighter's attack. Cannon shells ripped past us as he overshot. Either he lost us in the dark or found another target in a better position to follow up. We breathed a sigh of relief, but only a brief one. Even a short let-up in vigilance could be costly; once you were targeted, your chances diminished. In this case, though, they must have lost us, traded us for another bomber in the stream, or run out of fuel or ammunition. Thank God for us, no other nightfighter came at us. We were able to complete the operation and return to base without further interruption. These two attacks on Emden were far from successful. A large share of the bombs fell on Osnabruck, eighty miles away, the first night, and only part of the force located the target on the second night. The losses, however, dipped to 4 and 5 per cent respectively.

On June 25, we were excited to be able once again to take part in a major assault. That time we had 1067 bombers laid on to attack Bremen. The weather betrayed us. We arrived over the target to find it covered solidly by heavy cloud. During our search, we sighted Wilhelmshaven, another important port city, and clear of cloud. We were able to pin-point the docks and deliver an accurate attack. In this case, though, there was no saturation of the defences to provide us cover. We were pretty well alone in our attack. Though we didn't see any nightfighters, we were the object of the undivided attention of the entire searchlight and anti-aircraft gun defences of Wilhelmshaven. It was a rough ride to say the least. We were coned throughout our bombing run by the lights and peppered by flak all the time. Fortunately, we received no major damage and were able to drop our bombs accurately in the dock area and take a good photograph to confirm it.

In spite of the heavy cloud cover over Bremen that night, a large number of our bombers had considerable success dropping their weapons blindly. We lost 48 bombers and their crews that night. Taken in isolation, this was considerable, but it was a loss rate of just over 4 per cent, which was acceptable in the long run, if only statistically.

Chapter XXI

Following that series of attacks, two significant things happened: first, the squadron was taken off operations; and, second, I was considered to be tour-expired. The first event sort of obscured the second because I wasn't posted immediately, but remained, for the time, the squadron navigation officer and bombing leader. Rumours were rife as to the reason for our being stood down. It wasn't long, however, before it became evident that the squadron was being readied for a foreign assignment. The aircraft engines were being modified for flying in warmer climates. Since I was still navigation leader, at least nominally, it would be my job to prepare the observers for whatever lay ahead.

When I learned about the mission for which we were bound, a secret flight to the Black Sea area for a short period of duty in support of the Soviets, I didn't feel that we could prepare everything adequately before our scheduled departure. Much would have to be done after we arrived, and I felt strongly that it would be inadvisable to hand over my responsibilities to a new man on the eve of unfamiliar duties in strange territory. Besides, I was simply bursting to be part of this new venture. I therefore appealed to the squadron commander who agreed with me, and who arranged for me to see the station commander. At the end of the interview, I was given permission to remain on the job for the duration of the special assignment.

We had all been confined to camp, incommunicado, for a number of days when on July 5, notices posted on the bulletin boards of the messes advised the listed personnel to report that same afternoon to the station hospital. We gathered there and found the MO quite literally rolling up his sleeves, surrounded by an array of containers and hypodermic needles. As the syringes were being loaded, the MO said in a voice somewhat lacking in bedside manner, "Sorry chaps, but there just isn't enough time. I'll have to give each of you the lot in one shot, Doc's cocktail you might say!" With that, he took each of us in turn and injected the potpourri, of every serum required by regulations for travellers to the east, into our upper left arm. One huge bloody great shot. Just to prove it, I still have a floating nodule at the exact spot where that shot was given.

Despite that unwholesome injection, and possibly only because of our excitement and enthusiasm at the prospect of a new and different experience, we were all up with the dawn, eager to be on our way. At 0700, our tropical gear stowed with us, we were airborne and setting course for Gibraltar. What a feeling of happy intoxication there was as each aircraft thundered down the runway, heavily laden not only with its air and ground crew, but also with a share of spare parts and ground handling equipment which would be required for maintenance in a foreign environment. In addition, each aircraft carried a full fuel load for the long over-water flight from Leeming to Gibraltar. There would be no safe alternatives along the way if any of us ran into difficulties.

It was more than a bit of an anticlimax, therefore, when we had to land back at base one and a half hours later with an unserviceability. But we were airborne and on our way once again by 0930. After an uneventful, but watchful, flight across the Bay of Biscay, we landed at Gibraltar, nine hours and fifty minutes later.

Landing on "The Rock" was quite a challenge, particularly for the first time, and was made even more so by the load we were carrying. The landing strip ran across, that is only the width of, the thin neck of land which joins it to Spain. The length of the runway was, therefore, strictly limited. It had been built up out of the water on both sides of the neck by rock fill from the excavations which the army were making within the Rock itself. Although work to extend it was almost continuous, it was still too short for our large and heavily-laden Halifaxes. The hot weather and the position of the runway, lying as it did in the lee of the Rock, subjected it to unpredictable wind shears. If landing there was hazardous, it paled by comparison to the perils of taking off at maximum all-up weight. The aircraft skeletons marring the clarity of the waters off both ends of the strip paid mute testimony to the risks involved.

The flight from Gibraltar to Egypt was expected to be difficult and hazardous. We were required to fly down the middle of the Mediterranean in order to stay clear of the German and Italian air defences to the north and those of the Vichy French to the south. All of them could be expected to attack us if we strayed within their range. We were also under orders to avoid Malta, except in dire emergency, because the arrival of RAF heavy bombers there would only draw intensified assaults on that already battered island. Besides, the small reserve of fuel there had been delivered at a bitter cost in men and material, for survival of the island and not for our use. The flight would also be at the limit of our safe range. There would be little, if any, reserve for evasive manoeuvres, bad navigation, or poor engine handling. If we succeeded, W/C Bennett's persistent efforts to maximize our aircraft and air crew performance would be more than justified. Judicious use of revs and boost would have to be the aim of each crew to achieve Bennett's target of one air mile to the gallon.

All the aircraft made it safely to Gibraltar. We spent the next few days working on them, preparing for the Egyptian leg, and adjusting to life on the Rock. It was a very sad place for many of its residents. The non-commissioned ranks of the army personnel were, in many cases, men of the regular army who had been on the Rock since before the war broke out. They had few privileges, and no opportunity to leave their fortress prison. A stone's throw away in Spain, La Linea, and its many bordellos was frustratingly out of bounds. And once the Spanish workers returned home at the end of each day, there were no women on the island other than the commissioned nurses. The only available outlet for these unfortunate Rock Hounds was the plentiful booze. The bars, however, could be dangerous places for the unwary when the stir-crazy army types or some visiting navy crews were venting their frustrations. Being a "Brylcream Boy" was no protection, as one of our Canadians found out to his discomfort. He took a couple of heavy boots in the face, while being held by two of his assailants' buddies in the dark alley behind one of the bars, after a drunken argument. The next morning, along with his hangover, he sported two of the finest shiners I have ever seen. But, the fresh fruit, the warm clear waters, and the excellent beaches were welcome diversions and compensation for our incarceration there.

Our main daily topic of conversation was how best to get our Halifaxes airborne on that short runway, in the heat of the late afternoon, with maximum all-up weight. Each of us knew it would be touch and go and the arguments waxed hot and heavy in the messes on the merits of various schemes. One of the pilots, an older and very humorous New Zealander, claimed to have the sure-fire method. He refused to disclose his idea because he said it was so novel he first had to try it for himself.

We happened to be watching the take-offs when it was his turn to go. Like everyone else, he taxied down to the extreme end of the runway, turned, and revved up his engines to maximum power before letting off his brakes to start rolling. His speed began to increase as he rolled down the runway, his tail lifting. He had reached better than half his take-off speed by the time he crossed the road to La Linea, which intersected the strip about midpoint. But no sooner had he crossed the road than he began a violent swing. The side of the runway past the road was doubly lined with 45 gallon steel drums, filled with aviation fuel! The Halifax rumbled thunderously on without seeming to pick up any more speed, but swinging further and further towards the edge of the runway and the lines of fuel drums. Finally, and well before it reached the end of the strip, the Halifax smashed into the drums, sending them scattering like pins in a bowling alley. And then, it fell out of sight off the side of the runway.

When we saw the swing take hold, we had already started to run towards them. We were racing by the time the Halifax disappeared over the side, hoping against hope that there would be something we could do. When we reached the edge of the runway and could look down toward the harbour, there she was, barely at sea level, flying ponderously among the ships and trying to maintain flying speed as she struggled to climb out of the crowded port. Before long, we saw her circling overhead, crossing the Rock with her undercarriage still down and setting course for Egypt. Much later, we discovered that the scheme had called for the flight engineer to put on flap halfway down the runway with the object of lowering the speed normally required to get airborne. That flap manoeuvre might just have saved their lives although the violent swing had not been part of the plan. Fortunately for the rest of us, he had not shared his novel idea for take-off from Gibraltar. Unfortunately for him, it seems he did not remember to lift his undercarriage until he had wasted an unnecessary quantity of fuel. He had to crash-land, out of fuel, in the shallow waters off the coast of Egypt, where a British Eighth Army patrol picked them up.

Because all of the aircraft were not able to leave at the same time, we had to wait in Gibraltar. It was oppressive. But on the 13th, one week after our arrival, we were serviceable and briefed to go. We managed to take off without incident but didn't have time to enjoy our success. Within an hour we were back on the ground, unserviceable again. We repeated that overloaded, grinding take-off on the 18th. That time we remained airborne for all of two hours before we had to land back at Gibraltar again! Before we finally succeeded on the 12th of August, we saw everyone of our squadron crews leave for Egypt. We were the only Halifax left on the Rock. Throughout our wait, we had no news of the fortunes of the others and we worried that we'd never make it to the Black Sea in time.

After a flight that lasted twelve hours and thirty-five minutes, we at last landed at Heliopolis Airport near Cairo. We had left in the late afternoon and landed on the morning of the 13th. We breakfasted while the aircraft was refuelled and were then dispatched to a forward landing field known only as LG 224. From there, we were again re-directed to Fayid, an airfield in the Nile Delta of Egypt. It was noon of that day when we finally joined up with the rest of the squadron.

Counting in wartime days, our isolation from any information while we had been forced to stay on Gibraltar made us very eager to get caught up. Besides the one aircraft ditched on the beach, two had elected to land at Malta for refuelling. They had immediately been taken care of and hustled off the island, but not before they experienced an abortive air raid. They claimed that there was more risk of injury from the rain of shrapnel from spent anti-aircraft fire than there was from enemy action! We also learned that W/C Bennett had been removed from the crew lists just prior to our departure from Leeming. By the time we reached Fayid, our "A" flight commander, Seymour-Price, had been promoted to W/C and command of the squadron. His post went to newly promoted S/L Ray Gouldston. It began to look as if we were to remain in the Middle East as part of the Desert Air Force; our mission to the Black Sea evaporated into thin air, as did our belief that we would be away only a few days! The arrival of a similar number of Halifaxes from 76 Squadron, another in 4 Group, seemed to confirm the change in plans, or at least the plans as we had known them. We were to combine as 10/76 and finally as 462 Squadron. The latter was actually an Australian squadron number in the Commonwealth numbering system. Apparently, we had been sent there to fulfil the role of heavy bomber support for General Alexander's coming campaign in the Western Desert.

Chapter XXII

Life and operations in the desert were very different from what we had experienced in the European arena. It wasn't simply the obvious differences of desert life and generally uninhabited terrain. In England, we had been operating within a highly organized and efficient centralized command within which our squadron was a single, efficient element among other like elements. And we operated against an equally highly organized and efficient defensive structure set in some of the most urbanized areas of the world. Suddenly, we were the only heavy bomber unit in the new Desert Air Force, bereft of the intricate logistical and technical support infrastructure which had maintained and sustained us. Although we were operating in a strange and naturally hostile environment, the only active defences we faced were those which defended vital targets. There were no area defences, no concentrated belts of flak, searchlights, and fighters to penetrate on the way to our targets. We had only to contend with the actual point defences and the occasional unenthusiastic Italian Air Force Macchi fighter.

For the observers, it was even more pleasant. The skies were rarely obscured. The heavenly bodies were always there for astro sights. And, although it was generally devoid of any identifiable features, the ground was almost always visible. The predictability and reliability of meteorological conditions were an added bonus. Of course, the heat and the ubiquitous sand played havoc with the air-cooled Merlins and with us. Black Halifax airframes, looking like toothless pachyderms, their empty engine cells like gaping cavities, began to dot the desert scenery. Salt and pepper shakers dispensed flavoured sand on our food and made us fear that we might be equally toothless before long. Bully beef, which had been a virtually non-existent luxury during our stay in England, quickly became a bore in the desert. We ate it daily, in every conceivable form, hot, cold, fried, stewed, etc. Oh yes, things were different, from khaki shorts and short-sleeved shirts, to emptying your shoes every morning before putting them on, lest a scorpion had chosen one for a nest.

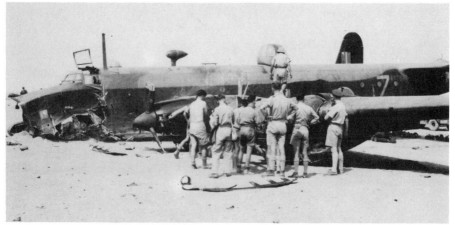

Crashed Halifax after engine failures.

Domestic side of desert operations.

The desert assignment had other perks. Sometimes you had to look beneath the unfamiliar crust of the oriental facade, but the pleasures were there. One of them was Cairo and it certainly had its crust, of filth, poverty, and teeming population. The youngsters who pestered you on every busy street to shine your shoes were a particular nuisance. They were only too likely to hold you to ransom for a higher fee after polishing only one of your shoes, or to threaten to flick their wet black brush at you if you rejected their services. Pickpockets flourished in the crowds. Even a fountain pen clipped in your breast pocket was fair game for the light-fingered, fleet-footed rascals. And on every street corner, the purveyors of pornography abounded. The Eastern flavour and the exotic atmosphere of this historic city, however, more than made up for its filth, its ragged shoeshine boys, its predatory thieves, and its omnipresent beggars, so often pitiably crippled or grossly deformed by leprosy.

But beneath this overlay were luxuries we only dreamed about in England. I well remember my first visit to the city when we went to Groppis, a marvellous restaurant and ice cream parlour. After our long spell of RAF cooking and wartime rationing, we felt like kids just released from school. We had a wonderful steak, followed by fresh strawberries and cream! The war certainly didn't seem to have reached that establishment. We were almost salivating at the anticipation of a nice cup of coffee to finish our meal and were completely taken aback by the thimble-sized cups which the waiter placed before us. Even more so by the black, muddy-looking ooze he proceeded to pour into them. The smell said that it was coffee all right, but the taste and the consistency were anything but. Not even English coffee was that bad! To be honest though, no one had told us how to drink "Turkish Coffee," allowing the grain sediment to settle on the bottom of the cup and slurping the steaming liquid off the top.

Halifax awaiting N.F.T. at Fayid.

In the desert, the squadron had already begun operating before we joined them at Fayid. It was, therefore, essential that our crew become familiar with the operational practices and procedures of the area. But before my crew was ready, I was able to take part in an attack on Tobruk with P/O John Kenny and his crew. His observer happened to be ill that day so I filled in for him. John had already been to Tobruk in an earlier raid, so this provided me with an excellent opportunity to catch up on local conditions with an experienced crew. As might have been expected, we had no difficulty navigating to the target area. With such clear visibility and a coastal target to boot, we were able to line up for the run well out from the aiming point. We turned onto the bombing run and headed across the built-up area to drop our weapons on the primary target, the docks. The searchlights and flak were active and accurate, but not particularly concentrated. We made an excellent run and dropped our bombs right in the dockyard. It was exhilarating to be able to use one's navigational skills under such ideal conditions and to be able to attack the enemy when his defences weren't so thorny.

For me, that was the beginning of the Tobruk Milk Run. As the only "heavies" in the Desert Air Force at the time, our efforts were devoted to Tobruk, almost to the exclusion of everything else. Though we were not privy to the strategy being applied at that time, it did seem clear that we were part of the preliminaries to a final assault on the Axis forces in the Western Desert. The Royal Navy was doing its part, sinking as many ships as possible en route; our part seemed to be that of denying them those supplies which succeeded in reaching the harbour.

Following that first flight with John Kenny, I took part in attacks on Tobruk on the 23rd, 25th, and 28th of August, and again on the 3rd of September. By then it was quite clear that we were in the desert to stay. The dream of a few days' special assignment in the Black Sea was becoming more like a nightmare to some. For those of us who came from overseas, it meant relatively little. The operational theatre in which we fought was simply a matter of chance. But our sudden and secret departure from England had created serious problems for many of our British members. No messages of any kind had been

Relaxing at Fayid after a swim in the bitter lake. John Kenny is centre front.
Ray Gouldston is second left at rear.

permitted during those last few days while we were confined to base prior to departure. We had simply disappeared, leaving families, wives, and children in difficult circumstances. Mail was neither prompt nor reliable. So, for many weeks, there was an agonizing period of strain until communications were restored. We officers had the added task of censoring outgoing mail and were often concerned and disturbed by the tone of those letters going back home. Occasionally, of course, we had a hearty laugh from the turn of an earthy phrase or two of those who kept their sense of humour despite the strain. There was one of the British flight engineers, an often colourful crowd, who wrote in one letter to his wife, "You'll think some one dumped a bowl of hot porridge in your lap when I get home."

In view of the uncertain, but presumably long, period of time we might be facing in the desert, it was generally agreed among us to give operational priority to the newer air crew members of the squadron in an attempt to bring all members to tour expiry as quickly as possible. Those of us who were at or near expiry would operate less frequently, and crews would have to be broken up more often than usual because of the differences in individual operational experience levels. In my own case, this would mean few, if any, more operations, since I was supposed to have been screened before we left England.

Despite this policy, and because of the illness of another observer, I was able to participate in another attack on Tobruk on the 20th of September. This time I flew with Sgt Wyatt, the same RAF pilot who had participated in the Filey Bay fiasco with the abortive test of the Tirpitz mine. Again, but in an unusual attack on Tobruk, I was able to fly with Wyatt and his crew on the 12th. We were required to attack and engage the defences for one and one half hours by bombing and strafing. Wyatt and I made a number of bombing runs that night, at much lower altitudes than usual, dropping only a couple of bombs at a time. On each run we strafed the searchlights and the flak batteries as they tried to engage us. While we kept the defences occupied, our forces were carrying out an amphibious assault. We got a tremendous boost out of our part in this attack. It broke the monotony of the Milk Run, provided our gunners with a unique opportunity to hit back at the enemy for a change, and introduced a new and distinctly offensive flavour to our war.

It was at about this time that the RCAF was urging the RAF to take action on the promotion of the many Canadian airmen who were serving in their squadrons. One manifestation of this took the form of a directive to our base commander to consider a selected group of Canadian NCO air crew for promotion to commissioned rank. The names had been passed down from higher HQ, presumably having originated in Ottawa or RCAF Overseas HQ in London. Our base commander at the time was anything but popular, having no wartime operational experience and being generally considered a leftover from the prewar RAF overseas personnel policy. His interview with each of the selectees followed the same pattern — some trick mathematical problems, a few searching questions regarding literature, music and the classics, and finally, a summing up of his assessment. As it turned out, only one selectee, a very fine bilingual undergraduate of McGill University, merited his approval. Even then, his assessment was, "I will be pleased to recommend you for commissioned rank *when you get your pilot's course*." This was the assessment made of a very capable wireless operator in the midst of his tour of operations in the

Middle East, with about as much chance of getting a pilot's course as the proverbial snowball! It was a very unhappy and bitter group of Canadian NCOs who gathered in their mess that night.

There was nothing we could do at the base about this kind of treatment. But, not long after, when I was spending a few days in Cairo, I discovered that Canada House had established a post for a senior RCAF officer in the Middle East and was fortunate enough to meet W/C Kennedy, who had been assigned to it. He was distressed to hear about the incident and took the names of those who had been involved, promising to seek some sort of redress. Although it took a while, we were all pleased to learn that future promotions to commissioned rank would be effected at RCAF HQ and then promulgated, not subject to RAF approval, even for those serving in RAF units. The RAF could, however, promote personnel in their units to acting ranks to fill established positions, as had happened in my case.

Whenever I visited Cairo, I stayed at a place called Wellington House, a large penthouse apartment which had been donated to the RAF for the duration of the war. It was run by a F/L Howard, Leslie Howard's brother, who was himself an actor in peacetime. It was a delightful place to stay, clean, well-run and, very economical. If you were lucky on your visit to the city, you might meet one of the South African WAAFs who helped staff the HQ in Cairo. They did a magnificent job of helping the soldiers, sailors, and airmen forget the horrors of war and the loneliness of being far from home, at least for the few hours of their womanly company. They were billeted in one of the Cairo hotels, and it was not at all unusual to find all three of the services represented in the hotel lobby, from generals to privates, each happily looking forward to the appearance of their uniformed date. It was during one of those encounters that I met a Long Range Desert Patrol crew. What a magnificent group they were. It was a pleasure to join in their fun on a number of occasions and to be able to contribute some suggestions on aircraft navigation techniques and equipment to assist them in their forays into the desert.

On the 2nd of November, I found myself in an unusual and uncomfortable situation. An undesirable practice had become evident during our frequent runs on Tobruk. As each aircraft arrived in the target area, instead of attacking immediately, they had begun to circle outside the range of the defences, waiting for someone else to make the first assault and bear the brunt of the enemy resistance. The less daring then followed in his wake as closely as possible to take advantage of the engagement of the defences. Such a practice reflected a loss of confidence and dedication within the crews, and it was also contributing to premature release and wasting of bomb loads. The squadron commander's suspicions had focused on one crew in particular, and he asked me to fly as their observer to check on their operational suitability. I didn't like the assignment, but I was well aware of the suspicions involved and their deleterious effect on air crew morale. I therefore agreed to the CO's request and found myself as the observer in that crew the night we were to attack the airport at Maleme in Crete. Though we weren't aware of the significance, this attack was to be another nail in the coffin for Rommel's supply line. With his sea transport compromised, it was time to cripple his air transport.

The major portion of the flight was over the sea from the Egyptian coast to the island, and it was more like a navigation exercise than a combat operation. We flew under clear skies, in shirt sleeves, below 10,000 feet, and unencumbered by wearisome oxygen masks. Everything was smooth and predictable as we made our landfall at the southwest tip of Crete, on the ETA we had planned. We then set course to approach Maleme across the western end of the island. Having set our course for the target, I left the navigation table and lay down in the nose of the aircraft at the bombing panel, letting my eyes adjust to the darkness around me. As I lay there, I fused and selected the bombs and set up the Mickey Mouse, our name for the automatic clockwork device we used to drop the bombs in a stick at predetermined intervals. All of this was done in the darkness so I would have maximum night vision for the run. By that time, I was ready to pre-set the bomb-sight for drift, ground speed, and altitude. But I was finding it difficult to keep my head up! Just the effort of raising it to read the bomb-sight from my prone position seemed to be a physical strain. Even the mental effort involved was suddenly taxing me almost beyond my capacity. I was rapidly losing interest in what I was supposed to be doing when I looked at the altimeter to set the height on the bomb-sight. It read 19,000 feet! Despite my feeling of exhaustion, it was sufficient to alert me to the fact that I was suffering from hypoxia!

I was shocked out of my lassitude to say the least. And I was also very angry. It was either standard procedure for this crew to climb to maximum altitude before attacking, and I had not been told, or the pilot had advised the rest of the crew about what he was going to do while I was off the intercom for the short time it took me to change positions. Either way, I couldn't have cared less about the details at that moment. I was boiling mad. By then we were approaching the target and I had put my oxygen mask on. I let the target approach continue and intentionally took them on a dummy run, over the airfield, across the harbour, through the defences, and out to sea before turning them around and completing an attack on the second run, through the flak and the searchlights. It was foolhardy, and perhaps a little cruel, but I had to vent my anger somehow. We made several more runs as I dropped the load in short sticks on the airfield beneath us, determined to make the best of a bad deal.

Needless to say, we had successfully attacked the primary target before we finally turned for home. The aircraft was strangely silent on that return flight. Apologies were finally offered, and accepted. However, there was no doubt in my mind about the mental state of that crew. Had they remained in Europe, and survived, of course, they would have been screened by then. But, because of the unusual circumstances in the desert, they were being extended beyond their limits. Not everyone has the same capacity. This crew badly needed a rest, and that is what I recommended to the CO as strongly as I could on our return to base that night.

Two days later, I was operating with Sgt Wyatt again, on another change of venue, a maximum effort against El Alamein. We were directed to fly at low level in support of the ground forces, bombing and strafing enemy troop concentrations from Ras al Kanayis to Matruh. It was awe inspiring to watch the flickering artillery flashes reflecting from the ground in uncountable numbers across the still, dark landscape. We tried to imagine what it must have been like to be at both the firing and receiving ends of that overpowering barrage. But no effort of imagination could possibly fully grasp the hell and fury of such an onslaught on the senses of the soldiers down there on the battlefield. We were happy to be above it all yet exhilarated to be playing such a direct role in what was clearly, even at that point in time, a major 8th Army offensive.

Chapter XXIII

While I was in hospital after my birthday dunking in the Mediterranean, Air Marshal Edwards, the senior RCAF officer overseas, had made a tour of the Middle East from his London HQ. With him was W/C Rod McInnis, his senior public relations officer. They learned of my escapade and met me when they toured the facility and I found myself invited to join them on some of their visits as well as for Christmas dinner at their hotel.

Rod was an excellent PRO who had flown operationally quite a few times to obtain better coverage of the air battle and to experience for himself the conditions faced by Canadian airmen. He had justifiably earned the confidence of the airmen through his understanding, his level of knowledge, his experience, and his integrity. I wasn't to grasp the depth of his comprehension of operational life and his dedication to his job until I had returned to England with my squadron.

Once there, I had to report to RCAF Overseas HQ where I discovered that the RAF Air Ministry had authorized one month's home leave for me as an escapee. I was already booked to sail for Canada almost immediately on the *Queen Mary* out of Greenoch in Scotland, and a F/L PRO from Rod McInnis' group was going to accompany me. I was so delighted with the chance to see family and friends again that I failed to see the possibility of Rod's kind hand in these welcome, but unexpected, arrangements. It just seemed to me to be a fortunate, but entirely natural turn of events. As one must appreciate, everything and everyone was taken at face value in those days, at least in squadron life. And I had still not learned to look behind or beyond the scenes for any other meaning than the obvious.

In comparison with my earlier trans-Atlantic crossing, this winter passage was uneventful. We landed in Halifax on the 27th of March and left immediately by train for Ottawa. When we arrived at Ottawa Union Station, I was amazed by the crowd of people who filled the waiting room. My PRO escort was with me as we came off the train and entered the rotunda. Immediately, a young, exuberant P/O dashed up to us, came to heel-clicking attention, and snapped a drill book salute. Both of us were completely taken aback, but were saved from embarrassment by his introduction as a junior member of the HQ PRO Staff who had been detailed to meet and greet us. We were accommodated in the nearby Chateau Laurier Hotel where reservations had been booked in our names. He advised us that a press conference had been scheduled for the next morning, after which we would be free to proceed on leave.

When I reported to the press conference, I found there were three more besides myself who had just returned from overseas: F/L George Casey DFC, P/O Bruce MacNab DFM, and P/O Warren Wortley DFM. We had been brought together to tell the assembled reporters about our ex-

Ottawa press conference. MacNab is seated.
Wortley, Casey and self are standing behind.

periences and to respond to their questions as best we could. Although there were very many Canadians involved in the war, it was being conducted at such a distance from home that very little information was getting back. Hence, the great interest in our arrival from the front and, quite possibly, the real reason why we had been sent home on leave.

Before I had left London for home leave, I had visited my friendly pub in Piccadilly Circus and been shown a copy of a Canadian photographic news magazine, a sort of *Life* or *Look*. The reason I was shown this particular copy was the centrefold picture; it was a full page portrait of Evelyn, the lovely Maritimes girl I had met while waiting in Montreal for the trans-Atlantic flight. She was featured in this particular issue as a sort of Miss Canada. An air force friend, who was also an habitué of the same pub, had recognized the picture of Evelyn while on home leave, and kindly brought the magazine back with him.

At the end of the press conference, memory of her refreshed, I decided to head to Montreal and Evelyn before heading home. I was on the train before I realized that one of the correspondents had followed me to see if he could purchase the rights to my story. I really had no idea what was involved or what he was willing to pay. I wasn't interested and said so.

I had first met Evelyn at Dinty Moore's restaurant so, as soon as I arrived in Montreal, that was where I headed. As I might have expected, there had been many changes in the staff, but I did find a couple of waitresses who had known Evelyn and recognized me after I spoke to them. One finally admitted that she knew where Evelyn was, but was unwilling to tell me. She seemed disturbed by my persistence and tried to talk me out of finding her, saying that she wasn't worth pursuing. However, after much persuasion, and with obvious unwillingness, she told me Evelyn was living at the Hotel de La Salle.

Hurrying over the few blocks that separated us, I registered at the hotel and asked for Evelyn's room number. When I called at the room, I found that she was sharing with another girl of about the same age, but dark where Evelyn was fair, attractive, but not as lovely as Evelyn. The welcome was all I could have hoped for, despite the shock of my sudden reappearance. There were tears of joy and warm embraces after which followed some embarrassing moments as the facts of her living arrangements were disclosed. Like so many of the young girls who had come to the big city to make good, she had fallen into the trap of living beyond her means, buying on credit. The vultures had moved in when the time was ripe, when her credit had run out, and the bills had to be paid. Because she was beautiful, she had been rescued by a benefactor, a benefactor who then became her provider in exchange for other privileges. She and her room-mate were being kept by two shrewd businessmen who shared the expenses to cut down on the overhead. Even that was probably on their expense account!

At the hotel, I met a young Montreal businessman who seemed to have plenty of cash on hand. He seemed also to be quite at home with the girls, but I never did discover if he was paying any of the tab. He certainly didn't resent my being there. When he learned that I had just returned from overseas and was planning to leave for Hamilton, he first tried to encourage me to stay in Montreal and, when I resisted his suggestions, offered to lend me a car and as many gas coupons as I needed, assuring me that the tires were in good condition.

I had left home, barely out of school, full of ideals and believing in the justice of what I was doing. My vision of the war and the men with whom I was serving had been idealized, despite or perhaps even because of the losses which had befallen so many with whom I had served. The fact that there were men in my own country who were enjoying the profits from the sacrifices of such youngsters was deeply disturbing. To be confronted by one such profiteer and to be offered openly to share in the fruits of his crimes was revolting. Though my disdain and my revulsion must have been apparent, my forceful rejection of his offer probably didn't even dent his thick skin.

I returned to my room and decided to leave for Hamilton in the morning. I was upset by what I had discovered. A girl whom I might have grown to love under normal circumstances was another man's mistress. Graft, corruption, disregard for the law, and flagrant profiteering seemed to be flourishing in Montreal while good men were risking and losing their lives in a struggle against a common enemy. I had a great deal of thinking to do as I sat on the train heading home. The seeds of feeling uncomfortable in my own country had been planted.

It was wonderful to see my mother and sister again and to see that they were able to deal with the problems my being overseas had created. Mother had sold our home and was living with my sister and her family. My sister was working, so my mother had more than enough to keep her busy, looking after the house and the children. As usual, she was able to find others less fortunate than herself who could use her help and her skills as a seamstress. There was, however, no room for me, so I accepted the kind invitation of a very good friend from my pre-war days at the Firestone Rubber Company, Bill MacDonald, and used his apartment as my base. He was equally generous about allowing me to use his car whenever I needed it, and when he could spare it.

I looked up many of my old friends, particularly those from my old neighbourhood, and some of my previous girlfriends. It was good fun, but it was also quite obvious that you could never bring back the past. I never consciously thought about it but, if anyone had asked, I would

With mother and brother.   *With brother and uncle.*

have instantly and honestly replied that I was absolutely normal, that my experiences overseas hadn't changed me in the least. Inwardly, that's how I felt. Outwardly, it was apparently not so. Others saw me as a person on edge, not able to sit still for any length of time. My host was always amazed whenever he served drinks; my glass was empty before he could sit down to enjoy the first sip from his own. This for a youngster who hadn't touched a drop before joining up! On top of that, since all my overseas time was spent in the company of RAF mates, it was inevitable that my accent and choice of expressions had changed. In the RAF, I had always been one of those bloody Canadians, a Colonial, as we so often jokingly referred to ourselves. Now, at home, I was being accused, albeit in a friendly way, of being a bloody Limey! There just wasn't much common ground with the folks at home at that time. My past was history and my concept of the war was far more personal and intense than that of any of my old friends. I probably made them feel uncomfortable at times, certainly never intentionally, but I was feeling less and less at home and less and less at ease in their company.

When my leave was over, I was ordered to report to the Air Observers' School at Malton where I had taken my initial navigation course. I had been expecting to be sent back to Britain after my leave, not to be an instructor. My mind was geared to returning to squadron life. The mere thought of becoming an instructor was abhorrent. Anything other than returning overseas was incomprehensible to me, and I lost no time in acquainting the staff at the school with my feelings. My complaints and my request to be sent back to the front were heard by my CO who promised to forward them to HQ in Ottawa. In the meantime, however, I was to go to Rivers, Manitoba to attend the next navigation instructors' course. In my mind, the course was another nail in my coffin. But there was little I could do about it short of finding myself in serious trouble for disobeying an order.

At Rivers, I made another formal complaint and request for overseas posting. Their promise to investigate the circumstances seemed more promising, as the value of any instructors' course to an unwilling student was doubtful. Fortune smiled on me this time, and I think for the school staff as well, for I would have been a thorn in their side had the decision to put me on the course not been changed. I was posted to Toronto, not to go overseas as I had hoped, but to take part in the Fourth Victory Bond Campaign. At least, I had evaded the immediate prospect, or should I say threat, of becoming an instructor.

On my arrival at the Loan Campaign Office in Toronto, I learned that F/L George Casey DFC and I had been paired together. We were billeted in the Royal York Hotel and, to kick off the campaign, our first assignment was to address the Toronto Board of Education and their staff. There had been some publicity about George and me taking part in the drive, and the Toronto Star had carried a rather flattering picture of the two veterans who were helping out during their home leave.

For a young fellow whose schoolboy speeches had been agonizing beyond belief, the idea of addressing the Board of Education was terrifying! I knew practically nothing about victory bonds and I had never participated in any kind of public campaign. It was impossible to prepare anything ahead of time, or even to have something committed

With George Casey about to start on victory bond campaign in Toronto.

to memory as an opener. When the time came that evening and I stood in the middle of the rotunda, looking around at the faces which were all focused on me, I was not quite as paralysed as I thought I would most certainly be. It suddenly occurred to me that they were there to listen to us tell them about the war, something about which we knew far more than any of them. Once launched into my theme, I became exhilarated rather than frightened and I knew there was no problem to public speaking as long as you had something positive to say and you knew what you were talking about.

There were numerous other bond rallies for us to attend in the Toronto area, but it wasn't long before the campaign manager in Hamilton took exception to one of their city's heroes campaigning in and on behalf of Toronto. He requested, and obtained, my services for the Hamilton campaign. Thus, I found myself heavily engaged in the Hamilton area, appearing at many rallies, including one at the Firestone Tire and Rubber Company, my employer just prior to my joining the RCAF. That was quite an experience in itself. I had left, as a 19-year-old scheduling clerk, and found myself welcomed at the door by the President and Vice-President themselves, to give a speech to the assembled work force on the need to support Canada's war effort by buying victory bonds!

By then, I was speaking as many as four times a day, every speech refreshing memories of events that might better have been forgotten. I was becoming emotionally involved in my appeals, and slowly, growing more aggressive in the tone of my remarks. The campaign staff in Hamilton, including one of my prewar football mentors, Sam Manson, began to look upon me as their hardball hitter, the one to send in when they sensed there would be reluctance to give adequately for the troops. Occasionally, I was called back to Toronto for appearances at places like Victory Aircraft or other major wartime production centres.

On the final day of the campaign, I was once again recalled to Toronto to take part in a monster parade and rally which was to end on the steps of City Hall. I was to report to the campaign office on arrival and take my place with the dignitaries assembled at City Hall for the review of the troops on parade. After the various VIPs had made appropriate remarks to the crowd and the troops below, I was shocked to find myself introduced as the final, and guest speaker. Fortunately for me, unexpected but long-awaited news came when I had reported that morning. I was able to keep my remarks brief before I held up a message that I brought out of my jacket pocket. "Ladies and Gentlemen, this is the last day of the Fourth Victory Bond Campaign. In closing this rally, I want to tell you that I have been advised of my re-posting overseas. As soon as I leave this square, I will be reporting to the embarkation depot. I want to take with me a message to my comrades overseas, a message of your unstinting support. Take this Victory Bond Campaign over the top. There can be no better or clearer message."

It seemed to be a fitting climax to my involvement with the campaign, and the response of the crowd that day eliminated any bitterness which might have been building up in me and left a good taste in my mouth. My posting was another of those fortunately-timed elements that were shaping my life. The emotional crisis which had been building within me as the campaign evolved was totally and naturally vented. I was able to close out on a high and positive note, and escape the atmosphere I sensed was doing me no good.

I returned to Hamilton to pack up my clothes and say goodbye. Fortunately, my time was short. My mother would have been happier for me to stay, but she made no attempt to influence me or make my decision any more difficult. It was hard to say goodbye again despite my conviction that I was doing the right thing.

I had time to stop in Montreal on the way to Halifax. I wanted to say goodbye to Evelyn too. I stayed the night at the hotel and Evelyn stayed with me. She was confused and uncertain. Though the circumstances were difficult, she remained loyal to her benefactor while, presumably, trying to show me that she loved me in her own way. It wasn't an easy time for either of us, but it did make it easier for me to say goodbye in the morning and board the train for Halifax.

Chapter XXIV

After a short stay in the embarkation depot in Halifax, I joined a small air force draft and we were sent by train to New York. There we boarded the *Queen Elizabeth*, bound for Britain. The vast majority of the personnel aboard were American servicemen, mostly from the US army. We were sailing from an American port and thus were under American rules. This meant that the ship was "dry," no alcoholic beverages being allowed on board. This wasn't a particular hardship, but it was the first of my three wartime crossings in which there was no bar, and I must admit it made the trip much more boring. The dominant presence of the US army and their unusual, at least to us, approach to discipline and decorum placed an additional damper on our spirits. But, the variety of personnel in our own draft provided sufficient stimulus for good conversation — two doctors, one of whom had served his internship in a mental hospital, a pilot whose father was Basil Rathbone the British and Hollywood actor, and two of us who were returning overseas with previous operational experience.

There was still plenty of U-boat activity in the Atlantic but, apart from occasional changes of course, we saw no indication of their presence. Presumably the admiralty was feeding the *Q.E.* intelligence on U-boat activity and location. We raced unchecked across the menacing waters, cutting a marvellous bow wave at top speed towards Scotland. There wasn't a spare bed on board. Our bunks were stacked so close together that you could not sit up straight without risking a fractured skull, especially if you were lying down when the boat drill sounded! The kitchens never stopped; the dining room fed its passengers in regular shifts around the clock. It was the closest example of perpetual motion one could imagine, a far cry from that first crossing on the *Aurania* with the RN.

The *Q.E.* arrived safely in Scotland and, without any fanfare, the thousands on board disembarked to swell even further the mass of military might which was being assembled in Britain. Our draft was put on a train and sent to the south of England, to Brighton, where the RCAF had established a reception depot in some of the larger coastal resort hotels. If one had to sit and wait, the site couldn't have been better. Brighton was a very attractive resort city with ample recreation facilities geared to handle thousands of tourists. Although most of the usual tourists had disappeared with the advent of war and the threat of invasion by sea and by air, the diminishing likelihood was beginning to draw some of them back. And then, of course, there was the large number of Canadian airmen. Many of the tourists were hard-working girls from the industrial Midlands with money in their pockets and looking for a good time. If there was a young man to share it with, so much the better. As I said, if you had to sit and wait, Brighton was certainly an ideal place to put in time.

As soon as it was possible, I travelled up to London and reported to RCAF Overseas HQ. I was fortunate enough to find one of my former squadron mates from the desert, F/L Ted Greenway, on the staff of the personnel section. I wanted to find out what the immediate future held for me and was asked what I wanted to do. "Go back on operations," I answered. Ted made a quick mental calculation and replied, "OK, Jack, it's six months since you last flew on operations in the desert. That would constitute the required rest tour, so you should be able to be posted back on operations. Just go to Bournemouth and wait for a posting message. We'll make the arrangements as quickly as we can."

As promised, my posting came through. I was ordered to report to the Heavy Conversion Unit (HCU) of 6 RCAF Bomber Group at Top-cliffe in Yorkshire, not far from my old base in Leeming. I was placed on supernumerary strength to await the formation of a new RCAF squadron. All of the northern Yorkshire bases, which had been in 4 Group when we left for the Middle East, had been combined in 6 Group. They housed the bomber squadrons of the RCAF which had been formed while I was away. While I waited at HCU, I learned about the formation of the Pathfinder Force (PFF) and its role in the locating and marking of the aiming points for the main force of Bomber Command. This was a major development and an innovation which called for significant changes in bomber tactics.

I also learned that my former squadron commander, W/C DCT Bennett, was the air officer commanding Pathfinders! Not only was he the AOC, but he was also one of the men responsible for its very inception. Having been involved in the original proposal to establish a hand-picked force of bomber experts to find and mark the targets for the rest of Bomber Command as a means of improving the effectiveness of the bomber offensive, he had been selected by A/M Harris to assume its responsibility when the concept was approved. I believe that Bennett's original idea was to use 10 Squadron as the nucleus of this band of experts, and to expand the squadron to three flights with volunteers from among the best crews in the command. However, the group commanders of Bomber Command had foreseen such a collection of the cream of available crews concentrated in one squadron as a potential problem. The typical rank structure of a squadron would have to be inflated to accommodate so many experienced fliers. There would also have been an unusual proliferation of awards for bravery within such a unit. The normal distribution of personnel of the top echelon in leadership and proven courage in each of the bomber groups would have been seriously disrupted, possibly to the detriment of squadron morale and operational effectiveness throughout the command. The results, which were so important to the future of the bomber offensive in Europe, might well have been counter-productive. The inherent benefits of the Pathfinder proposal might have been needlessly squandered.

The alternative, which was selected, was to establish a new group within the command to which each of the other groups would contribute one squadron and continue to support by providing volunteer personnel to keep that squadron fully manned with experienced crews. They hoped that this would maintain the individual group identity within PFF and thereby minimize the risk of resentment building against an elite within the command. When Bennett was taken off 10 Squadron, just before we left for the Middle East, it was to be promoted to group captain and begin the organization of what was now 8 Group, the PFF of Bomber Command. By the time I returned to England, he had been promoted to air commodore and was the AOC of the then operational group. I had, of course, known nothing of all this when we left for the Middle East. Such is compartmentalization of global conflict that none of these developments filtered down to us during our tenure with the Desert Air Force.

My request to serve in PFF was flatly refused by the senior personnel staff officer (SPSO) of 6 Group. I was being programmed for a flight command in the new squadron. He did, however, agree that it would be sensible for me to attend a familiarization course at the Navigational Training Unit (NTU) of PFF so that I could be brought up to date on the new tactics. Thus, I found myself enrolled in the NTU at RAF Wyton, part of PFF and close to its HQ.

I had completed my course as a navigator at the NTU and was prolonging my stay by enrolling in the bomb aimers course when I received an unexpected telephone call. It was W/C Shepherd, who had been our station intelligence officer at Leeming and who was now the group intelligence officer at PFF HQ. Bennett had arranged for his promotion and transfer to the PFF staff when the new group was being formed. Shep was calling from PFF HQ to say that my presence at the NTU had just come to the attention of the AOC and that the AOC wished to see me. Remembering the clashes of opinion I had had with Bennett when he had taken over command of 10 Squadron, I hesitated in my reply and then said, "Oh, come on Shep, you know as well as I do how we clashed." Shep laughed, "Yes, I remember. But he has mellowed since then, particularly since he put up that wide band. And I can assure you Jack, he sincerely wants to see you." I must admit that I was flattered and a little curious to see Bennett again. So, Shep arranged to send a car for me the following morning.

We met on the outside stairs of PFF HQ when I arrived and he escorted me to the AOC's office, leaving me with the WAAF officer who served as Bennett's secretary/assistant. When I was ushered into his office, A/C Bennett was sitting at his desk, looking just as I had remembered him, whippet-slim, dark and vibrant. I still had the same impression of him as when I had first met him in the Montreal AT-

FERO office, a highly-bred race horse, whose every quality emphasized the job for which he seemed to have been created. Shep was right, though, he had mellowed. As I entered, he rose to his feet, came quickly out from behind his desk, and met me in the middle of the room, his hand out and a warm smile on his face. He put me right at ease and, as he waved me to a seat and sat beside me, said, "How good it is to see you, and looking so well. I read of your exploits in the desert and wondered how you had fared. Tell me, are you fit?" I assured him of my well-being and answered his queries as to my present status with the new group. I also mentioned the fact that I had volunteered for PFF, but had been turned down. At this, the A/C interrupted to ask me who had turned me down. When I answered, he signalled for me to wait and picked up the telephone, asking for W/C Mahaddie, presumably his SPSO. The A/C briefly explained the situation to him and closed the conversation with a terse directive, "Yes, he's in the office with me now. Call me back."

When he put the telephone down, he swung around to face me and resumed our conversation as though nothing had intervened. We talked about old times and old names and drank tea in a most agreeable way. Then the telephone rang. The A/C picked it up, listened, responded with the occasional, "Yes" or "No," and with a "Thank-you," hung up, resuming our interrupted conversation once more. Then he said to me, "Oh, by the way, Jack, you are now in PFF. 6 Group has agreed to post you to their PFF 405 Squadron. However, now that you are in PFF, I will decide where you can best serve and I have a job that I want you to do. You will join 109 Squadron." And that was as close as I ever came to serving in the 405 or any other RCAF squadron.

My new squadron was based on a prewar, permanent station in Norfolk County at a site known as Marham. It was a grass airfield in beautiful countryside, renowned for its estates and fine shooting. The squadron had only recently been formed from a test and development flight which had been involved earlier in the detection and disruption of the guidance beams the Luftwaffe had used in their night bombing of Britain. The more recent development of a new RAF system of accurate blind bombing, in which this flight had participated, had reached operational status. To operate this new system, code-named "Oboe," 109

Squadron was formed and Tactical Light Bomber Squadron, 105, was converted. At first, the choice of the name "Oboe" seemed rather strange but, according to definition, the instrument produces a sound "having a high, penetrating, melancholy tone." The more I learned about the system, the more I realized how very appropriate its name was. The tone for which the navigator had to listen was indeed melancholy, but not nearly as sad as failing to hear it would be.

Before reporting to the squadron, I was sent to the group navigation officer, S/L Eric Bagnall, DFC, who briefed me on the technical aspects of Oboe and the observer's role. The accuracy of the bombing itself depended on the instrument flying skill of the pilot, combined with the faultless operation of the very complex equipment on the ground and in the aircraft. It was also quite apparent that the success or failure of the airborne operation of Oboe depended upon the skill, the accuracy, and the timing of the navigation. I learned later that the first group navigation officer in PFF had been Angus Buchan, our station navigation officer at Leeming who had joined Bennett when PFF was being formed. But I was not to have the pleasure of seeing him again. He had returned to operations for his second tour and was posted missing before my return. Angus had been an excellent navigator, a fine leader, and a man with exceptionally high principles. His was a sad loss to all who had known him.

The Oboe system required two ground stations in England, near the coast to maximize their line of sight range over enemy territory, yet far enough apart to provide a baseline for a decently sharp triangulation cut of their arcs over the selected targets. Each ground station used a cathode ray display to measure the distance of the responder in the aircraft from that station. One station, selected for its geographic suitability vis-à-vis the target, would act as the tracking station. Its display would reflect the fixed-range arc which passed directly over the release point, precalculated precisely for the height, air speed, and wind effect, so that the weapons would fall on the pinpoint target. The other station acted as the releasing station with its display correlated with the fixed arc of the tracking station on a distance/range basis, with the exact distance along the predetermined bombing track calculated for the release of the weapons.

In the original system, only one aircraft at a time could be tracked. Not until the aircraft had received release, or had been keyed off because of some technical or flying failure, could the next aircraft be called in. The aircraft were individually timed, in a ten minute sequence, to reach waiting point, fifteen minutes from the target along the bombing track. Unless you were first on target, you reached the waiting point on your appointed time, turned down the bombing run, tuned in the antenna, and listened to the aircraft ahead of you. You then made any adjustments to your timing as might be required, so that you reached Point A, ten minutes from the target, when the aircraft ahead released and switched off, and you were called in.

This was the crux of the Oboe operation for the individual crews: when you were called in, and you switched on the transponder, you had to be where the ground station expected you to be. The narrow beam which the stations emitted left no tolerance for any error in location, and there was no slack in the system to allow the stations time to search for an aircraft that wasn't in position. If the ground station could not pick up the return from your transponder, they had to key you off and call in the reserve aircraft. Otherwise they would lose the essential continuity in the marking of the target and risk disrupting the entire raid sequence. Accurate navigation was the key to Oboe's success. And it was hoped that Oboe-marked targets would be the solution to Bomber Command's search for strategic effectiveness at night and in any weather. Navigational errors could not be hidden or glossed over, and it was clear that they could not and would not be tolerated.

When I reported in at Marham, I immediately felt at ease, a sense of comfort that I had not felt for some months. It was like returning home after a long absence. I suppose the feeling was really that of belonging again, of sharing and of being in harmony with those around me, in spite of the fact that I knew no one at the station. The kinship I felt was not based on friendship or nationality; it was based on a commonly-shared commitment, one for which each and every person was prepared to risk their life. Who knows maybe the war had changed me after all. I knew I was back where I belonged.

Chapter XXV

Every member of 109 Squadron was a veteran. Most of the pilots and all of the observers were on their second tour. The few pilots who were on their first tour had flown many hours, particularly on instrument flying, on such duties as instructors in blind landing. They had all, without exception, been selected for their flying experience and their above-average skills in the air. It was a squadron of the elite and an outstanding example of the quality of personnel to be found in PFF.

All the PFF air crew were volunteers, a fact that played a significant role in the executive decision which had to be taken on one of the first-tour pilots selected for 109. He was an excellent pilot who had converted to the Mosquito easily and quickly. On his first night exercise, however, he had run into trouble, unexpected trouble. He and his navigator were flying a simulated operation in which they had to climb to 28,000 feet after take-off. The take-off and climb had progressed without incident, with the pilot concentrating on his instruments to the exclusion of everything else, until they reached operational altitude and levelled out. For the first time since take-off, the pilot took his eyes off the instrument panel, lifted his head, and looked out. He was shattered. The stars were below him! Never having flown at such heights, particularly at night, he immediately became severely disoriented. Stars were supposed to be above you, not below! In spite of all his flying experience, in spite of the hours of instrument flying and the normalcy of the preceding climb, he blurted out, "My God! We're upside down!" With that, he flipped the aircraft over onto its back. The navigator, of course, fell out of his seat and hit the roof of the cockpit screaming, "For Christ's sake! You're upside down now! Turn over!" This violent rotational manoeuvre was repeated several times before the poor pilot was able to regain control and his own equilibrium. By that time, they had lost so much altitude that the horizon had once again become a familiar reference, and the pilot was able to resume flying on a visual basis. There was absolutely no chance for them to complete the exercise by then, so the navigator steered them back to base as quickly as he could, and they were able to land the aircraft safely.

It was subsequently decided that the pilot would never be suitable for Oboe operations after this experience. However, because he was such a fine pilot otherwise and was so keen to become operational, he was kept on Mosquitoes and transferred to 2 Group where he would fly low-level, daylight operations. There was no cause for embarrassment on his part; he had shown no lack of courage and would have plenty of opportunity to prove himself in daylight sorties.

My introduction to 109 Squadron was most pleasing. I was greeted by the adjutant, F/L Jones, a World War I pilot. He took me in to meet the squadron commander, W/C Harry Bufton DSO DFC AFC, who made me feel most welcome, though slightly apprehensive. I got the impression that he had received some sort of personal briefing from PFF HQ about my joining the squadron. Had it not been for his good nature and ready sense of humour, I might have felt that he resented my arrival, or at least the remarks which had been made about it. Fortunately for me, I was not privy to what had been said, so there was no presentiment or embarrassment on my part to complicate matters.

Although Harry was a stranger to me on my arrival, I came to know a great deal about him. The more I learned, the more my respect for him grew. He had been shot down earlier in the war on a night bomber trip, but had bailed out successfully. He had made his way into France where he made contact with the Underground. They smuggled him into Paris, then south over the Pyrenees into Spain where he was imprisoned for some time. He was finally released to make his way to Gibraltar and, at last, back to England. It had been a harrowing and physically demanding ordeal. Yet, there he was, back on operations, a strong and vibrant leader whose behaviour was always exemplary and whose demands were always tempered by humanity.

From his office, I was taken to the navigation office where I was introduced to S/L Findlater DFC, the RAF squadron navigation officer, and given my navigation kit. Then it was to "A" Flight where I met the flight commander, S/L Dick Cox AFC, a Canadian serving in the RAF, and was given my parachute harness and pack and my Mae West and assigned my locker. Shortly thereafter, I met F/L Peter Sooby DFC, also a recent arrival to "A" Flight, who was not yet crewed up. Peter was a tall, dark, handsome, sophisticated, and slightly older Englishman. He had joined the RAF on a Short Service Commission just before the war, after serving briefly in the London constabulary. Peter had been awarded his DFC after a distinguished tour on heavy bombers during which he had flown the ill-fated Manchesters, the twin-engined predecessor of the much more successful Lancaster. His wife, a WAAF he met during his service, and their two young children did not live near Marham, but his parents lived in nearby Swaffam, Norfolk, where his father was the local veterinary surgeon.

Peter and I both lived in the Officers' Mess, though we did not share the same room. My room-mate was a gangly Australian pilot who seemed to be quite a rake. He suffered from a persistent dry cough that seemed to be irritated by the high altitude flying associated with Oboe. The cough didn't create any friction between us because it wasn't long after I arrived that he was admitted to the station hospital where TB was diagnosed. He had to be transferred to a sanatorium for treatment, which put paid to his high flying and his high living too.

Peter and I hit it off right from the start. He had a dry, slightly caustic wit, and viewed the world with a somewhat superior air, blaming this jaded outlook on his experiences with human nature while a London bobby. He was certainly more worldly than I, but I suspected that a good deal of his cynicism and seemingly lazy indifference was a facade. At this stage anyway, Peter was as keen as I to master Oboe technique and to become a full-fledged Pathfinder.

The following day, September 30, I came face to face for the first time with the DeHavilland Mosquito, that wooden marvel which was to prove as vital to the success of Oboe as Oboe was to Bomber Command. Peter and I took one of them up for a test flight. We flew for an hour and fifty minutes so that I could familiarize myself with this aircraft. The next day we flew another test, but only for forty minutes. That same night we took it on a cross-country navigation training trip. The very next day we flew another test followed by a night exercise which simulated an Oboe operation without leaving friendly territory. The exercise was a success; we completed it within the prescribed accuracy and time limits. We were considered to be ready for operations.

For the fourth day running, Peter and I flew an air test and that night, October 3, we took off at 1930 hours for our first operation together. Our squadron was still in the process of developing and proving the Oboe system which was optimized for attacks on the Ruhr, that vital target which had proven so difficult and so costly in the past. There were twelve Oboe aircraft in this raid on Knapsack, a virgin target near Cologne, where we were to attack the power station with high explosive bombs. We escaped without loss and twelve Oboe aircraft repeated the attack the following night. Peter and I were on both of these operations and were able to deliver our bombs on target, and on time, each night. Subsequent reconnaissance of the target revealed bomb damage which correlated extremely well with the calculated results of the individual Oboe bombing runs as recorded at the ground stations.

Experience during this test and development phase proved conclusively that the bearing and distance of each attack from the exact aiming point could be calculated from the data provided by the ground stations, and that the experienced crews could consistently achieve accuracy within the maximum of 200 yards. And this was while operating at high altitude without any visual reference to the ground. Frequently, the margin of error was within 20 yards of the aiming point but this accuracy could not be assured on any one bombing run. Although we were already achieving such results, Oboe was still considered to be in a proving stage of development. We had permanent, resident representatives of the Technical Research Establishment, our "boffins," who were responsible for the Oboe equipment in our aircraft. They became as much a part of our squadron as the air crew, their emotions clearly showing their personal involvement in every operation we flew and their concern for the performance of the equipment for which they were responsible. Our debriefings dealt more with the technical functioning of the Oboe equipment than with enemy resistance. Priority at this stage was clearly on the development of a blind bombing system which could guarantee target accuracy independently of weather, visibility, or diversionary tactics. Within its range, Oboe showed by far the greatest promise of achieving this enviable goal.

Our sister Oboe squadron shared the Marham base with us. We naturally developed an intense, but productive, rivalry. The Technical Research Establishment improved Oboe by providing a second channel which permitted two aircraft to operate independently and simultaneously on the same target. One channel was assigned to 105 and one to 109. This resulted in a sort of head-to-head competition in any attack in which both squadrons participated. I, like all of my squadron mates, firmly believed that 109 was the superior squadron, but I am not at all sure we ever proved it to the satisfaction of 105. Since 109 had evolved from the special testing flight which had been engaged in similar activities for a long time, we felt that we had priority rights to Oboe, and we looked on 105 as interlopers. It was probably just as well that we felt this way because 105 was a squadron with a long and illustrious record as a low-level, tactical bomber squadron whose past commanders included such outstanding flyers as G/C Idwald Edwards VC while 109 had no operational record at all.

We often expressed our squadron rivalry in games of field hockey and rugger matches. Rugger was the particular favourite. Our commander had played rugger as a forward for the Harlequins before the war. He was still fit and very competitive, ready to don his rugger gear any day on behalf of his squadron. When they found out I had played the North American game of football, but not rugger, I was drafted immediately. Our Scottish doctor, F/L Liddell, who played hooker for the team, suggested that I learn the game by beginning to play alongside him in the front row of the scrum, where he could brief me as we played. After a couple of games propping up the hooker, they decided to move me to the position of lock, the man in the centre of the rear rank of the scrum, where I could break out as soon as the ball cleared the scrum and join the line-out. From there, it was finally decided to move me to the wing forward position where my speed and agility could be fully utilized. For the rest of my rugger-playing time, I played as a winger and enjoyed both the running and the tackling which this position provided in plenty.

Rugger proved to be a marvellous game for those of us who played on the station. It was an excellent outlet for the energy, drive, and combativeness of the young air crew and it produced a healthy state of physical rather than nervous exhaustion. We organized a station team that included English, Welsh, Scottish, and Australian players, and one lone Canadian. We played matches against other RAF Stations, Cambridge University, the 8th Army, and Bedford School. The game with Bedford School was particularly appealing. We, of course, were older, bigger, and stronger than the schoolboys, but nowhere near as fit. It was inspiring and discouraging at the same time to see those young lads bounce back from tackles or from being muscled off the ball, and to watch them keep coming back for more. Their condition and their spirit almost overcame our advantages of size, weight, and experience. They had our backs to the wall by the end of the match.

Afterwards, we joined them for tea in their dining room, we in our beribboned and slightly scruffy RAF uniforms, and they, pink-cheeked and scrubbed, in their neat school uniforms. It was both a pleasure and an embarrassment to witness the respect with which they viewed us and the thrill it had given them to play against us. Most of us weren't much older than the oldest of those boys, in terms of years anyway. Playing against us probably made those lads feel bigger and better; it made us look back over the short distance in time, the long time in experience, which separated us from what we had left behind us. We drove back to the camp that afternoon, feeling tired, but better in body and mind for our efforts.

On the night of October 8/9, Peter and I took off at about midnight for our first marking flight. Bomber Command was attacking Hanover with a force of 504 aircraft. Since it was beyond the range of Oboe, we were unable to mark the target, but we were able to assist the heavies by laying down accurate route markers as an additional means of keeping them on track and in concentration. RAF Bomber Command attacks had become more concentrated, better planned, and more precise ever since the 1000 raids and during my absence in the Middle East. Oboe's role in this particular raid was to provide accurate turning points on the way to the target within the interior of Europe, where the chances for navigational error among the heavies were the greatest. Our markers would give their navigators accurate reference points not far from the target, from which they could make their final bombing run with more confidence than would otherwise have been the case. This role wasn't as risky for us as marking the actual target would have been, but it did make a valuable contribution to a most successful raid which left Hanover in a badly damaged state. Unfortunately, our efforts did nothing to reduce the loss rate. Twenty-seven of our bombers failed to return, a loss in excess of 5 per cent.

I felt strange at first, sitting in the cockpit, feeling rather naked and vulnerable with my head almost touching the top and only glass surrounding me. When you were trapped in searchlights, they seemed to flood the cockpit with dazzling light, making everything inside brighter than day, but blinding you to the outside like a blanket. Only heavy anti-aircraft guns could reach the high altitude at which we operated, but each of those heavy guns was individually radar-predicted and astonishingly accurate. It was intensely nerve-wracking to sit through fifteen minutes of straight and level instrument flying in the target area, the last three minutes of which were as precise and smooth as an approach for a blind landing. During the first five minutes of your run, you were treated to the spectacle of the Oboe aircraft ahead of you, flying through the concentrated defences of the target in the final minutes of his run. In almost every case, he would be pinned in a cone of searchlights like a moth in a candle flame, the bursts of heavy flak blossoming around him like fireworks. The completion of his run was marked by a sudden termination of the flak and searchlight activity up ahead, and the breathtaking beginning of your turn. As if of a common mind, searchlights and flak switched their efforts immediately, and you became their target. It was fascinating, in a hypnotic sort of way, to be there, the proverbial sitting duck, so obviously vulnerable, and watch the searching fingers of light and the exploding flak reach out for you on the radar prediction of your height, track and speed, all of which were, as you well realized, both precise and predictable. You knew where the next burst was going to be as the flak moved progressively closer and closer as you approached the target. Our RAF slang was expanded as a result of such experiences! One spoke of a "ring twitch" and your "pucker string" in reference to the feeling of vulnerability in your lower regions as you sat over that threat of molten metal exploding beneath you. Your sphincter may not have "twitched" literally but, assuredly, it tightened involuntarily on those occasions when you felt certain that the next burst must be a hit.

As I became more familiar with the Mosquito and the equipment with which I had to work, my mind became less than totally absorbed and less oblivious to my surroundings. There was room for my imagination to come into play. I became constantly alert to any warning lights in the cockpit, to any change in the rhythm of the mighty Merlins which powered us so swiftly through those dark, unfriendly skies. The flash of a warning light, a falter in the smooth revs of the engines, was enough to raise the hairs on the back of my neck, and to revive the memory of those final moments of my fiery, screaming plunge into the Mediterranean.

It wasn't pleasant during those times, struggling to regain my confidence, to repair that emotional armour, and to resume that inner detachment and insulation that had combined in the past to preserve me in the face of danger and against the loss of so many comrades. This was a battle within a battle, and no less of a bitter struggle because it was private and personal. I had to overcome my expectation of trouble and my fear of plunging to earth again like a fiery comet. There was really no alternative. I was back where I felt sure I belonged; I just had to make the necessary adjustments to become comfortable again.

Chapter XXVI

Since I had missed an earlier invitation to Buckingham Palace, I was delighted to discover that I had been included in another investiture there. I was available this time and was given leave to travel to London.

A wartime investiture must be the epitome of investitures — the monarch of the realm presenting the nation's highest awards for gallantry and service to the defenders of his nation. The potential is certainly there; all the ingredients of a memorable experience are present. Unfortunately for the recipients, their very numbers detract from the excitement of the event. The ubiquitous queue of wartime Britain was inescapable even there, when the civilian and military recipients and their guests arrived for the investiture. The main queue divided initially into two streams, one for guests and one for recipients. The former were guided into a long hall lined with rows of gilt chairs facing a red-carpeted, railed dias which stood in front of some doors and was flanked on each side by a ramp. The recipients gathered in a large reception room where staff officers and stewards divided them first by awards, then by service and, finally, alphabetically by last name. The various award groups were then marshalled into separate waiting rooms in alphabetical order. The sequencing of the recipients took far longer than the seating of the guests, who must have been sitting for an hour before the national anthem was played and the king arrived on the dais.

There must have been at least two hundred awards that morning. As a recipient of the DFC, a member of the junior service and a "W" to boot, my turn came late. Still, as I marched into the hall, up the ramp, halted, turned to face and salute the king, I was thrilled beyond belief. But as I stepped forward to have my medal pinned on my breast, I could see the pallor and fatigue under the light make-up the king was wearing. My heart bled for him as I felt the tremor in his hand and witnessed his determination, despite his difficulty, to say something personal to me about Canada. With my medal pinned over my heart, I stepped back, saluted, turned and marched off, free to depart. The hour and a half ceremony had been reduced to something less than a minute's personal involvement! Yet I felt sure that every recipient felt as I did, as each left the dias — inspired by His Majesty and pleased to have been so honoured.

Although I didn't remember it, my mother had apparently said, when I left for overseas the last time, "See you in the comics." It must

Membership tokens for the three clubs, Winged Goldfish, Caterpillar Club and Late Arrivals.

have been an expression current at that time. What brought it to mind was a letter from my mother reminding me of her remark and enclosing a page from one of the American comic books that were flooding the Canadian market. The page was headlined, "OUR HAT IS OFF TO," and contained six photographs. Five of them were of decorated US servicemen and the sixth was of me. My escape in the desert and my membership in the three clubs, the Winged Goldfish, Winged Boot, and Caterpillar, were mentioned in the caption. The picture was an official PR one that made me look pretty chubby. It decided me to use my investiture trip into London to get a better picture for Mother. I looked around the Regent Palace in the West End, where I was staying, and found the Michael Curzon Studio at 5 Strand in WC 2. The photographer was a young, pleasant, and somewhat delicate-looking man. I was in uniform, of course, and he seemed to be pleased I asked him to photograph me. He took great pains with the session and chatted in a friendly fashion all the time he was working. When he heard that I had been to the investiture and was on my own in London, he invited me to join him for a drink at his club that evening. It seemed a typically generous invitation of a "Colonial" by a local, so I agreed. It was my good fortune to discover later in the day, from my pub friends at the Devonshire Arms, that the White Door Club, where we were to have met, was a notorious homosexual meeting place. My photographer friend had probably misinterpreted my choice of his establishment or my remark about being on my own. I, in turn, had not recognized his proclivity. But, I was not yet worldly nor suspicious of people's generosity. I passed up the invitation and what I

Curzon Studio's flattering portrait.

feared might be an embarrassing or distasteful situation. The photographer did, however, produce a most flattering picture, proving again the fallacy of that old saw that pictures don't lie.

On one of my later trips to London and my old stomping grounds the Regent Palace, I was surprised and pleased to meet a group of old school friends from Hamilton. There were three: Harry, Gord, and Alan. Harry and Gord and I had played football, and Alan had been the team manager. They had joined the same army unit in Hamilton as second lieutenants, and had come overseas together. We had not seen each other for two or three years, so it was a joyful, though brief reunion. Because of conflicting commitments, we separated, but made arrangements to get together later in the hotel. I cannot recall whether I had a girl with me at that later gathering, or even how many girls were there. All that I do remember is the striking girl that Alan brought with him. Her name was Sandra. She was as tall as Alan, with a great figure, pale creamy skin, black hair, big dark eyes, nice teeth and a warm smile. I feel sure that I didn't do anything to embarrass Alan or myself that night, but I did manage to make sure, before we parted, that Sandra knew I was remaining in the hotel after the others returned to camp and that I would love to see her again.

I believe Sandra called me the following day, or the next. We arranged a rendezvous and began the most enjoyable and warm relationship I could have wished. I discovered that she was a part-time model, that Sandra was her professional name, that she was of Russian/Jewish extraction, and that she lived with her grandmother in London. I also discovered that she had few inhibitions and a healthy enjoyment of sex. She seemed to be quite independent and was always well, even if colourfully, dressed. Hotel accommodation was hard to come by in London, and my room was a single. Because of hotel rules restricting visitors after ten o'clock, we were somewhat restricted in the time available for bedroom activities. Though she seemed to be more than willing, it was simply impossible to arrange for her to stay overnight. Instead, we looked forward to and planned for my next leave, when I could arrange for suitable accommodation and when she would not have to catch the last train home.

It was becoming apparent that Peter and I were a good team and a reliable crew. We continued to fly together and to achieve good results in both accuracy and timing. There were frequent test flights for aircraft and numerous equipment trials. It was now November, and we were experiencing winter conditions at high altitude for the first time on Mosquitoes. "Coring" became a problem that caused a fair amount of grief. The first indication of trouble in flight was a sudden, inexplicable rise in the oil temperature of one or both engines when we were at operational altitude. There was never any warning, or gradual rise; the temperature just jumped from normal to dangerous levels from one instant to the next. To have continued, without curing the problem, would have caused the engine to seize. It was discovered that the oil in the cooler began to freeze in the extreme conditions and, once it started, the coring restricted oil circulation and enlarged the freezing core of immobile oil in a rapid, multiplier fashion. Closing the cooling gills on the cooler was totally inadequate once the condition took hold. The only cure was a razor's edge: preventing the oil from cooling while keeping it within safe operational temperature range to prevent overheating.

This problem was something like that of the oxygen supply being cut off when the bomb bay was opened at altitude. The airflow in the bay interfered with the functioning of the oxygen regulator. We were never sure what these problems had cost in crews lost before they were discovered and cured. It would have been naive to believe that they were detected the first time they occurred.

In spite of these winter flying technical problems, Peter and I took part in three successful attacks on Bochum in November. On the 5th, twelve Oboe Mosquitoes attacked; on the 13th, eight; and on the 29th, ten of us went in. The target was the same in each case, the blast furnaces of the massive steel mill, in an attempt to achieve strategic results while Oboe was still under development without resorting to the use of the heavy bomber force. Peter and I also flew one of seven Oboe Mosquitoes which attacked Dusseldorf on the 7th and again on the 12th. All of these raids were on targets in the Ruhr where the Oboe equipment was working at optimum range. Each aircraft carried four 1000 lb high explosive bombs to inflict as much damage to the targets as possible with such a small force. During the same period, on the 18th, we carried out an unusual type of attack. Peter and I, along with five other Mosquitoes, dropped our bombs on Aachen and then proceeded to a second target site where we dropped route markers for the main force. They were out that same night in an attack on Ludwigshaven/Mannheim, a target well beyond Oboe range. There were 395 heavy bombers in that attack, and 23 were lost, mainly to the nightfighters which were becoming increasingly persistent and increasingly effective in the defence of their homeland. Navigation of the Oboe aircraft on this dual operation was much more demanding than usual. The need for accuracy was just as great at both target locations, and there was no slack to compensate for any time lost on the first operation. It required a high standard of crew discipline over a longer period than we had faced on any of our earlier Oboe sorties.

Our Mosquitoes, with their superior performance and Oboe equipment, provided us with many more opportunities to attack the enemy than had the heavies. This meant that our crews, including Peter and me, were able to operate more frequently than had been the case in the earlier days of the heavies. Not only had the tempo of our operations increased significantly, but we also found ourselves frequently operating independently of the main force.

Peter and I experienced our first abort during that same month of November. We had taken off at 1745 for an Oboe attack on Krefeld in a Mosquito we had flight tested earlier in the day. We were back on the ground within thirty minutes with an unserviceable aircraft. However, we managed to switch to a reserve Mosquito and were back in the air by 1845 with an adjusted time on target. When we reached altitude and were on course over the North Sea, we began to experience a most unnerving problem. The aircraft refused to settle at height and started an uncontrollable hunting-for-height action. The longer we persisted, the worse the hunting action seemed to get. With such a control problem, we knew that we could never meet the precise instrument flight requirements of the bombing run even if we reached the target. And that seemed doubtful at this stage of the flight. There was no recourse but to abandon the operation and return to base, if we could. With the operation aborted, we no longer had to maintain our high altitude and as we descended into the warmer air of lower altitude, the control problem disappeared. We felt that some element of the longitudinal control cables must have frozen, but why it had affected this particular aircraft that night, we were never able to determine. We flew that same Mosquito later in the month of January without any difficulty. I must confess, though, that I was very relieved to turn back and to descend to warmer levels that troubled night. There is nothing quite so unsettling as a struggle against the unknown or against the forces of Nature. You can fight an enemy, match your strength, your skill and your resolve against his, but how do you fight the unknown, unseen, immeasurable?

During our development flights, we carried a normal bomb load of four 1000 lb high-explosive bombs in our bomb bay. The Mosquito, however, had been designed with wing tip fittings for carrying external loads, either additional fuel pods or additional weapons. It was decided, therefore, to increase the destructive potential of our attacks by carrying an additional bomb under each wing. This added load proved to be no problem for the versatile Mosquito. We could still get airborne, climb to our operational height, and maintain speed and manoeuvrability for the attack.

Everything seemed to go according to plan on the first attack that we carried the extra, externally-mounted bombs. Everything, that is, until one of the pilots called the control tower after he had landed on the flare-lit, grass runway, to say that he had seen bombs on the airfield! The rest of the aircraft, which were en route home or circling for landing, were put on hold and a vehicle sent to investigate. Sure enough, the pilot was right; there were bombs scattered on or around the runway in use! These were hastily removed by the armament section duty staff without incident, and the waiting aircraft were instructed to land and proceed with caution. Four came in, one after the other, touched down and taxied to their dispersals. The fifth arrived, touched down a little hard, bounced up, and as it touched down again, was flipped over on its back in a violent explosion. The sky lit up with lurid colour. Men and vehicles rushed to the crash site. There was no chance of reaching the pilot trapped in the wreckage of the blazing cockpit, but the navigator had, by some freak of explosive force, been ejected out of the burning mass and was lying on the grass, one leg trapped under the blazing starboard engine. At considerable risk to themselves, the rescue party was able to lift the engine high enough for others to pull the navigator free. He lost his leg, but was otherwise unscathed.

No more aircraft were permitted to land. The few who were still circling were diverted. The next morning, a ground survey revealed a number of unexploded bombs on the perimeter of the airfield, but no more on the runway. It wasn't difficult to determine what must have happened. When the aircraft reached the target, after flying at high altitude in sub-zero temperatures and in and out of cloud, the bomb doors had been opened, the bombs fused and then released over the target. As on every operation, the electrical equipment check would have been made by the observer to confirm that all of the bombs had been released, before the bomb doors were closed. What had not been experienced before was the use of externally-mounted bombs in high altitude attacks. When the bomb release was activated, the bomb suspensions had opened to allow the bombs to fall free. To this extent, everything was normal, and the after-release check of the system would have indicated all bombs gone because every suspension was open. However, under the conditions in which we had been flying, ice had accumulated around the external bombs and their suspensions. Although the suspensions had opened satisfactorily, the bombs had hung up under the wings simply because they were frozen there. The flight back to base in warmer air had softened the ice by the time the aircraft reached base, so that some bombs had fallen off as the aircraft circled the airfield and others hung on until landing. These latter bombs had fallen on the runway and caused the alarm. Those aircraft had obviously enjoyed good fortune. Their bombs must have fallen horizontally balanced and landed safely beneath them. The one unfortunate crew must have dropped one nose down, with the resultant explosion under their wing. It was one more of the costly incidents in the development of a weapon system under hurry-up, wartime conditions. The price in this case was a valuable crew; an experienced and capable pilot was dead, an experienced and skilful navigator crippled. The fault, however, could be overcome. We would be able to continue using those external bombs, and the Mosquito would fly with increased effectiveness, once the necessary corrective measures had been taken.

Chapter XXVII

On one of our operations, Peter and I were flying at our operational altitude of 28,000 feet over occupied Europe on the way to a target in Germany. It was a clear night above the dark land mass beneath. We were nicely on track and well within our planned time. For a change, I could afford to sit back briefly and to look about me. As I scanned the area, my attention was drawn to a flickering light on the ground directly ahead of us. I pointed it out to Peter and kept my eyes on it for the entire time that it was visible, because it was somehow different from anything I had seen before, and because it must have been very bright to have been noticeable from such a height. I decided to record the exact time and location at which I had first seen the light which, by then, had disappeared. While I was doing this, we were rocked about violently as if we had been struck or as if we had flown right through the turbulence of another aircraft nearby. Looking around as the aircraft shuddered, we were amazed to see that we seemed to be flying through a corkscrewing, vertical contrail! We were mystified by what we had seen and were experiencing. Seemingly, though, we had not been damaged by the turbulence. We did wonder whether our antenna might have been damaged, but there was no way for us to test it prior to starting our run into the target when our turn was called. If it had been damaged, we would just have to abort. But until then we would have to carry on in hopes that we were still serviceable.

As it turned out, we were able to make a successful Oboe attack that night; our antenna was functional. Such concern might seem a bit farfetched, but we were aware of a somewhat similar incident involving one of our squadron aircraft only a few nights before. That crew had returned to base after the ground stations reported that they had not responded when called in to attack. The crew reported that everything had been normal until somewhere over occupied Europe at their operational height, they had been suddenly and violently shaken up. The aircraft had almost gone out of control. Fortunately, the turbulence had been short-lived and control quickly re-established. Little loss of height had resulted from the brief shake-up, and they were able to resume their flight to the waiting point. During their run from the waiting point, they had heard their call sign and switched on as required. It had quickly become apparent, however, that the ground station was not seeing them, and they heard the reserve aircraft being called in to replace them. They had no choice but to abort and return to base. On the ground, while they were being debriefed, it was discovered that the antenna under the aircraft had been sheared off and that the underside of the fuselage showed numerous longitudinal streaks and scratches in what was normally a clean, smooth, painted surface. It was fairly obvious that they had been flying directly over another aircraft on the same track and at the same altitude. In any flight at our altitude, there is a small degree of "humping" in what is considered to be level flight. There must have been a moment when the two aircraft brushed against one another in this gentle humping action. The aircraft which aborted and returned to base was obviously the one on top. It came through the encounter with only scratches and the loss of its antenna. The other never made it back. It was the second of our Oboe craft which failed to show up on the ground station that night.

This experience was uppermost in our minds after we had recovered from our own little bout with turbulence. However, that possibility had been eliminated by our successful attack. We were, therefore, somewhat surprised by the interest shown by the intelligence staff in our report of the incident. We were taken aside after completing our normal debriefing, and I was asked for a more complete description of the incident and as precise a location as possible for the ground position of the light we had seen. No explanation was offered to satisfy our curiosity about their interest, and we were left to wonder what was so interesting about what we had witnessed. It was a long time before we discovered that we had seen one of the test launches of the V2 rocket and had unwittingly flown through its turbulent wake as it climbed almost vertically to its apogee. How close we came to colliding with it, I will never know, but the severity of the turbulence and the density of the corkscrewing condensation trail through which we had flown were strong evidence of a very near miss. To have been inadvertently shot down by an experimental V2 would have been bizarre to say the least.

Shortly after that, I was sent off for a few days' operational leave, the first since meeting Sandra. As planned, I made reservations, this time for a double room at a smaller, family-type hotel in Cadogen Square, rather than at my more familiar haunt in Piccadilly Circus. I had the pleasurable experience of being able to behave like a young officer sharing his leave with his lovely young wife in London. Whether the hotel staff was taken in by this deception or not, I do not know, but nothing was done to discourage our play-acting, nor to make us feel anything less than welcome in their establishment. It was a relaxing and exciting break from the monastic, dedicated squadron life which otherwise absorbed me to the exclusion of all else. Sex was never an indiscriminate activity for me but, with a girl like Sandra, to whom I was emotionally and physically attracted, sex did provide relief from the tensions operational flying built up in me. Thank goodness Fate hadn't seen me enlist in the navy!

By that time, I had adjusted to flying over Germany once again and was able to overcome my imagination. I was no longer haunted by memories of that plunge into the Mediterranean and my insulation from involvement in the events around me had been restored. Along with it, my confidence had returned. My enjoyment of life and its pleasures hadn't lost any appeal; it simply fell back into second place in my priorities again. My main motivation was the job at hand, the development of Oboe and successful bombing of German targets.

Whenever the squadron was on operation without you, you instinctively listened for the sound of returning aircraft, no matter what the time of night or day. One night, we all heard the Mosquito approaching the airfield, its Merlins at full throttle. The roar of those engines grew to an ear-straining pitch as the aircraft came closer. At first we could not see it, then it flashed overhead at high speed, too close to the ground. The sound diminished as the aircraft flew farther away, only to increase again as it began a second approach. The engine pitch never faltered, the throttles must have remained fully open. Suddenly, in a roar of power, the Mosquito reappeared at the edge of the airfield, this time right at ground level. Within a moment, it was hurtling along the grass, propellers flailing at the ground, twisting like spaghetti. It must have touched down at 200 plus miles per hour. Quick action by the crew to shut off the fuel flow, and a goodly portion of luck, prevented an outbreak of fire. As the speed of the initial, and seemingly suicidal, landing slowed down, the top hatch of the aircraft flew off, jettisoned to prepare for crew evacuation. Just before the remains of that redoubtable Mosquito ground to a halt, the navigator and pilot emerged from the hatch to jump down to the ground, unscathed.

The aircraft had suffered severe damage from heavy flak during its bombing run and had tumbled out of control. There had been considerable doubt that they would be able to regain it. The engines had not been damaged, but they discovered that every time their speed fell below 200 mph, the aircraft again became uncontrollable; they would tumble and have to build up their speed again to regain any semblance of control. Even at high speed, control was minimal, with little or no aileron response. They had, therefore, flown at high speed all the way back to base, letting down slowly to reach the airfield at low level. They had purposefully overflown it and, unable to bank the aircraft, had flown a wide, flat circuit, still holding their high speed, to come back to base for a belly landing. As the navigator said after escaping from the wreckage, "I didn't mind the landing. It was the bloody running to keep up after we rubbed the bottom of the aircraft off!"

As might be expected, the weather in December was far from suitable for the heavies. Peter and I were full-fledged Pathfinders by then, and proud to wear the albatross on our left breast pocket flaps below our flying badge. We flew a couple of test flights and some equipment development flights for the boffins, but we were able to fly only three operational missions that month. On the 12th we flew in a force of twenty Mosquitoes in an attack on Essen. In addition to bombing a key element of the Essen Works, taxing the air defences of the Ruhr once again in the drive to wear down their efficiency and forcing the population to take to their shelters while playing on their fear of another massive air attack were significant side benefits. We lost one of our most experienced crews that night, presumably to the heavy flak that responded to our attack. On the 22nd, we took part for the first time in an attack on two of the V1 sites situated between Amiens and Abbéville, an ideal location from which the Germans could launch their unmanned weapons against London. It was a very short flight over the Channel, not far from Dieppe, where we dropped markers for the 43 heavies which were to bomb the two sites. We had provided eight Mosquitoes to mark the targets. Because of the brief penetration required to reach them, we were able to carry out the attacks without loss to ourselves and with at least one of the sites destroyed.

Those of us who had been to London around that time had seen the V1 in operation, and some of us had experienced its destructive force and its emotional effects on the population. The unique sound of its pulse jet engine, the knowledge that it was unmanned and undisturbed by any opposition, made it eerie and unnerving. Then, the ominous silence, as the motor shut off and the silent glide began, made you hold your breath as you waited for the inevitable explosion. It seems a strange thing to say in such a bitter war, but the lack of human involvement and the seemingly inexorable, mechanical effectiveness of the V1 made it seem unfair. It was, without a doubt, a psychological weapon, and we were delighted to be able to strike at its heart.

As Christmas approached, the Officers' Mess decided to try to forget about the war by planning a big party for all of the officers, their wives and girlfriends. It was to be as close to a peace-time party as could possibly be arranged. Peter, of course, was bringing his wife, as were many of the other married officers. I decided, with Peter's encouragement, to bring Sandra. He had heard enough about her, but had not yet met her. Being something of a ladies' man, he was determined to correct this oversight, and even offered to use his car for the chauffeuring which would be required. I wrote to Sandra, received her enthusiastic agreement, and reserved a double room at a lovely country hotel in Swaffham, where Peter and his wife, Penny, would be staying with his parents.

I was really looking forward to Sandra's arrival when Peter and I took off on the 22nd for the attack on the V1 sites. I was suffering with a mild head cold that day and probably should not have flown. However, the nature of the attack, and the fact that we had not been able to operate since the Essen raid, were too much for me to turn down. The flight had gone well and we had dropped our markers accurately and on time. I had felt a little discomfort during the flight, particularly on the descent, but I had encountered no serious problems. The next morning, however, was a very different matter. I had a high fever, a severe headache, and what proved to be a very badly infected throat. After a verbal dressing down by the doctor, I was rushed into a hospital bed and tested for diphtheria.

As I lay in the hospital, my greatest concern was for the Christmas party and Sandra's imminent arrival in Swaffham. I didn't want to cancel any of the arrangements, but I certainly didn't want her to find me in hospital. That afternoon, the two RAF doctors, one of whom was my Scottish rugger friend and mentor in the scrum, Dr. Liddell, popped into my room to discuss my treatment. They were well aware of my dilemma and my anxiety for a quick cure and, as it turned out, were quite sympathetic. They asked me if I wanted to be a guinea pig. They had just received a supply of a new drug with which neither had any experience and for which they had been given very little clinical guidance. The drug was penicillin. In 1943, it was new and relatively unknown, even in the medical world. My two doctors had heard of its miraculous curative powers against infection. They were anxious to try it and — I had thought that they were just being sympathetic — they needed a guinea pig. But I was just as anxious as they were for a miracle cure.

When they began discussing dosages and speaking in thousands of units, I began to wonder whether I had been wise or just hasty in agreeing to be their test case. After my initial injection, I was somewhat shaken by the doctors' remarks about being totally in the dark as to what my reaction to the drug would or should be. They agreed to monitor me frequently, and personally, to watch for any reaction. For the rest of that afternoon and evening, one or the other made an hourly visit to see me and ask how I was feeling. Since I was feeling no ill effects at all from the injection, I began to find it quite amusing to watch the quizzical expression on their faces as they peered around the door on each visit, wondering what sort of reaction might greet them. By the next morning, it was apparent to them, and to me, that it was indeed a miracle drug. One further day of treatment sufficed to eliminate all traces of the throat infection and the fever. The diphtheria test was negative. I was released from hospital but barred from flying for at least forty-eight hours. The doctors saw me off the premises, throwing a little cold water on my growing excitement by saying that they hoped there would be no unfortunate physical side effects of their drug that could spoil my Christmas!

Sandra arrived the day of the party. I met her at the train and took her to the hotel. That evening, Peter came by in the car to pick us up for the drive to the Officers' Mess. I was in the lobby downstairs to greet him, and Sandra was upstairs in our room putting on the last touches before making her appearance. And what an entrance it was. She came down the stairs, slowly and gracefully, as a model would, wearing a striking, close-fitting, long, sheath-like dress and a gold-coloured turban encasing all of her hair. With her slim height, full breasts, creamy pale skin and those big dark eyes, she was a sight to behold as she descended those circling stairs into the lobby of that quiet country hotel. The dramatic silence was shattered by Peter's involuntary, but loud and awed, "Jesus Christ!"

We had a wonderful party that evening and a most enjoyable, though brief, stay in the hotel. Penicillin proved to have no noticeable side effects. However, some disturbing developments did manifest themselves during this idyll. Sandra brought some of her family background into our conversations. She told me she was the seventh child of a seventh child which, in the folklore of her people, foretold great things for her firstborn. This, true or not, seemed to me to be a subtle introduction of the subject of marriage into our relationship. It was a subject for which I was not psychologically prepared, at least not then. Sandra was a lovely and sexually exciting woman. But there was no future in this relationship. I wasn't psychologically ready to settle down. Operations were my life; sex was a welcome diversion. It would be better to break cleanly rather than prolong matters which, inevitably, would have become more difficult for both of us later on. Our parting at the railway station was, therefore, "Goodbye," and not, "Au revoir."

On the 28th, we were back on active crew list and included in an Oboe attack on Hamborn, not far from Essen. This was another thrust against the Ruhr defences to keep the population off balance, and off work at the same time, and to hit vital small targets in the key factories in the area. The timing of the Hamborn raid, however, was planned to provide cover and distraction for the large force of heavies which was attacking Berlin that night. More than 700 bombers were involved. Twenty failed to return. Although this was a lower loss rate than usual, it was not possible to say whether our efforts had contributed directly or not to that improvement.

Chapter XXVIII

The new year started on January 1 with another attack on a V1 site. This launching platform was in the Cherbourg Peninsula near a village called Bristillerie. We marked the target for a small force of heavies and were back at base in less than three hours. On the 4th, we were part of a force of twelve Oboe Mosquitoes and sixty-eight heavies attacking two V1 sites in the Pas de Calais area and another in the Cherbourg Peninsula. In each case, the launching sites were accurately marked and successfully attacked. Again, on the 27th, as a tiny force of nine Mosquitoes, we attacked, on our own, another V1 installation at Herbouville in the Pas de Calais area. There was no question that we were having reasonable success in our bombings of the V1 sites, but the German ability to recover seemed equally efficient and possibly less expensive overall than the bomber effort being expended upon them. We did, however, reduce the rate of buildup in the V1 attacks and we succeeded in buying time for other defensive measures to take hold.

In between our attacks on the V1 sites, Peter and I took part in an all-Mosquito raid on Duren, on the western side of the Ruhr. There were thirty-seven of us involved in attacking six different pin-point targets within the Duren area. Though it was a complex operation for the ground stations, with six different target coordinates to set up in rapid succession, for the individual air crews it followed normal procedure. The whole operation reflected the growing confidence in Oboe's reliability and accuracy. Each of the six aiming points was hit and without loss to the Mosquito force.

On the 30th, we were included in another of the all-Mosquito attacks. This time there were twenty-seven Oboe Mosquitoes in the raid on Elberfeld, a target which was a little deeper in the Ruhr and an added test of the range and accuracy of the Oboe system.

About mid-month, Peter and I had been called in to see the squadron commander, now G/C Bufton, who told us we had been promoted to the rank of squadron leader. When he told us, I was very surprised by his apology for the promotion having taken so long. It seemed that the telephone call from PFF HQ, which had preceded my arrival, must have included the information that I had left a squadron leader's post in 6 Group to join PFF. G/C Bufton had been trying to have me promoted ever since I became operational in the squadron. His attempts had been thwarted by the limitation of the squadron establishment until then. It was doubly satisfying for me that Peter was promoted at the same time since, by then, we were a team, and a damned good one at that. Besides, Peter had been a squadron leader before, was quite senior and could use the extra money to meet his family expenses.

Winter was providing us with the longer, dark nights needed for bomber operations. The weather, however, was often a limiting factor, particularly for the deeper penetrations beyond Oboe range. H2S provided the heavies with a radar ground mapping capability which was not inherently limited by range. However, despite the significance of the development of H2S, the picture it provided was far from exact and not particularly well-defined. It required a great deal of expertise to use it effectively. The results it provided required good correlation with accurate navigational data for confirmed interpretation. It was, without a doubt, a definite aid to navigation, and on some occasions, an aid to general target location. But it was not of much assistance in pinpoint accuracy for blind bombing. Winter was still a perverse paradox for Bomber Command; it brought the long hours of darkness which were essential for the deep penetration of unescorted bombers, but it also brought the climatic conditions most inimical to flight and accurate navigation.

It was on one of the deeper attacks in the Ruhr, when Oboe Mosquitoes had to fly at maximum altitude, that an incident occurred which might have accounted for some of the losses we had suffered while our aircraft had been on their bombing run and were being received by the ground stations. The problem was revealed when one of our crews, which had been lost by the ground station while on its bombing run, returned safely to base, but badly shaken by their experience. The navigator, in particular, was still visibly shaken when they arrived for debriefing. Their run into the target had been quite normal until they were well down the run. After they had reached the halfway point, they had opened their bomb bay doors in accordance with standard procedure, and had settled down for the more precise portion of the target run. Before they reached the release point, however, the navigator was horrified to see the pilot slump over the control column, pushing it forward and forcing the aircraft into a steep dive. They had been flying at 30,000 feet, but began losing altitude at a great rate and picking up speed at the same time. There really isn't much room in the cockpit of a Mosquito, and no duplicate controls. There was, therefore, very little chance for the navigator to take over control. The only alternatives were to bail out or to stick with the pilot and accept the consequences. The navigator chose to stick with his pilot. Though he couldn't lift the pilot clear of the controls, he could ease the pressure of his weight on the control column. As the aircraft reached lower altitude, the angle of the dive lessened, and the pilot began to recover. The pilot had no recollection of his collapse, but was able to recover control and level out. They realized there was no longer any chance to complete the attack, so they set course for home.

An investigation revealed no technical failure in the aircraft systems. However, it was quite apparent that the pilot had suffered severe hypoxia, oxygen starvation, which, at that altitude in an unpressurized aircraft, is swift and deadly. Fortunately, it had not affected the navigator, possibly because at that phase in the attack, the physical demands were less for him than for the pilot. The easing of the dive and the availability of the more oxygen-rich air at lower altitude had allowed the pilot to recover before it was too late. Further investigation and flight testing established that opening the bomb bay doors at high altitude could create air currents within the confined space of the bomb bay which affected the operation of the economizer valve in the oxygen system. The result was that the valve pulsed at a high rate instead of working on demand as the crew breathed in and out. This created an effect similar to that of heart fibrillation. The faster the rate, the less efficient the pumping becomes. In this case, it was oxygen being pumped instead of blood or, more to the point, was not being pumped.

Most of us had been through high-altitude training in decompression tanks, and I, for one, had completed a high altitude operation with a faulty economizer valve. It had drastically reduced my oxygen supply, but I had realized what was happening and had warned Peter to be alert for possible consequences in my performance. I had been able to work in spurts and rest in between, sufficiently to keep from losing my efficiency. We had completed the operation successfully, but I paid the price the next morning with a splitting headache which featured the beat of the economizer pounding in my head. We all knew the dangers of hypoxia at the altitudes we were flying, and we were aware of its insidious effects. To have reworked the oxygen system of the Mosquito would have taken a great deal of time and effort. It probably would have meant taking the aircraft out of service while the modifications were being made. At this stage in the offensive, such a penalty was unacceptable. Instead, we worked out a simple, quick fix. It became standard procedure for the navigator to switch the oxygen system to "Emergency" at the start of the bombing run. This by-passed the economizer valves and provided a steady flow of oxygen from the pressurized tanks, ensuring that no crew member would suffer from oxygen starvation while the bomb bay doors were open.

It was at about this time that I walked right into the first, and only, disciplinary incident in my career. We happened to have a very young Welsh navigator in the squadron. He had, without a doubt, one of the most brilliant minds I have ever encountered. He had been born and brought up in poor economic circumstances in a Welsh mining community. Early in his education, his brilliance had been recognized and a scholarship took him to an excellent public school that would otherwise have been beyond his reach. He had volunteered for the RAF as soon as he was old enough, and while he was still in school. He must have been commissioned because of his academic performance and his good schooling, because he was the least prepossessing officer you could possibly meet, and a rebel to boot. Even his navigation technique was unorthodox. His log and chart work were almost non-existent, and what was there was just about indecipherable to anyone else. He seemed to do his navigation in his head, making little, if any record of his activities. Despite this, he was remarkably proficient. So, he was tolerated by the RAF, a service which showed surprising tolerance for the unusual character, at least in wartime, and as long as he was good at his work.

Taffy, for that was his name, was also inclined to drink to excess whenever he wasn't flying. He either had a great capacity for fluids or a low tolerance for alcohol, because he inevitably achieved a state of inebriation on every occasion he drank. His behaviour when he was drunk was disturbing to the mess staff and to the cleaners of his room. He was, as a result, constantly on the Commander's "Shit List," and probably only survived because of the good offices of his squadron commander.

Anyway, be that as it may, Taffy and I were together one night when the bar closed. Taffy was still ambulatory, though pretty well under the influence. I was sober, but hungry, as usual. He said to me that one of the WAAFs on night duty in the kitchen was a girlfriend of his and that she would feed us for sure. Taffy had seemingly made this late feeding a regular practice. So, in spite of knowing that the kitchen was out of bounds, we made our way there and, true to Taffy's prediction, the girls on duty sat us down to toast, jam, and tea. It was a friendly foursome that the station administration officer encountered that night when he came into the kitchen! We suspected that he, too, had come in for a late snack. But, on seeing Taffy and me already at the table, he had assumed the pose of a responsible station officer finding officers out of bounds and illegally consuming rations. Our names were taken, and we were advised that we would be reported to the station commander.

The following morning, G/C Bufton called me into his office to tell me that I was to report to the station commander at 0930. Buff had a pretty good idea of what was involved and asked me to report back to him when I was dismissed by the station commander. As soon as I stood before the CO, he said, "Watts, do you know why you have been brought before me?" "Yes, Sir," I replied, "I do." "Well," he said, "I am very disappointed in your behaviour. You should know better. Do you see any reason why you should not receive the same punishment as your companion received?" "No, Sir," I replied, "I don't know of any reason why I shouldn't." "Right, then," he said, "you are barred from using any of the mess common-rooms for four weeks, except for meals in the dining room, and your bar privileges are cancelled for the same period. Dismissed."

When I reported back to Buff, he was indignant at what he considered an unjustified and unreasonable punishment. As far as the loss of my bar privileges was concerned, the punishment was of little consequence to me. I had been making little use of my bar bill anyway. For an officer living far from home, though, the denial of the mess common-rooms was much more punitive. If it hadn't been for the fact that I had made Buff a promise to escort his sister-in-law to a party in the mess, I wouldn't have been concerned at all. Still, I hadn't objected when the opportunity had been provided. Someone else would have to look after the young lady on this occasion.

In February, the weather was even more restrictive. Peter and I were limited to three operations that month. On the 11th, we were in a group of 11 Mosquitoes which attacked a target in Ruhrfort. On the 15th, we were part of a group of 23 Oboe Mosquitoes that attacked the airfield at Venlo in Holland, near the German border. This airfield was one of the major nightfighter fields, and our attack was timed to divert attention from and to support an attack on Berlin by 891 heavies, of which 43 were lost. Sixteen of us attacked the Twente airfield in Holland on the 20th; it was another nightfighter airfield close to the Ruhr and our attack was in support of the heavy attack on Leipzig by 823 aircraft. Losses were heavier in that attack; 78 bombers failed to return. In each of those raids, we lost one of our Oboe aircraft as well. The nightfighters had become the enemy's most effective air defence weapon when measured in terms of kill rate. Improved passive defence measures were being developed by the RAF to be employed against the nightfighters to make their task more difficult, and more effort was being devoted to counter the nightfighter success. Our attacks on their bases were just one of the means employed. It was a diversion from Oboe's primary role, but one which was justified in the struggle to gain the crucial bomber versus fighter supremacy.

We were all very sorry when G/C Bufton left us. He had seen the squadron through its growing pains, had seen Oboe and the high-altitude Mosquito through their technical development, and had moulded the men and the machines into a first-class operational unit of Pathfinders. His leadership had been a very important, if not an essential, element in the success of 109 Squadron. Dick Cox, the Canadian in the RAF whom I had first met when I reported to "A" flight the previous September, took Buff's place.

Although there was never any decrease in Peter's application or determination when it came to bombing or marking targets, he did seem to be tiring and to be less enthusiastic about operating as frequently as we might. As a result, in March, I operated four times; twice with Peter, once with a Canadian, F/O Pattison — the first RCAF pilot with whom I had operated — and once with an Australian, F/L Jacobe. During the same month, I also flew one night flying test with a New Zealander, F/O Dray, and one with an RAF pilot, S/L Kleboe. For one reason or another, those latter tests had not materialized into operational flights. When I look back, the unusual span of Commonwealth representation in my pilots that month was quite impressive; British, Canadian, Australian, and New Zealander. This was the beginning of a trend that was to persist for the remainder of my operational career which by its close would involve my flying with twenty-three different pilots.

The first raid in March was an Oboe attack on the Le Mans railroad marshalling yards by 6 Mosquitoes. We marked the target for a small force of heavies and we used sky markers instead of ground markers because of the cloud cover over the target. Despite that, heavy damage was inflicted on the yards. No aircraft was lost on this occasion. On the 13th, Peter and I, along with 29 other Mosquitoes, returned to the Ruhr in an Oboe attack on Dusseldorf. We stirred up the usual hornets' nest and, hopefully, created more panic in the surroundings as we bombed our assigned targets. I flew with Pattison on the 23rd in an Oboe attack of 22 Mosquitoes on Oberhausen, in a diversionary raid to draw the enemy defences away from an attack by 816 heavies on Frankfurt. The latter was highly successful even though 33 aircraft were lost in the raid. On the 29th, I flew with Jacobe. We were a small force of four, on a pin-point target in Cologne. In spite of our number, the defensive reaction we provoked was out of all proportion. The searchlights were concentrated and persistent, and the flak was heavy and deadly. Regardless of the damage we were causing in these Oboe-only raids, we were achieving much greater benefits than the costs involved. In terms of effort expended by the enemy to defend against our attacks and in terms of the effect on the morale of the population in the Ruhr, the entries in the ledger were clearly in our favour.

On the 13th, when Peter and I had climbed into the aircraft for the attack on Dusseldorf, we had closed the hatch and were starting to stow our gear before starting the engines, when we heard a knock on the hatch cover at my feet. This was most unusual. Once you had buttoned up, you were on your own and ready to leave. With considerable curiosity, therefore, I leaned forward, unlatched, and lifted the hatch cover. There, in the dim, reflected light of the cockpit, was the face of one of the RAF ground crew, holding something metallic in his hand and saying, "Excuse me, Sir, but is this yours? I thought I saw it fall to the ground as you climbed in." What he held was my bracelet of Canadian nickels! One of the links had snapped, possibly after it had snagged as I climbed in with my gear in hand. I was quite shocked. That bracelet was the one item which had seen me through all of my operations to date. Though not consciously, it had become my talisman as well as my link to home. The idea that, except for the sharp eyes and concern of that unknown airman, I would have been airborne and on my way to face the enemy for the very first time without my bracelet was a little unsettling. Had we taken off without my becoming aware of its absence, I obviously would not have been concerned. But my reaction to the thought that I might have left without it, ruffled me more than I expected. I thanked the observant airman, put the bracelet in my left breast pocket where it remained for the balance of my operational tour, and took off, feeling easier in mind that it had been only a near miss after all.

Being stationed at Marham had many advantages. The countryside was beautiful and relatively undeveloped. It was marvellous hunting country and there was a very large estate bordering on the airfield itself. A few of our RAF types didn't worry about doing a little poaching on the old admiral's estate. They even had the nerve to accept his invitations to join in the official shoots! One of them used his duty shift as the night flying duty officer to take the small van onto the grass airfield after take-offs had been completed to make a tour of the open grass area. The rabbits and hares which sat up in the grass, apparently hypnotized by the dim van lights, were knocked off by the front bumper of the van as he aimed for them. He would stop, run behind, pick up the dead animals, toss them in the back of the van, and send them home the next day to supplement his family's meagre rations.

My being crewed up with Peter had some side benefits as well. With his father's position as the local veterinary surgeon, Peter had a natural entrée to the local population. Peter and I became regular visitors to the local doctor's home where he and his wife always made us most welcome. Being a country doctor, he was often paid for his services in kind. Every time we were guests of the generous doctor and his wife, it was to enjoy a marvellous dinner. I was never there when he did not have pheasant, grouse, or hare hanging in the out-house, aging for the pot.

Peter and I were always most appreciative of the opportunities of getting out of the mess for a while and enjoying the feeling of being in a happy and comfortable home. However, we began to feel embarrassed at being guests so often when we had next to no ability to return their kindness. Peter and I arranged, therefore, to provide the amenities for the next party at the doctor's. It happened to be the right time of year for suckling pig. So, Peter and I set out one morning for the village pub which stood close to the open farmers' market. It was the regular hangout of the farmers whenever they were in town for sales. As soon as we walked into the dimly lit, low-ceilinged, raftered room of the bar, a deep rumbling voice said, "Good day, Master

Sooby," in a slow Norfolk drawl. Waiting for a moment while his eyes adjusted to the light, Peter peered around and then said, in an equally slow, broad Norfolk drawl, "Hello, George. You're just the man I wanted to see." After an invitation to join in a pint of the local brew, we got down to business. Yes, George's sow had recently had a litter and yes, George had, as usual, protected a couple of the piglets in his report of the litter to the Ministry officials. Not only had he a couple of piglets unaccounted for, but yes, he could also spare one for us.

Alcoholic beverages were hard to come by and beer had become the common drink. So, this was included in the rest of the supplies we were able to provide. It was a very enjoyable party with the suckling pig playing the starring role. Although it could never really compensate for the many evenings we had enjoyed at the doctor's, at least it made us feel better knowing we had made the effort.

Chapter XXIX

Those March raids marked the end of our operations from Marham. The grass airfield would not be able to meet the requirements of aircraft planned for the future and, as a permanent RAF base, it would need concrete runways. The future was already beckoning, so the two Mosquito squadrons were being transferred and the airfield decommissioned for hard surfacing. Our squadron was to be based at Little Staughton in Bedfordshire, a wartime airfield situated between Bedford and Cambridge. It had been used since its construction as a vehicle park for the US Army but was returned to the RAF for use by PFF as an air base for 109 Squadron and 582 Squadron, a squadron of Lancasters only recently formed. As a wartime-built base, it was a far cry from the comfortable prewar regular force bases. It had draughty Nissen huts for quarters, chilly, centralized ablutions and hutted mess facilities more reminiscent of a summer camp than an RAF Officers' Mess. However, none of us was there for pleasure and, though it might have seemed a poor trade by material measure, the move had absolutely no effect on the attitude or morale of the squadron personnel. There was even a positive factor in the move, as it produced a healthy, competitive relationship between the two squadrons.

We flew our aircraft from Marham to Little Staughton on the 2nd of April while our ground crews made the trip by road. I flew with the Australian, Jacobe, that day and on a night flying test the following day. On the 4th, Jacobe and I took off for our first operation from Little Staughton. It was an all-Oboe attack on a V1 site in the Cherbourg area, a simple assignment with minimal risk. It did illustrate, however, how quickly and efficiently the change in bases had been made. The move had had almost no effect on our operational availability, costing no more than one day at the most.

Six days later, I flew my next sortie, an attack on Essen. That time there were forty Mosquitoes in the attacking force, and my pilot was the Canadian, Pattison. Although he was an experienced pilot, this was his first tour of operation. We were in a new Mark of the Mosquito which we had been air testing over the past couple of days. It was one of the latest models with an enlarged bomb bay capable of taking a 4000 lb "blockbuster," and on this occasion, we were carrying the big bomb.

The flight proceeded uneventfully in the early stages, and our Oboe equipment was working well as we began our run to the target. As we went in from the waiting point, we could see the aircraft ahead of us in the concentrated cone of searchlights and the bursts of heavy anti-aircraft fire that seemed to surround it during the final minutes of their run. Then came the moment we had been waiting for, when our hearts beat a little faster and our sphincters tightened in nervous anticipation, the pause when the enemy defences ceased their concentration on the leading aircraft and swung over to us. We were called in to attack. It was as if we could hear the silence while we waited for the assault to begin.

I sort of "became aware" of Pattison, who was quite a bit shorter than I, scrunching down, lower and lower in his seat, until his head was below the level of the cowling. He had to look between his hands on the control column to even see the instrument panel! He simply couldn't see outside, presumably reflecting that "What you can't see won't hurt you" philosophy of a not-so-long-ago childhood. His low profile made me feel even more conspicuous, my helmet brushing the top of the glass cockpit, as I watched the anti-aircraft shells exploding ahead of us in a precise, straight line, coming closer and closer. Pat, to give him his due, kept us straight and level towards the target and towards the line of shells. It was a race between our accurate run straight to the bomb release point and the gunners who would try to hit us before we could drop our bomb. As it turned out, it ended in pretty much of a tie. We received our signal to release; I pressed the bomb tit; the line of anti-aircraft bursts reached us. There was a violent rocking as a shell struck under the aircraft. I felt light tugs at my right knee and on the right sleeve of my battle dress as slivers of shrapnel blasted through the floor of the fuselage. The flight instruments ceased to function and the starboard engine began to stream the billowing white cloud of escaping glycol.

We veered violently to avoid further hits and had to feather the starboard engine immediately to prevent it from seizing and becoming even more of a drag. By the time we had levelled off, we found the windscreen completely frosted over. We were blind, we could not see outside. Except for the simple needle and ball and liquid compass, we were totally without instruments. Our generator was on the dead engine, so we had to minimize the use of power to save the batteries for communications and emergencies. This meant turning off all non-essential electrical services, including my nav aids.

The hasty and violent manoeuvres we had just engaged in had made the liquid compass temporarily unreliable; the liquid was too agitated for the needle to settle into a reliable magnetic reading and it would take some time for it to be of any use. We would have to steer a steady course somehow until the compass was functional. Without other instruments to guide him, and blind to outside, Pat was having difficulty holding a steady course long enough for the compass to settle. I scratched a hole in the ice on the windscreen, and by sighting a star and using it to guide him, we were able to hold a heading long enough for me to obtain a compass reading. I was able to calculate, roughly at first, how many degrees of change in heading we needed, to port or to starboard, to get on a course for home. Each turn had to be estimated and then made on a time-rated basis. Then, the star-sighting procedure had to be repeated each time to reduce the degree of change required to achieve our final course to base.

To avoid looking like a cripple and an easy kill for the nightfighters, we maintained a reasonable speed on that one engine while over enemy territory by initiating a slow rate of descent. This also brought us into warmer air, and as we flew out over the North Sea, the frost disappeared from the windscreen. We were breathing a little easier by that time, and I could at last begin to wonder just where on the British coast we would make our landfall. Theoretically, we were headed for our base in Bedfordshire, but I would not have taken any bets.

With the final result still very much in doubt, there was little conversation. When we reached the point where I calculated we were within fifty miles of the coast, we switched on the VHF set and began to call on the emergency frequency. What a relief to find that we had no difficulty in reaching and alerting the emergency service. As we flew on, no longer losing any altitude, we were thrilled to see searchlights, three of them, coned in the sky right ahead of us. We felt sure that these were airfield lights, probably those of an emergency airfield on the English coast. We flew straight on and passed over them, confirming that it was indeed one of the coastal crash dromes, Bradwell Bay, about fifty miles south of where we would normally have crossed the coast. There was a short-lived debate in the cockpit whether we should proceed on to base or land at Bradwell Bay. It seemed pointless to me, at this stage, to press on when we would be navigating with minimal aids and when we were no more familiar with our new base than with Bradwell Bay. Besides, to my way of thinking, a bird in the hand is worth two in the bush, and the sooner Pattison put me on the ground, the happier I would be.

We circled the airport as we prepared to land and, as we turned into final approach, Pat let the wheels down. We had maintained our height over the North Sea and as we crossed the coast because we had not known where we were going to land. As we turned into the final leg and put the wheels down, it was apparent that we had too much height. At first, Pat put the nose down more steeply as we approached the runway, but it wasn't long before we crossed the threshold, still much too high. We were halfway down the runway, still far above the ground, too high to touch down. It looked very doubtful that we would be able to land at all before we ran out of runway. Then, it was emergency power on our one engine as we struggled to regain speed for at least level flight to try to go around again. Wheels up was selected to reduce drag but, willing though the Rolls Royce was, we could not sustain flying speed as we turned away from the end of the runway. The control tower had witnessed our abortive approach, had heard the engine roar at full throttle and then had lost sight of us as we turned. We had dropped below their line of vision by the time we had made less than a quarter of our turn.

The tower alerted the crash and rescue crews which had been standing by, and sent them in the direction where they estimated we would be crashing any minute. Suddenly, we reappeared, clearing some trees on the airfield boundary, to come barrelling in at ground level and at a right angle to the runway! The landing gear had only partially retracted and it readily collapsed as we hit the ground. We skidded across the grass on our belly and then across the concrete strip. This particular runway was equipped with FIDO, the acronym for RAF terminology "Fog Installation, Dispersal Of" and consisted of two steel fuel pipes running along the sides of the runway for burning fuel oil when necessary to raise the temperature and disperse any fog. We certainly hadn't planned on a belly landing, but it seemed to be a happy, if accidental-solution until we hit the steel pipes. When we climbed out of what had been a new Mosquito Mk XIV, it was a very sorry sight, a complete write-off, its back broken, both engines damaged, and the propellers twisted like pretzels. We had come through it though, alive and well, without injuries. It was bad luck about the aircraft.

An Oxford from the squadron picked us up the next morning, the 9th, and flew us back to base. I was on operations the following night, but with Peter once again. He was somewhat indignant about my "free-lancing" and suggested that my close call on the 8th was retribution for venturing forth without him. We flew an unusual operation that night and marked two separate targets for elements of the Main Force to attack. Both of these were railway facilities. The first was the yards at Aulnoye on the outskirts of Lille and the second was the yards at Villeneuve-St-George. Both targets were well marked and heavily bombed, and it was a bit of a relief for me to be on a target that was not in the Ruhr after the experience of the previous night at Essen. There were 11 Oboe Mosquitoes on Aulnoye to mark for 228 heavies. One was lost, so only 10 of us carried on to mark Villeneuve-St-George on the outskirts of Laon for the second element of 215 heavies.

Again, on the 27th, Peter and I were among the 8 Oboe aircraft which marked the railway yards at Montzen in France for 136 heavies. The marking was continuous and accurate, the bombings well concentrated and on target. One more of our aircraft was lost in the marking. On the 30th, I flew another scrounged trip. That time, with an RAF pilot, S/L Foulsham, and we were one of 8 Mosquitoes marking another attack on the French railway system, the yards at Somain for 134 heavies. The results were excellent, but for the loss of one more aircraft.

Our station commander at Little Staughton was G/C Collins. He was a big man, in all directions, but he was a very experienced flier, a former test pilot with many types of aircraft in his log book. He had, however, never flown a Mosquito. This led to an encounter in the bar one lunch hour and to a subsequent commitment on my part to fly with him on his initiation flight. One of his claims to fame was a press story which featured him as the test pilot who was too fat to bail out! It was this story, and his tendency to bait people, that had led me into the trap of flying with him instead of one of our experienced pilots. Although he didn't look the part, particularly as I pushed from below to help him get through the hatch in the floor of the Mosquito, he turned out to be an excellent pilot who could fly the Mosquito as expertly as any of our most experienced pilots. We flew a short cross-country while he checked himself out on the aircraft, and then made as smooth a landing as I could have asked for.

Chapter XXX

April became a very special month in my life. It brought my meeting with Norma, the English girl in the WAAF who was to become my wife. I had only just arrived at Little Staughton and that particular day was unusually warm and sunny. As I walked along the station road towards the flight offices, I caught sight of a WAAF corporal in shirt sleeves, cycling along the perimeter of the airfield. The WAAF uniform was a far cry from the creations of the Paris couturiers. The skirt was strictly utility, straight, snug and slightly short, and jackets were not required dress that day because of the warm weather. The combined results in this case were marvellous. The skirt rode up, unavoidably rather high, displaying a most pleasing length of leg in spite of the lisle stockings. And the shirt, which was equally utility, was doing its best to cover, but in the end only emphasizing, an excitingly swelling bosom. The hat seemed to perch perkily on a dark head of hair which curled neatly around it, well clear of the collar. What was in her mind at that moment I did not know, but it must have been pleasant because she was smiling prettily to herself as she sailed across the road ahead of me, completely unaware of my attention, or even of my existence at the time.

The world of an operational station is pretty small. It didn't take me long to find out my WAAF corporal's name and to discover that she was one of the control tower staff, a radio-telephonist who gave us our take-off and landing instructions. I also learned that the WAAFs in the tower, who had to work shifts to cover our night and day flying, had a small tea room on the ground floor of the tower where they could make up meals on a hot plate when they were unable to get to the dining hall at regular meal hours. They were soft touches for a cup of tea and a piece of toast from their rations for any of the air crew types who dropped in. The number of those who took advantage of their generosity was fairly small, but every one of them seemed to be friendly with one or other of the girls. I decided that I should include myself in this group. My efforts to ingratiate myself were fruitful right from the start, but with the wrong girl! I found myself being warmly received, in fact sort of adopted, by Nikki, a nice little thing, but not my bicycle-riding corporal. It began to look as if Nikki was taking a somewhat possessive stance every time I showed up in the tea room. This, in turn, was resulting in Norma's disinterest, particularly since she was in charge of the shift of WAAFs in which Nikki worked. My planned campaign was being short circuited. Something decisive was needed if my intentions were to succeed. Fortunately, for me and for our children, persistence wore down resistance.

Despite the early obstacles to my getting together with Norma, it wasn't long before we became quite close. Our first date was in a foursome with Peter and another WAAF friend. It was on April 5, and we celebrated Norma's birthday with a visit to the lovely coaching inn, the White Horse, at Eton Socon, just a few miles from the airfield.

Like so many other aspects of life at the front in wartime, personal relationships evolved very rapidly. To someone who was not there at the time, it may sound melodramatic, or even apologetic, but there was always that unspoken and perhaps even unconscious feeling that life's opportunities had to be grasped when available. Tomorrow could be too late. Our relationship blossomed rapidly, perhaps in part because of this prevalent atmosphere but also in spite of the restrictions imposed on such a relationship by the service.

On occasion, when I was on operations and Norma was on the night shift at control, she would sit in my old Vauxhall car on the airfield after flying control had shut down, and wait for me to come out of debriefing. If she had been fortunate in her scrounging from the local farmers that day, she might have a bottle of fresh milk to offer to her tired and thirsty airman. It was springtime, and Norma would listen to the beautiful song of the nightingales in the trees as night slipped into dawn while she waited. Never again would she be able to hear those early morning sounds of an English spring without remembering the vigils she kept for her flier.

During Norma's scrounging trips when she cycled around the local farms in search of such delicacies as fresh eggs or milk, she was fortunate enough to become friendly with one farmer's wife, Mrs. Brown of Brown's Farm. Besides being very generous with their small surpluses of fresh foods, they became interested in meeting Norma's boyfriend, the main reason for her frequent scrounging from them. It was agreed that we should visit them for tea one afternoon when we were both free. As it turned out, tea was served with scrambled eggs on fresh asparagus, my favourite vegetable. I must confess that my image may have been permanently and irreparably damaged when I literally licked my plate clean.

Although our relationship hadn't started out to be anything unusual, and, for my part, had resulted from an entirely unexpected but appealing sight of an attractive WAAF on a bicycle, it wasn't long before the unusual, for me, began to manifest itself. With the exception of the interlude with June in Harrogate, in which her youthfulness and sexual naivety had prevented any slide into sexual freedom despite some steamy moments, all of my previous liaisons had clearly been of a sexual nature. Though the opportunities for tasteful sex between a squadron leader and a corporal on a bomber station were few and far between, I developed a distinct unwillingness to allow our relationship to grow along those lines. Not that there wasn't plenty of evidence of mutual desire! It just seemed, this time at least, that my intentions were, as one might have said, honourable. Somehow, perhaps a reflection of some forgotten part of my earlier upbringing, there was an instinctive feeling that, if this girl were to become my wife, then I should not soil our relationship by premarital sex. Such a resolution was sorely tested at times when passion and purely sexual desires were almost overwhelming. Youth nearly had its way on numerous occasions.

Norma and I decided to get away from the airfield for a break, to discover a little more about ourselves away from the confines of service life. We organized a weekend pass and took the train to London.

As usual, hotel space was at a premium, and we were looking for two single rooms. The taxi driver at the railway station gave us a knowing look when we hired his cab and asked him to take us to a hotel where we could get rooms. He delivered us to the Mapleton Hotel in Leicester Square in the West End. It certainly wasn't five-star accommodation, and the woman who greeted us in the somewhat seedy lobby didn't look much like a lady. She told us she didn't have two vacant singles, but she did have a suite. Not being at all confident, we had asked the cab driver to wait while we looked at the suite before registering. One look was enough. We were afraid even to open any of the drawers or closets for fear that the cockroaches would come spilling out.

We hurried back to the lobby and took the waiting cab. I couldn't think of any alternative, so we headed for the Regent Palace where I presented myself at the registration desk. Without reservations, I was really at the mercy of the reservation clerks. Fortunately, one of the girls there had become quite friendly with me during my earlier visits. She greeted me with a warm smile, that is, until she saw Norma. In the end, she found one single room, for me, but made us wait until the last hour of check-in time had expired before she came up with the second room for Norma. The total irony of this didn't get to me until I called for Norma at her room that evening. My room was on one side of the hotel and hers was on the other, the side which faced the direction from which the V1s were coming. One had struck the building just across the street and had exploded at roof-top level. The window of Norma's room had been boarded up, and shards of the glass which had been blown out of it were still embedded in the opposite wall, over the head of the bed. My room was on the protected side of the hotel and in perfect order. Was there a message there? This was one of the occasions when my resolve to avoid intimacy in our relationship was most sorely tested.

It is impossible for an airman such as myself to be dramatic about life on a bomber station. It was simply our job, and we were good at it. Individually, we were too impersonal, too dedicated to the war and too professional in our attitude to dwell on the drama. And yet, it abounded on a bomber airfield. There was a dramatic intensity in watching the crews being driven to their aircraft dispersals, hearing the roar of the Merlins starting up in the far corners of the field, seeing the aircraft taxiing out onto the airfield perimeter track heading for the runway as the daylight faded, watching the heavily-laden bombers begin their ponderous run, one by one, as they picked up speed, lifted their tails, took off, circled the field, then disappeared on their night course for Germany. All that was left was the enveloping silence, the mute testimony of the operations board in the flying control room with its list of aircraft call signs, captains' names and times of take-off, a poignant vigil for the departed aircraft and their crews. Everything and everyone on the airfield waited, sometimes for long hours, for the sounds of their return and the opportunity to fill in the waiting blank spaces reserved for the time each aircraft landed back at base. For the watchers, and particularly for the girls in flying control, there was nothing impersonal about it. And for the day shift whose duty was to wipe it clean, the landing time entries still empty on the ops board the next morning were painful reminders of those who failed to make it back. The last operation would be erased and another would take its place.

Perhaps it was the change in the weather which accompanied our transfer to Little Staughton. A good deal of Bomber Command's effort in the succeeding months was devoted to the V1s and then to the railway system in occupied France. The nature of the war seemed to be changing as the Allied Powers' activities began to reflect an intensified and generalized move to the offensive. Thoughts were turning more and more to the possibility of an Allied invasion of Europe. The tempo of operations began to pick up, and I was able to fly nine operational sorties in May. On the 2nd, Peter and I flew in an all-Mosquito attack on Leverkusen. This was pushing Oboe to its limits and we had to fly above 30,000 feet to maintain line of sight with the ground stations. We had 29 aircraft out that night and were heavily engaged by searchlights and flak. The extra height, however, may have added some safety from the nightfighters for we were able to complete the attack without a loss.

On the 5th, Peter and I had to fly some calibration tests on a new ground station which had been sited to provide us with added coverage of continental targets. On the 7th, we took to the air to mark the airfield at Nantes for a small force of 93 heavies. The marking was accurate and the bombing very well concentrated. The hangars and the runways were severely damaged, but we lost one aircraft. Attacks on French occupied territory were definitely becoming more frequent. The emergency created by the V1s seemed to have started it, but now it appeared to be dictated by a change in priorities, and logistical facilities in the French coastal region bore the brunt of our attacks. More and more signs were pointing towards the buildup for an invasion. There was a growing feeling of optimism and anticipation among the crews as well as a renewed eagerness as the role of Bomber Command became more tangible.

Early on the morning of the 9th, while I was at the flight office, I was surprised and elated to learn that we were being called for a daylight raid. I had flown only one daylight raid before and that seemed so long ago that I was bursting to go on this one. Peter hadn't arrived at the flight but I was able to get assurance from the operations staff that we would be included. No sooner had I received that news than I tore out of the office and ran to billets to find Peter. As it turned out, he was still in bed, not at all excited about my news nor well enough to fly. I ran back to the flight and was able to crew up with F/O Emmerson, RAF, whose navigator wasn't available either for some reason. We had three targets to mark that day, all of them on coastal guns. Each target was marked by 7 or 8 Oboe Mosquitoes and then attacked by 30 or more heavies. All three targets were successfully marked and attacked, but the results were difficult to assess even in daylight because of the built-in nature of the targets. Only one aircraft was lost, despite the fact that 116 were involved in the operations. This was encouraging to those of us in Bomber Command. Day or night, our marking would not be more or less accurate, but the concentration and accuracy of the bombing by the heavies would be considerably improved in daylight. In addition, they would be much less likely to be misled by dummy markers laid down by the Germans to confuse visual identification by the bombers.

On the 11th, I teamed up with another Australian, F/O Grant. We were one of 8 Mosquitoes to mark the railway yards at Boulogne for

127 heavies. That was a night attack in which we lost two aircraft, but in which a good concentration of bombs was dropped on the target. Before returning to base that night, Grant and I had to carry out some equipment tests on the new ground station. On the 19th, Peter and I took off for an attack on Cap Gris Nez which turned out to be abortive. We were, however, able to take part in a daylight attack on the 21st. There were eight targets, all of them in French territory. Five were railway yards, two were heavy gun positions and one was a radar station. A total of 790 aircraft participated of which only 6 were lost. All of the assigned targets were successfully marked and attacked except for the railway yards at Amiens where the master bomber, who was directing the attack by the heavies, called off the attack when the target was obscured by clouds and smoke. He was not willing to risk the heavy loss of French civilians which would have been incurred if the bombers strayed from the yards and dropped their bombs in the nearby residential area.

On the 22nd, Peter and I were among the 14 Oboe Mosquitoes which marked Dortmund for a force of 361 heavies. It was the first time Dortmund had been attacked in more than a year. Bomb concentration was very successful and much damage was inflicted. But we lost 18 aircraft in that raid, and the euphoria we experienced in the earlier less-costly operations against French targets was somewhat dampened. Raids into Germany were proving to be as costly as ever. On the 27th, Peter and I were in the air again, in a group of 8 Oboes, marking the Aachen railway yards for a force of 162 heavy bombers. The target was accurately marked and the heavies dropped their bombs on target within a total raid time of twelve minutes! The destruction within the yards and the immediate area was very severe. The searchlights, the flak and the nightfighters, however, combined to bring down 12 of our bombers. If we needed any, that was further proof that the German air defences were not weakening. To close out the month, Peter and I went on another marking assignment for the main force. That time we marked the railway yards in Tergnier with 4 Oboes for a force of 111 heavy bombers. The railway yards suffered extensive damage and our losses were confined to two in the main force.

The bomber offensive was clearly applying pressure on Germany. When the Oboe squadrons were not marking for the main force, they were attacking selected pinpoint targets with high-explosive bombs including the 4000 lb Block Buster. Another group of PFF Mosquitoes, known as the Light Night Strike Force, was making almost nightly attacks, mainly on Berlin, to add to the disruption of life in Germany and to undermine morale in the civilian population. When you thought about all of the bomber raids, including those of the main force and those of the daylight formation raids carried out by the US Army Air Corps, you just had to think that the end was within reach in spite of the continued German resistance. Bomber Command was stretching every sinew to the limit and utilizing ingenuity to the maximum to hold their loss rate down to an acceptable level.

Fighters had shown their mastery over the day bombers early in the war. The toll they were exacting on the night bombers by this stage of the war was growing significantly. Anti-aircraft fire had always had a deterrent effect, but only a limited kill capability. It was the night-fighter that had achieved the larger percentage of our bomber casualties. The ebb and flow of offence vs. defence and measure vs. countermeasure fluctuated throughout the entire air war. The results always varied, but the constant throughout remained the lives lost; sometimes more, sometimes less. But for the individual, no matter what the cause, it had only to be one to be the final count. Could the end be in sight? We all felt that something had to break soon — the second front perhaps — ever since spring and the increasing frequency of the targets in France.

I hadn't taken any leave for some time, hoping that whatever it was would break. When June came, and no invasion, the CO suggested that I take some leave while I could. It was quite a shock, therefore, when I was awakened in my room at the Cumberland Hotel on my second day in London, by the room maid with a cup of tea and the remark, "Ooooh, Sir, it's happened!" "What has happened?" I asked. "The Second Front, Sir. The Allies landed in France this morning." I jumped out of bed, called Norma's room, grabbed my clothes and asked the maid to bring me some breakfast right away. A shave, breakfast, a quick call to the railway office and to the squadron adjutant and we were on our way back to Bedford Station. We were met by one of the squadron officers, wearing a side arm, who had come to meet us with a van. With the onset of the invasion had come the order for greater security, hence the side arm to be worn by all officers and the use of a daily password to enter operational sites. Hence also, the need to have an officer greet me and escort me back to base. It was quite impressive, as was his story of the all-out effort being made to support the invasion and the amazingly successful security and decoy measures that had preceded it.

Chapter XXXI

As soon as I reported in I was able to get back to work. I operated on the 7th with F/L Grant, the Australian, in an attack on the vital six-way road junction at Forêt de Cérissy, between Bayeux and St-Lo. There were large fuel dumps and tank units based there which were critical to the German defensive actions. We had 10 Oboe Mosquitoes marking the target and 112 heavy bombers to attack it. The operation was a success and only 2 aircraft were lost. On the following night, I flew with a different RAF pilot, F/L Gatrill. A force of 483 aircraft was launched that night to attack the rail facilities at five different sites to prevent reinforcements from being moved from the south into the Normandy area. The Oboe squadrons supplied 28 marker aircraft, and our particular target was the railway yards at Alençon. All of the targets were successfully attacked and out of the total force, only 6 aircraft were lost. Again, on the following night, this time with Peter who had returned from leave, I flew in an attack on German airfields situated just south of the Normandy battle area to counter the German air activities directed against our invasion forces. There were 401 aircraft engaged in these attacks, of which 20 were Oboes to mark the four airfields. The marking and the attacks were a success and only 2 of our aircraft were lost. The joy of operating in direct support of the invasion troops and on such short-range targets was almost overwhelming. Morale rose to a fever pitch in the Command.

Before the Alençon operation, W/C Grant DSO DFC, our squadron commander and a Canadian in the RAF, had called me into his office. He asked me to fly with Gatrill, who was on his first tour of operations. Despite the fact that he was inexperienced operationally, he must have been considered an exceptional pilot, particularly in the field of instrument flying, to have been selected for Oboe. However, some question as to his suitability for the PFF role must have been raised during his earlier operational flights. W/C Grant wanted me to fly with Gatrill on this occasion to assess his operational suitability. I couldn't help but think back to my experience when I had been tasked with the assessment of the New Zealander and his crew on the Maleme airport attack in Crete. In spite of that disturbing memory, I could see no reason why I should not accept such an assignment again.

The operation that night had been completed successfully, despite its considerable complexity. Gatrill had flown the aircraft expertly and without hesitation throughout the operation. His instrument flying during the bombing run had been steady and precise, and our results commendable. To make matters more difficult for Gatrill, the weather had deteriorated drastically on our return flight. We had to be just as precise in our return as we had been to reach the target, and we had to make an instrument landing in heavy wind and poor visibility on reaching base. Gatrill had handled his part of the operation in exemplary fashion.

When we reached the locker room, however, and Gatrill removed his flying suit, I couldn't help but notice that his jacket underneath was soaked in sweat, in spite of the cold in which we had been flying. In the discussion which this stimulated, I discovered that he had never aspired to be a pilot and that he felt no natural aptitude for flying. He had been a very successful athlete, a competitive diver in school, and he had responded well enough to the efforts and encouragement of his instructors in the RAF training schools to have been retained in the training system after receiving his wings. He said, and I believed him, that he had no particular fear of being killed on operations, but that he did fear being found inadequate in his flying and of being responsible for someone else's death because of his inadequacy. It was this fear that beset him during operations and made him sweat so profusely.

The following day, I had no hesitation in recommending to W/C Grant that Gatrill be retained on operations with the squadron. I commended him on his flying skill and on his performance in the attack as well as the instrument landing we had had to make on our return.

I added, however, that it would be essential for Gatrill to be crewed up with an experienced, second-tour observer, preferably one who was a little older and definitely phlegmatic. Such a crew mate would serve to bolster Gatrill's self-confidence, particularly in difficult circumstances, if he could witness the lack of visible concern in the observer sitting beside him and the man's obvious confidence in his pilot's ability. Happily, these recommendations were followed, and Gatrill and his veteran observer became a regular crew in the Oboe force.

All of those last attacks had been carried out in direct support of the invasion. But on the 12th, our attention was diverted back to Germany. We flew with 16 other Oboe Mosquitoes to mark Gelsenkirchen for a force of 286 heavy bombers. Unfortunately, we lost an engine over Germany and were unable to maintain the extremely high altitude required by our Oboe equipment. We had to abort the trip, but the rest of the force attacked the Nordstern Synthetic Oil Plant in Gelsenkirchen which was the primary target and the beginning of a campaign directed against the oil industry in Germany. The success of the attack was due, in part at least, to the improved version of Oboe with which we were then equipped.

Daylight attacks were still something of a novelty in RAF Bomber Command. But on the 15th, Peter and I were able to participate in another daylight operation, in a group of 12 Oboes marking the flotilla of light naval vessels which the Germans were amassing in the harbour at Boulogne. There were 285 heavy bombers in the force following our markers that day and they wreaked a tremendous amount of damage in and around the harbour. It was really exhilarating to be able to fly over enemy territory in the clear light of day, to see the stream of bombers converging on the target below us and watch the bombs rain down upon the area.

On this particular occasion, we had a little more excitement than we would have preferred. As we turned onto our target run, I was keeping a wary eye for fighters coming from the inland side. This meant that I was looking across Peter through the window on the port side. No sooner had we turned than I picked up two dark spots which quickly, much too quickly, blossomed into the head-on silhouettes of fighter aircraft approaching from the enemy area on what looked like an interception course! They were a little below our altitude and, having alerted Peter, I watched them grow, ever so rapidly, into Messerschmidt 262s, the twin-engined jet known as the Swallow. It was the first German jet we had ever seen. At that moment, however, we weren't admiring its sleek beauty or its obvious speed. As usual, we were unarmed, so there was no thought of fighting off an attack. We were already committed to our bombing run to mark the target. Any violent evasion manoeuvre on our part would have resulted in a failure of the Oboe run and a break in the continuous marking. There really was no alternative but to press on with our target run.

The Messerschmidts made no move to climb the few thousand feet which separated us. The closing rate seemed to increase as the range decreased and the fighters grew larger in our vision. Suddenly, they passed out of sight from the port side and vanished beneath us. I swung around in my seat, straining to catch sight of them as soon as they reappeared for the attack. Once they committed themselves to an attack, presumably from the rear, and as long as I could see them, we might be able to turn inside their angle of attack, using our propellers to reduce speed much more quickly than they could and making them overshoot. It would be an unequal match, but not an impossible struggle to avoid becoming a sitting duck. We continued our run, as though we had not seen the fighters, and were seemingly undeterred. I felt certain that they had seen us, simply because they couldn't have missed us. My skin crawled, knowing how blind and helpless we were from behind and beneath. I couldn't help anticipating those traces of cannon fire coming from behind. Yet, once they had passed out of sight, they disappeared completely. We flew on methodically, keeping to the Oboe pattern which had become so familiar to us and wondering what had happened to them. Why hadn't they attacked? We had certainly been a juicy target! Maybe they were on a training mission; maybe they were unarmed. Who knows? Whatever the reason, we were overjoyed to be able to complete our run and drop our markers on the target. Just the same, it was a tremendous relief to break off that straight and level run which had been growing more and more oppressive by the second after we lost sight of those jets.

On the 21st, I teamed up with F/L Hunter, RAF, when we flew with 8 other Oboe Mosquitoes to mark another target in the campaign against the German oil industry. The target was the synthetic oil plant in Scholven and the attacking force was 123 heavy bombers. There was heavy cloud cover when we arrived, but we were prepared for such conditions and were able to mark the target with sky rather than ground markers. Weather conditions like these would have thwarted any attack in earlier days, but Oboe had put those days behind us. The bombing was accurate and severe damage was inflicted on the plant. The air defences in German territory, however, were just as intense as they had ever been. We lost 8 of our bombers in the attack.

Peter and I joined forces again on the 27th for another daylight operation. A force of 300 plus heavy bombers was assembled for attacks on three of the V1 sites to relieve the strain on the southern part of England where the major support for the invading Allied forces was located. We provided 15 Oboe Mosquitoes, which were divided between the three sites, to mark the launching platforms. Our V1 site was near a village called Les Hayons. The weather was clear and we had no trouble marking the target. The bombers were able to place their bombs on the launching platforms and in their immediate vicinity, putting them out of business for some time. The fact that the attacks were delivered without loss made the whole operation doubly satisfying.

Support of the invasion had become the top priority for Bomber Command at that time. We were marking more and more targets in occupied France in direct support of our ground forces. Among some of the strategic bombing purists there may have been some dismay at this change in policy direction, but it was never shared by the operational crews. The natural feeling of relief from the hazards of deep penetrations into the improving air defences over Germany was understandable. But, of equal import, was the feeling of satisfaction in being able to play a direct and visible role in defeating the enemy after years of waging an almost invisible and intangible strategic battle inside Germany. None of us ever questioned the tasks we were assigned, nor the wisdom of them. We didn't resent the casualties which we had to suffer throughout the campaign. Yet, there was no denying the excitement and the anticipation felt by the crews now that they could actually see the effects of their efforts. The daylight raids added significantly to those feelings when the crews could see for themselves the destruction their bombs were wreaking in the enemy's camp. It was a little like finally seeing the enemy after struggling against him at long range, quite literally in the dark, never knowing if the blow you struck was crippling.

First April, now June became an important month. Besides the long-awaited invasion which marked the real turning point of the tide in Europe, June included Norma's and my engagement which took place on the same day as the invasion, June 6. Our engagement hadn't made Norma's shift in flying control any easier for her. Every operational sortie was an emotional strain on the girls in control. They knew so many of the crews personally that it made their waiting a long and trying time, clearing each returning aircraft for landing and hoping that the rest of them would make it. And this went on night after night for those girls. To have your fiancé included in the crews for whom you held vigil, and to have to suffer the agony in silence, must have been hellish. Fortunately, it wasn't for long. At the end of June, I was ordered to report to PFF HQ.

I was taken immediately to see the AOC, now A/V/M Bennett. His greeting was both familiar and friendly. After an exchange of pleasantries, he asked me how I was enjoying life in 109 Squadron and, almost without pause, how I felt about leaving it. I had already said how much I enjoyed flying in 109, but went on to assure him that I realized I wasn't there primarily to enjoy myself and that I was prepared to go wherever my services were required. It was, apparently, the right response, because his reply was, as usual, prompt and to the point. "It is just as well you feel that way, because I have another job which I want you to do. You are to remain here at HQ for a few days to learn more about the technical aspects of Oboe, and then you will be posted to your sister Oboe squadron, 105. I am not satisfied with their performance and I feel that the navigation section is the key to their improvement. You are to take over the navigation section and effect that improvement." There was no sympathy about my having to leave Peter in the lurch, or about having to break off the squadron relationships which I had naturally developed over the past ten months. However, knowing my AOC fairly well by that time, I really didn't expect any such consideration. And I must admit that my own character must have been somewhat similar, because I didn't consider that either.

I spent a week at HQ working with the group navigation officer, the operational staff and the Oboe technical staff. By the time I reported to 105 Squadron at Bourne, near Cambridge, I had learned enough about the Oboe system to function as the senior operations officer at briefings and debriefings and to fulfil the duties of squadron navigation officer. I had to endure the uncomfortable feelings of someone who has been parachuted as a stranger into an otherwise homogenous group. To my intense relief, there was one familiar and friendly face at Bourne, that of G/C Harry Bufton DSO DFC AFC, my former squadron commander at 109. He was then the station commander at Bourne. Although he maintained an intimate acquaintance with the operations which took place from his base, he never interfered with his squadron commanders in the day-to-day command of their squadrons. Regardless of our previous relationship, there was no doubt that I was on my own in 105, in taking over the navigation section and trying to raise their operational standards. Once again, but quite apparent to me this time, my arrival and my assignment had been preceded by precise instructions from PFF HQ.

My greeting and my welcome by the squadron commander, W/C Cundall DSO DFC, were pleasant and correct, if somewhat cool. My predecessor as navigation leader was still on the base, ready to hand over his responsibilities before departing. He was a very personable Canadian who had earned the respect and admiration of his navigators and who had also established an excellent personal operational record. His popularity was enviable, and I could not credit his having any responsibility for the AOC's opinion that the navigation section was operating at a less than optimum level. Nor could I see how I was going to be able to make any improvements. However, such deliberations took up very little of my time. We were all there to do our job to the best of our abilities, and I had been sent to take over the navigation section and to ensure that my navigators never contributed to the failure of any operation nor to the lowering of PFF standards of accuracy and timing. And that was what I intended to do, regardless of who had preceded me or how well the job had been done in the past.

I was only twenty-three at the time, mature only in the ways of a wartime airman, and a Canadian in a RAF squadron. I was particularly pleased then, and a little moved emotionally, when some weeks later one of my RAF navigators, an older and professionally qualified man in civilian life, said privately to me that he had fully appreciated the sensitivities of the situation when I had been posted in to take over. He, like the rest of the navigators, had felt some resentment. He went on to say, however, that he had never witnessed such a smooth and seemingly effortless take-over. He said that it seemed as if one day there was resentment, but the next time they thought about it, there I was, without having made any apparent effort, running the show with everyone supporting me. If it had been his intention to make me feel good, then he certainly succeeded. In my mind, I had ceased to be a member of 109 Squadron the day I left and had become a member of 105 the day I arrived. But it was a good feeling to know that I had been accepted as well.

Chapter XXXII

In July, the month of my arrival in 105, I was able to fly three day-light operations, each with a different RAF pilot. It was on the 6th that I flew with S/L Blessing to mark a V1 site at Forêt du Croc. Ours was one of five sites which were being attacked that day by a total of 525 heavy bombers and marked by a total of 26 Oboes. All of the sites were clear of cloud when we attacked and all of the launching platforms were seen to be hit, all, that is, except for the site at Forêt du Croc. Our target was under cloud cover. That didn't prevent the attack, but it did prevent our seeing the results. The following day was even more exciting for us night birds. I flew with S/L "Tubby" Wills to mark the fortified villages near Caen which were holding up the Canadian 1st and the British 2nd armies. There were two separate aiming points to be marked and attacked by 20 Oboe Mosquitoes and 447 Heavies. Both were well marked and heavily bombed. As a result, the Allied Armies were able to sweep down through the devastated villages the following morning.

I wasn't able to operate again until the 16th when I flew with S/L Channer in an attack on a V1 site at St-Philibert-Ferme. This attack introduced another novelty in our way of operating. There were 3 Oboe Mosquitoes involved, and each Oboe aircraft led a loose formation of 10 Lancasters. The target was cloud covered, and the Lancasters were briefed to close up formation on the bombing run and to drop their bombs simultaneously with the leading Oboe aircraft. With the accuracy of the Oboe and the pattern of bombs which would fall, the chances of hitting even such a small target as a launching platform would be optimized. Unfortunately, because of the cloud, we had no way of knowing how successful we had been.

In August, I was able to put in only three operations. On the 6th, with S/L Bignal RAF, I flew on a daylight marking operation of a V1 site at Forêt de Nieppe. There were 212 heavy bombers and 10 Oboe Mosquitoes attacking two sites, the second of which was at Bois de Cassan. We had no difficulty marking the target, but the bombing seemed to be more scattered than usual. It was difficult to assess the damage. Losses, however, were still being kept low. We had lost four aircraft in the attack on Caen and another three in the attacks on the 6th. On the 9th, I flew on another daylight with S/L Bignal. We were among five Oboes marking the fuel dumps in the Forêt de Mormal for 155 heavy bombers. That time the bombing was much more concentrated. When we left, the site was beneath a huge column of dark smoke. On the 12th, we returned to night operations. I flew with a different pilot, F/L Ackroyd RAF, in a group of five Oboes to mark a major road junction and a heavy troop concentration north of Falaise. The target was accurately marked and heavily bombed without loss to the force. It felt good to see the power of Bomber Command being applied so visibly and so effectively in what was clearly going to be the final battle for Europe.

It was about that time I witnessed another very disturbing incident. The squadron was test-flying aircraft for operational readiness one day when one of the aircraft failed to get airborne. A newer crew was flying the aircraft. For some unknown reason, they were unable to get sufficient power to reach flying speed. They persisted in trying until they reached the end of the runway where it crossed the road. They were still at full throttle when they came to the end. The roadway tore the undercarriage off and they crashed into a shed wall in the farm yard on the other side of the road. They burst immediately into flames. Despite the proximity and accessibility of the crash site, the intensity of the fire fed by the high-octane fuel prevented anyone from getting near. We could only stand and watch the two men in the cockpit be consumed by the flames. It was a very disturbing experience for all of us, even though we scarcely knew the crew. The thought of being burned alive in an aircraft crash was frightening enough; to see it happen in front of your eyes was sickening.

By September, G/C Cundall had left us and W/C "Slim" Somerville DFC AFC, one of our flight commanders, had taken over command of 105. Having already proven himself a capable and popular officer, Slim had no difficulty, as the new commander, earning the respect and admiration of all the squadron members. During that month, I was able to put in four operations, three of them daylights. Our efforts were being directed more and more to the battle in France where the Allies were making good progress, but in the face of bitter opposition. On the 10th, I flew with S/L "Tommy" Horton DFC, RNZAF, in a major attack on Le Havre. Eight separate aiming points were to be marked by 45 Oboe Mosquitoes for 947 heavy bombers to attack. Despite the size of the force and the fact that it was in daylight, each aiming point was marked and attacked successfully, and not one aircraft was lost to the enemy or to collision. With the number of individual bombers converging on one target, that was nothing short of miraculous.

A similar operation was mounted on the 17th against Boulogne where the garrison had been holding out successfully against our invading forces. I flew with S/L Harding DFC, RAF. As in Le Havre, there were a number of different aiming points within the harbour area. Forty-one Oboes marked and 721 heavy bombers attacked. The garrison surrendered before the assault by the ground forces began. On the 26th, F/L Taylor, RAF, and I flew on a third daylight attack of similar proportions. There were 45 Oboes and 677 heavy bombers to mark and attack three aiming points in Calais and four at Cap Gris Nez. Accurate attacks were delivered on all of the assigned targets, but we did lose two aircraft on each of the latter raids.

The following night we were back with one of our needling raids on Germany. Tommy Horton and I flew in a small force of six Oboes to drop our bombs on Heilbronn. This was a much deeper penetration than we had been able to complete before, and it must have been a test run for one of the new ground stations which had been located in France subsequent to the advance of our troops. This attack was followed by another night operation on Saarbrucken by four Oboes in which I flew with the Commander, W/C Somerville. It, too, was another development test under operational conditions.

In October, Operation Hurricane was planned by the combined RAF Bomber Command and the US Air Corps to demonstrate the overwhelming air superiority of the Allied forces. The plan called for the delivery of the maximum tonnage of bombs to be dropped on the Ruhr in the shortest possible time. The first wave, in which W/C Somerville and I flew, included 993 RAF heavy bombers with 20 Oboes to mark. The target selected for the attack was Duisberg. RAF fighters were to provide escort to the extent of their range. The sight of all those heavy bombers streaming in an unformed gaggle beneath us, dropping their bombs in an almost unbroken rainfall of explosives onto the city of Duisberg, was awesome. By the time we left the target area, 957 bombers had dropped their loads onto the city, a total of 3,574 tons of high explosives and 820 tons of incendiaries. The city appeared to be in desperate shape, but the air defences never slacked in their efforts to bring us down. We lost 14 in that raid. The same night, the RAF followed up with another attack of 966 heavy bombers and 39 Oboe marker aircraft on the same target. The Oboes proved to be somewhat redundant on this occasion as the fires and smoke from the daylight raid left little doubt where the target lay. The conflagration was visible for miles and the fires acted as guiding beacons for the new wave of bombers coming in from the North Sea. A total of 9,000 tons was dropped on Duisberg in less than 48 hours. The losses on the night raid had been seven aircraft, which made a total loss of 21 out of almost 2,000 aircraft in the two raids by the RAF. It was, without doubt, an awesome demonstration of the Allied air power — it was also a little sickening to witness such terrible destruction and, even more, to be part of it.

On the 23rd of October, Norma and I took leave to travel up to Coventry where her family resided. S/L Johnny Comar DFC, a Canadian pilot in the RAF and member of 105 Squadron, came with us to act as my best man. G/C Bufton, his wife Jean, and Tommy Horton and his navigator arrived the following day for the wedding and to see Norma and me off to Cornwall for a week's honeymoon. We stayed at the Treganna Castle Hotel in St. Ives which seemed to be about as far away from the war as one could get. Norma and I weren't the only ones who thought that St. Ives was a good place to get away from the

G/C Bufton, Jean, Tommy Horton,
and his navigator Haworth, arriving
for the wedding.

The bride and the groom
outside the church.

war. There was a goodly number of older ladies, dressed in long gowns, fur wraps and diamonds, who used to sit, in quiet solitude, in the chairs along the sides of the long corridor leading to the hotel's dining room. We used to refer to the walk down this imposing hallway as the Polish Corridor, as we passed by their critical eyes each time we went to dinner. Often, we felt like taking our wedding certificate with us and waving it before them to banish their suspicions. But that might have spoiled their mischievous pleasure in local gossip and innuendo, one of the few pleasures left for old and the lonely.

The sights and sounds of St. Ives and of Cornwall — the rugged coastline, the sea, the quaint harbour, the Sloop Inn and the Copper Kettle — will remain warm memories for the rest of our lives. When we rejoined the rest of the world, it was to go to Bourne where we stayed overnight with Buff and Jean before Norma had to return to Little Staughton and duty in the control tower.

On November 18 I resumed operations in a daylight marking with S/L Bishop. We were among 18 Oboe Mosquitoes which marked

Munster for the attack by 461 heavy bombers. One aircraft was lost but the bombing covered the entire city like a blanket. On the 20th, it was back to night operations once again. I flew with Bishop, and we marked the oil refinery at Castrop-Rauxel for a force of 255 heavies. The marking was accurate, the target was hit well and set afire. We lost four on this operation which, though saddening, was a low rate in view of the numbers involved. The next night, it was Hagen, with Bishop again, in an attack by 10 Oboes on a pin-point target. One of our Oboes was shot down at Hagen by the heavy flak of the Ruhr defences.

The frequency of operations was keeping me busy. I flew with Bishop again, on the night of the 27th. The target was Neuss, in the Ruhr. We had 18 Oboes to mark for 255 heavy bombers and we left Neuss ablaze when the raid was over. Then, on the 29th, W/C Somerville and I joined in a daylight formation attack on the tar and benzol plant in Duisberg. It had either miraculously missed being destroyed in the earlier massive attacks or had been repaired in the interim. In either case, we were one of three formations of Mosquitoes, each led by an Oboe Mosquito, and each targeted on the plant. This was the first time our Oboe aircraft had been used in co-operation with Mosquitoes from other commands. It turned out to be a bit of a farce as two of the three formations failed to link up and our single formation was inadequate for the job. Since the target was just as important as it had been when we made the first attempt, we had to repeat it on the following day, though I flew with Bishop, not Somerville. The experience of the previous day must have been a learning one because the three formations linked up in good time and we were able to make the attack in good form. But it was not without a great deal of nervous anticipation that we flew at the head of our nice tight Vee formation, straight and level, over the heavily-defended territory of the Ruhr. It felt even more like a live turkey shoot in daylight than it did at night — and we were the turkeys!

In late November, after I had completed more than one hundred operations, I was ordered to report immediately to PFF HQ. When I arrived, somewhat at a loss for the reason behind my summons, it was to find that the AOC, personally, wished to see me. I was, therefore, directed immediately to his office. Without any preliminaries, and in a noticeably acerbic tone, A/V/M Bennett asked me if I had been communicating with the RCAF Overseas HQ. When I assured him that I had not, he said something like, "Well, some one has!" The only suggestion I could offer was a recollection of a recent visit to Bourne by a RCAF public relations officer. The A/V/M, somewhat mollified, said, "OK, Jack, that probably explains what has happened. RCAF Overseas HQ called to say that they had discovered that an RCAF officer in PFF had completed one hundred operations and that this officer was to be screened from any further operations." Such a directive was an anathema to Bennett, a reflection on his leadership and a challenge to his authority. He had bridled at being told how to handle his airmen. He was, however, unaware of whether I was personally involved or not. Hence my order to report immediately.

Once my innocence was established, Bennett softened his attitude. Patting me on the back, he said, "Jack, as far as I am concerned, you have done all that I could ask of you. You can stop operating any time you wish. Just give me a call when that time comes. But, no one in RCAF Overseas HQ is going to tell me when to screen my crews!"

I was pleased by the AOC's consideration and by his willingness to leave matters in my own hands. As I had said to him at the time, I was in no mind to cease operations then, but would advise him when the time came for me to throw in the towel. There was no reason for me to tarry at HQ, so I returned to Bourne without further delay, in high spirits after the implied compliments of my AOC.

On the 4th of December, Bishop and I took part in another daylight operation. We were to attack the Erft River Dam to prevent the backed-up waters from being used to flood the areas into which the American troops planned to advance. We had three Oboe Mosquitoes, each leading a formation of nine Lancasters whose bomb aimers were directed to follow their Oboe leader in opening bomb doors and dropping their bombs. With the drastic differences in cruise speeds and handling characteristics of the two aircraft, it was very tricky getting the Lancasters assembled in formation behind a Mosquito. However, by throttling the Mosquito back to its slowest cruising speed, it was possible for the Lancasters to keep up and to maintain formation, and it was also possible for the Mosquito to fly its required precise bombing run. All three formations were able to make successful attacks which blasted the top off the dam, but which didn't breach it completely.

It was on a similar daylight formation operation against a supply depot in Cologne that one of my former squadron friends in 109 was awarded the Victoria Cross — posthumously. He had been flying an Oboe Lancaster, the only one of its kind, leading a formation of Lancasters. His deputy was flying an Oboe Mosquito which he had tucked behind the wing of the Oboe Lancaster in the run down to the target, to be in position to take over should there be a failure. The rest of the Lancasters were in formation behind them. In their run to the waiting point, the formation encountered a flight of German fighters which attacked with disastrous results. Many of the aircraft were hit, some of the crew members wounded, and three of the Lancasters went down. S/L Bob Palmer, who was flying the Oboe Lancaster, undeterred by the fighter attack, made a near-perfect bombing run with his aircraft aflame from the leading edge of the wings all the way back through the fuselage. His deputy in the Mosquito was still tucked in to his side behind his wing, blazing as well. There were only a few of the Lancasters left in their formation, but those who remained kept close to their leader until the aiming point was reached and the bombs were dropped. At that point, the leader exploded, the back-up Mosquito with him. There were no parachute escapes; they all went down with the wreckage of their aircraft. A few of the Lancasters in the formation made it back to England. That had been Bob's 110th operation.

Despite what the philosophers say, all men are not born equal, particularly if measured against a singular scale such as is the case in war. Most men react in a similar fashion to threats against life and limb, fear being the primary motivator. However, the individual capacity to withstand such pressure on a repeated basis is just that, remarkably individual. Some have the capacity to function effectively on an extended basis, others have difficulty coping with such pressures even on a short-term basis. Those whose capacity did not meet the "norm," which in Bomber Command had been defined as a tour

of approximately thirty operations, sometimes had to face the igno-
miny of being classed as "Lacking in Moral Fibre" or LMF, as it was
colloquially referred to in the RAF. Such a classification, which more
often than not resulted in demotion and the loss of flying category,
may have been justified in some cases. But, there must have been
many cases where justification for more considerate treatment
should have prevailed. No doubt, the fear that gentler, more compassionate treatment of such cases might have bred more instances of
that form of battle fatigue in the air crew ranks was the underlying
factor for such firm treatment. That sort of concern might have been
prevalent in the higher staff ranks, but I doubt that it would have been
supported within the operational ranks.

We had the sad experience of a case in the Lancaster squadron
with which we shared our base at Little Staughton. One of the Lanc
captains who had flown enough operations to establish himself and
his crew as regular members of the main force, though still a relative
newcomer, paid a formal call on his squadron commander one
morning. He requested that he be taken off operations, not to avoid
flying over Germany and thus demonstrate a lack of moral fibre, but
to be transferred onto some other type of aircraft where he would not
be responsible for a crew. He told the squadron commander that he
was certain he could not survive further flights in the Lancaster and
that he did not wish to be responsible for the death, or the loss, of any
of his crew members, who were in no way the cause for his certainty
that he would be killed before his tour was over. The Squadron Commander, who was both an experienced bomber pilot and a very
"press on regardless" type of airman, talked at length and sympatheti-
cally with the young airman, telling him that all operational crew
were frightened, admittedly, some more than others, whenever it
was necessary to fly on operations. And that every airman had to face
up to that fear and fly in spite of it. With that, he said the best thing for
the young captain would be to tackle the problem head on and that he
would place him and his crew on battle orders for that night's sortie.

Later, when all the aircraft were starting their engines and taxiing
out from dispersals, one aircraft did not start up and failed to answer
the tower's calls. The duty pilot raced out to the dispersal in his van,

in high dudgeon and ready to blast whoever was at fault. Aircraft were already taking off by the time he reached the silent hulk in its dispersal. The crew were there, in their flying gear, ready for take-off, except for the captain. The crew said that he had been there, but had said something about having forgotten some item which he needed and had gone back to get it. He had not returned. A search was made, but no one was able to find him in the dark. The crew were returned to the hangar, and their aircraft scrubbed from that night's operation, much to the disgust of the duty pilot and the squadron commander, particularly when he found out it was the young captain he had spoken to that morning. It wasn't until someone accidentally discovered the body behind the officers' Nissen huts the next morning that the full extent of the tragedy unfolded. When he had left his crew, he had gone to his quarters, picked up a revolver, walked behind the huts, put the barrel in his mouth, and pulled the trigger. He proved that he wasn't lacking in moral fibre, that rather than be responsible for the death of his crew, he preferred to take his own life.

Unfortunately, there were tragedies of the opposite kind as well. Those who found themselves, by some stroke of fortune, to be capable of withstanding operational pressures over the extended term also seemed to develop a form of addiction to operational flying. As in my own case, they only felt at home in an operational squadron, only satisfied while involved in flying against the enemy. For them, war had become a way of life, and would continue to be until either they bought it or the war ended, whichever came first. Unquestionably, airmen of this ilk would never have agreed to such an explanation. In truth, they would have denied any such definition. In their mind, they, and everyone in the squadron with them, were absolutely normal, which, unfortunately, was all too true if you restricted the norm to the active operational crews in elite squadrons such as ours. Such men were unusual, but by no means suicidal. They had learned to live with death at their side, ever present and always threatening, but they relied upon their experience, believed in their skill and ability to overcome the odds and continue with their work.

Sad to say, a significant number of these heroes were lost to enemy action. Typical of them was S/L Bob Palmer VC DFC and also Guy

Gibson VC DSO DFC, who was lost on yet another raid when he returned to operations after having survived the daring attack on the Moehn and Eder Dams, only one of the many raids on which he had flown since the early days of Bomber Command. Since such men seemed unable, or unwilling, to call it quits on their own, perhaps wiser heads should have prevailed and ordered them to stop before it was too late.

Among such men of skill and experience, with such dedication and devotion to the survival of their country, there must have been men who could have been future leaders and who would have continued to serve their country well in the difficult and trying times which were certain to follow the war. No country can afford to squander such talent. The tragic lessons of World War I, with its sacrifice of the cream of the youth of Britain and France, seemed to have been forgotten. In their eagerness to pursue the air battle to its fruitful conclusion, the British closed their eyes to the risks which were being taken by those veterans of Bomber Command. As long as you were willing to fly operationally, they were willing to let you — as long as you liked and as long as Fate would permit.

I had been like a brazen aerialist performing on the high wire without a net. Then, I met the girl who mattered and married her. I found myself no longer operating without a net. There *was* a future to think about. Nothing had seemingly changed, yet everything was different. The treadmill of flying sorties against the enemy on a never-ending basis, with no thought of anything except the next operation, was finished. I had never been irresponsible. But now my responsibilities had changed. They were no longer singular and dedicated solely to the successful conclusion of the war. I had taken on new responsibilities in the form of a wife and possibly, in the future, a family. My youth no longer seemed an infinite possession to be flaunted; the boy had become a man and had become mortal.

My bracelet of nickels had carried me through the perils of operational life for four years. The nightingales had brought me the girl and the love which led me away from that obsessive path and its almost inevitable conclusion. Now I began to think about a future.

On the 24th of December, it was densely foggy at Bourne, and almost everywhere else in England for that matter. Normally there would have been no flying. But, as it turned out, the pressure of the German breakthrough in the Ardennes had made air support essential for the Allied invasion troops. Bomber Command had a part to play. We were called upon to mark two airfields for attack by heavy bombers. Those airfields, located at Essen and Dusseldorf, were vital to the Germans in the movement of supplies to the Ardennes area. We provided 11 Oboe aircraft to mark the aiming points and 327 heavy bombers to attack them. W/C Somerville and I were to mark the Mulheim airfield at Essen. We dropped our markers accurately and saw the heavy bombers deliver a destructive attack which put the airfield out of operation and destroyed whatever supplies might have been stored there for the German Ardennes offensive. When we reached England on the return flight, we discovered the whole countryside covered by an impenetrable white blanket of fog. It was even more solid than when we had taken off, and even then we had not been able to see more than a couple of stripes marking the centre of the runway.

It was late afternoon and the light was fading rapidly by the time we were diverted to the only FIDO base in PFF. When we reached it, it must have been very late in the day. There were two columns of smoke rising above the top of the fog bank. We didn't know at the time, but they marked the sites of two aircraft which had not made successful blind landings and had crashed. We were given clearance to make our approach and, after a circuit, began to make our descent through the fog on the blind landing beam, looking for the runway. We were totally blind. There was no visibility, neither downward nor laterally. As we descended through the fog, it was as if we were flying in absolute silence, a feeling of total sensory deprivation. Suddenly, there was the runway beneath us. The heat of the burning fuel oil along the sides of the runway had cleared a strip all right, but over the time it had been burning, the cavern in the fog had moved slowly, but steadily to one side. When we saw the ground, the cavern no longer sat over the runway. This upset our approach completely. We put on full power and in a flash could no longer see the ground. There was nothing to be seen around us, nothing but white, as we frantically pulled up, instinctively holding our breath and hoping that nothing solid would block our escape. We broke out of that clinging fog into the clear air above and the welcome visibility of the low evening light. Airport control called us to advise that we would be allowed one more attempt to land, after which we would be diverted to Scotland. We were the last aircraft to be given permission to land that evening and, if it hadn't been the squadron commander flying the aircraft, I doubt we would have been given even that opportunity.

No time was wasted in our next circuit. Down into that blinding fog once again, searching for the runway, hoping this time to get our wheels down on the ground. Slim held to the steady signal of the beam approach as we descended and lowered the wheels and flaps, making ready to touch down. We were literally skimming the ground when the FIDO flames broke the fog in front of us. This time, we didn't fall for the cavern of visibility to one side of the runway. We put the wheels down on the hard surface of the runway with a firm thrust and held the Mosquito down on the ground as we sped along, finally coming to a stop while still on the strip. As we sat there, propellers ticking over, a vehicle came alongside and we were signalled to shut down and abandon the aircraft where we stood. Nobody was going to land after us! They were ready to tow the aircraft away, not trusting us to move it any further in the zero visibility.

The station commander, G/C Grant DSO DFC, one of my former 109 Squadron Commanders, came alongside the Mosquito in his car to welcome us and to tell us that we would be driven back to Bourne where a Christmas party was planned for later that evening. The drive was not much less of a strain than the landing had been, but there we were that evening, washed and changed, ready to join the party which was already in progress. Norma had come over from Little Staughton and was waiting with the Buftons for my arrival at the mess. Though she never said anything about it, knowing that I was operating that day and knowing how bad the flying conditions were, she must have been feeling the strain as they waited for news of our safe return. A little later, I felt a tap on my shoulder. It was Slim, glass in hand, and he asked me how I was feeling. When I said that I felt fine, he asked me how my legs felt. At that, I had to admit that my legs were aching for some reason. Slim laughed, and slapping me on the back, said, "So are mine! We sure must have been pushing the floor awfully hard on that last approach. But, you must admit, it wasn't a bad landing for a guy who hasn't made a blind landing in years!"

Only six aircraft were reported as being lost on those attacks. That, however, didn't account for those which crashed in the fog on their return to England. They weren't "lost" and were never included in the official loss figures. Unfortunately, even though such losses never entered the statistics as operational losses, their casualties were just as final as those who failed to return at all.

My pace of operations had slowed noticeably since I had completed my one hundreth sortie. However, my role as a duty operations officer had increased the demands on my time appreciably, and at very irregular hours, whenever the squadron was on operations. On the few occasions I could get away from base, I would join Norma in Staughton or in Cambridge, if she could free herself from duty at the same time. My extended tour of operations, the pressure of still being operational, the irregular and frequent periods of duty, and my desire to achieve some form of normal married relations were taking their toll. I was falling asleep at the wheel driving back to the base after seeing Norma. I was rapidly becoming fatigued; the elasticity of youth was wearing thin and losing its stretch. And along with it, my ardour to continue flying was leaking away.

On the 28th of January, I crewed up with F/L Litchfield in a major attack on Stuttgart. There were 602 aircraft in two waves. The first was targeted on the railway yards to the north of the city; the second on the aero-engine factory to the northwest. The individual attacks of 226 and 376 bombers were spaced three hours apart. The city was cloud-covered during the attack, but we had 28 Oboes dropping sky markers over the targets, through which the heavy bombers were able to drop their bombs accurately. We lost 11 aircraft in the two waves, another indication that the Germans were still vigorously defending their territory. Despite that, everyone felt optimistic about the future. The odds seemed to be clearly in our favour.

Again, on the 1st of February, I crewed up with Bishop for another major attack, this time on Ludwigshaven/Mannheim. We had 14 Oboe Mosquitoes marking the target for 382 heavies. In spite of cloud cover, sky markers once again allowed the bombers to deliver a concentrated and accurate attack. Although ground defences were most vigorous, their nightfighters were not much in evidence. Only six aircraft were lost on that operation. It looked as if the air war over Europe was in its final and, for us, successful phase.

When I landed back at base after that last attack, I felt certain that the bomber campaign was effectively finished, that what was left was only the wrap-up and that victory was assured. In addition, I realized that I was tired, that I could do no more and that it was time to return home. I had left home as a boy; I would be returning as a man, a married man. I could put aside my bracelet of nickels. I wouldn't need that kind of talisman any more. I wouldn't need a reminder of whence I came; I would be home again.

EPILOGUE

Only as I look back can I appreciate how absorbing had been the experience of war. From the moment I was sworn in, an undetectable but inexorable force took over my life. The press of events and the unceasing assault of new experiences, from the first day of training through at least my first tour of operations, left me no time for contemplation.

Your mental capacity was saturated with the infusion of new knowledge of a strange and different kind, along with the realization that there seemed to be no end to this learning. Intentionally or not, you became a programmed being, conforming to a specific mould, compliant yet responsive. Except for selective instinctive mores, you became a wheel in that machine that is war, and not just capable of wreaking mass destruction, but thoroughly convinced and determined to striving to achieve it more expertly than anyone else. Such conviction was based on the deep-seated belief that the cause was just — and that was as far as your thought process took you or needed to take you. Faith, loyalty, pride, and integrity in authority led you the rest of the way. Thank God we had wise and humane leaders. But, is that not what war is all about — the preservation of what we perceive as good leadership, be it that of government or individual?

Nickels and nightingales. The nickels had seen me through the trials of operational life and had kept intact the thread that linked me to my origins. The nightingales had sung their song to me at a critical point in my career of inflicting mass destruction on the enemy, and had started me back from that impersonal but dedicated life on the squadron to the life of the more humane and compassionate society we had defended at such terrible costs. It might take a long time to achieve normality again, to stop thinking we were living on borrowed time, and to begin thinking of the future. But at least, together, Norma and I were on our way.

Receiving the DSO and Bar to the DFC from the Lt Gov of Ontario.

For more copies of

Nickels and Nightingales

send $17.95 plus $3.00 for GST, shipping and handling to:
GENERAL STORE PUBLISHING HOUSE
1 Main Street, Burnstown, Ontario
Canada, K0J 1G0

Valour On Juno Beach $14.95
Black Crosses Off My Wingtip $17.95
Choco to A.I.F. $14.95
The Ridge $14.95
Trepid Aviator $17.95
Korea Volunteer $17.95
The Wing And The Arrow $17.95
In The Line Of Duty (Softcover) $39.95
(Hardcover) $59.95
Dragons of Steel $17.95
Ordinary Heroes $17.95
One Of The Many $14.95
Fifty Years After $14.95
The Canadian Peacekeeper $12.95
The Surly Bonds Of Earth $12.95
The Memory Of All That $14.95
No Time Off For Good Behaviour $14.95
To The Green Fields Beyond $14.95
Time Remembered $14.95

For each copy include $3.00 to cover GST, shipping and handling,
for *In the Line of Duty* include $6.00 to cover GST, shipping and handling.
Make cheque or money order payable to:

GENERAL STORE PUBLISHING HOUSE
1 Main Street, Burnstown, Ontario
Canada, K0J 1G0
613-432-7697   Fax: 613-432-7184
1-800-465-6072